The Ultimate Frontier

by

EKLAL KUESHANA

THE STELLE GROUP

Second Printing, 1970
Third Printing, 1974
Fourth Printing, 1978
Fifth Printing, 1982
Sixth Printing, 1984
Seventh Printing, 1986
Eighth Printing, 1986

ISBN 0-9600308-1-6

published by THE STELLE GROUP
P.O. Box 75, Quinlan, Texas 75474

PRINTED IN THE UNITED STATES OF AMERICA

THE ULTIMATE FRONTIER
by Eklal Kueshana

Author's Preface

The information disclosed in THE UTLIMATE FRONTIER comprises the first open discussion of the ancient Brotherhoods and their far-reaching influence in the civilizing of mankind. It may well come as a surprise to most persons that they have never heard of the Brotherhoods; but if the world had been aware of the work of these world-wide interlocking organizations during centuries past, they would only have suffered unwarranted suppression by political and religious factions in authority. The members and students of the Brotherhoods have traditionally withheld their identity from non-members in order to avoid certain persecution for holding highly idealistic views.

Despite these personal risks, the universal wisdom of the philosophy propounded by the Brotherhoods has long been successful in attracting the greater souls of the world into a magnificent, unified leaven of uplift for mankind. Paradoxically, the Brotherhoods have gathered their members from *all* the religions of the world as well as from among scientists, "free thinkers," and so-called agnostics. Persons of virtuous humanity, good-will, honesty, and philosophic integrity have been sought out as candidates wherever they may have arisen. This unlikely melange of intellects have found perfect unity, peace, and mutual dedication within the framework of the Brotherhoods' profound teaching, for it exceeds the finest in religions and appeals logically to critical minds. The students selected by the Brotherhoods have characteristically possessed the rare trait of mature individualism. Each was contacted by the Brotherhoods when he had sought more than his philosophy could provide; and in some cases the person had come to the point where his most cherished and tenaciously defended beliefs no longer completely sufficed, and he hungered for deeper answers. But it is also important to note that he had to be advanced enough in his philosophic objectivity to discard dogma and have the *courage* to embrace truth. That degree of truth which can survive every test is of a quality which can set men free to soar, but the rigorous reformation of personally entrenched beliefs needed in order to properly assimilate such truth demands an intellect of uncommon stamina and the faculty of adjusting upward.

It is to the credit of the many and varied students of the Brotherhoods that virtually none violated the code of esoteric secrecy. Each would generally continue his way of life to all outward appearances and respect his former allegiances and associations. However, his growth over the years in regard to his personal serenity, strength of character, courage, humility, and control of self while under the tutelage of the Brotherhoods generally aroused speculation among outside acquaintances as to what caused this man to become so outstanding. The student of many years was likely to have become regarded by his friends as an inexplicable but wonderful isle of wisdom, humaneness, and peace in this vast sea of frightened, grasping mankind. The singular success of these students in acquiring "that peace which exceeds understanding" reflects the exacting care exercised by the Brotherhoods in choosing candidates. For centuries they have quietly built their membership with the objective of superior quality rather than amassing large numbers. The activities of these scientist-philosophers would probably have remained forever undetected by outsiders if the urgency of the world dilemmas of our time hadn't made it particularly important that the Brotherhoods now publicly declare their position. The value of this unprecedented revelation will become evident in the early chapters of the book.

In effect, this book is an introduction to the activities of the Brotherhoods, and it has been cast as a biography because it allows me to quote directly from the mouths of several Emissaries of the Brotherhoods during their instruction of a young man referred to as Richard. His relationship with the Brotherhoods is a fascinating tale in itself, but his personal history is subordinate to the main subject material. Only those events in Richard's life which have bearing upon his conversations with the Emissaries are recorded here, and great care has been taken in verifying every detail. I can't claim verbatim presentation, but neither has any violation of content or intent been introduced. Fortunately, many especially knowledgeable persons have aided me in achieving exactitude in these matters.

Although the Brotherhoods' influence in Richard's life is exceptional, the account given here will provide the reader a sampling of the Brotherhoods' time-honored methods of enlistment and instruction. However, the publication of this book marks the beginning of a new phase in the Brotherhoods' work and manner of operation due to a grand, beneficent conspiracy of vital concern to an important segment of mankind. This segment will be drawn from people of all races and nationalities, and the information released in THE ULTIMATE FRONTIER is dedicated to them and to their reawakening.

Eklal Kueshana
March 31, 1961

CHAPTER 1

The Mysterious Dr. White

The strange meeting between the boy, Richard, and the mysterious Dr. White marked a climactic step in a series of arcane events encompassing many thousands of years. The outward circumstances of that meeting conveyed the impression of everyday normalcy as the youth and the elderly doctor strolled down sunny, quiet streets intensely absorbed in conversation. Yet despite their prosaic appearance, the ultimate importance of their conversation shall be measured by generations to come. Dr. White exposed Richard to ideas which profoundly affected not only the course of his life but which must also affect the course of mankind and its modern philosophies.

Richard enjoyed the appearance of Dr. White in his life only twice and then only for an hour or so each time. The first meeting occurred on August 15, 1939—the twelfth anniversary of his birth. The boy's view of life at that time was at its lowest point, and therefore his acceptance of Dr. White's wisdom was necessarily modified by this stage in his development. However, the evolution of Richard's philosophy was meticulously guided from the date of Dr. White's conversation with him.

Richard as a child was contemplative and perceptive. From the time he was a baby he had enjoyed the benefit of a handsome appearance which netted him easy acceptance by the adults he encountered. The youngster's winsome personality was enhanced by an inherent desire to please, a ready smile, and a natural good humor. Early manifestation of high-spirited nonsubmissiveness gave rise to a determined program of parental training in good manners, respect for elders, and consideration of others first until these characteristics were deeply instilled.

Because Richard was an only child, his mother, Melba, was able to devote more than average time to answering his questions about the world; and she gave, as fully as she could, answers to the detailed questions Richard would ask. His happiest hours were spent in discussion with some adult on subjects of widely varied scope. Perhaps his appeal to elders was his respectful acceptance of whatever they had to tell him. However, Richard privately decided for himself if what he was being told seemed reasonable or not. His decisions in this respect were not always correct, but at least they were consistent with his level of understanding.

Richard was pretty much protected from knowledge of the harsher realities of the world, which during the depression years might seem incongruous. But the children in his neighborhood were happy and normal, and everyone's father was employed. Richard's father, Rudolph, was part owner of a successful woodworking plant. The boy lived on the northwest side of Chicago in a clean and airy community of single residences with many empty lots in which to play ball, dig forts, and build tree houses. Between the ages of seven and eleven he was in the thick of boyhood activities. There were about a dozen boys all of the same general age as Richard, and every day, regardless of the weather, he and his friends were going full tilt until dark.

Beginning about the time Richard was eleven years old, disturbing elements began to threaten his placid world. He suffered a short but severe illness which resulted in his having to wear eyeglasses. Fortunately, he was able to enjoy perfect vision with proper lenses, and he completely regained his health in a few short months. But he soon discovered that he was no longer fully accepted by the boys at school. There was no planned ostracism by the children, but glasses and "sissy" were unquestioningly equated in their minds.

The boys in seventh grade were twelve and thirteen years old except for Richard who was only eleven because of his accelerated promotions in earlier grades. Richard did not share in the changing voices, downy chins, and hardening physiques of the seventh grade boys but was by far the smallest child in his class. He was unable to fit in during this critical year and was simply passed by. The easy social acceptance that had always been his suddenly became nonexistent. He later discovered that he could attract attention in class by making clever comments out loud which would often bring welcome laughter from his classmates, but this only earned him the open enmity of his teachers. Richard felt miserable, and he gradually developed a sour grapes attitude toward social acceptance. He became withdrawn, and he compensated his loneliness by developing an ardent interest in chemistry to the extent of collecting a sizeable portable laboratory. At this time, also, he acquired a clarinet and enjoyed learning the instrument, but he continued to impose an ever stricter isolation upon himself.

His schoolwork did not become better or worse but was regarded with his usual indifference toward studies. The assigned work was so easily mastered that it presented no challenge to Richard; and except for mathematics and science periods, he became restless and bothersome in class. As a result, he often became the butt of some teacher's sarcastic gibes. Any child thus out of grace with authority becomes a target for further hazards at the hands of his peers.

The circumstances gave rise to considerable introspection on Richard's part as he tried to understand what was happening to him. An eleven-year-old boy, however, is not given to personality analysis or to perceiving cause and effect in human relations, but it was clearly evident to him that there could be pain of a different sort than physical pain. It was about this time that he also became aware of the world's larger problems. The big news during the summer of 1939 was the impending war in Europe and the possible involvement of the United States. Richard began to take notice of public accusations against political personages which suggested the possibility that the best men didn't always win elections. He gradually came to perceive that many realities of life were much at variance with his mother's portrayal of our civilization as being the best of all possible worlds. His awakening observations built up into a sense of insecurity and consequent frustration at not being able to cope with the outrages of his heretofore neatly packaged concept of a moral, efficient, loving world. It was within the framework of such personal problems that Richard was to view the information divulged by Dr. White.

On the morning of the important though unexpected meeting, Richard awoke in a mood of happy anticipation with the realization that his birthday party was but a few hours away. This year he had informed his mother that he did not wish to have a children's party; so only the usual relatives were coming to celebrate in the cool of the evening. Because it was a special occasion, he was granted a day of leisure; and about ten o'clock in the morning Richard decided to go outside to see if anything of interest was going on in the neighborhood—and there usually was.

The day was warm and agreeable, and Richard stood a while in the sunlight deciding what he should do first. There were some boys about a half-block away playing roller-skate-hockey with a tin-can puck, and sounds of a dispute over a marble game were coming from the back yard of a house nearby, but he decided that he would first investigate the unusual activity of grasshoppers in the towering ragweed growing on the vacant property across the street from his home. About the middle of August the grasshoppers are quite large and present a challenge to anyone who seeks to capture one. Richard busied himself for a while catching unwary grasshoppers that were feeding on weeds bordering the sidewalk. Those he caught he would release by merely opening his fist palm upward, whereupon the insect would execute a mighty leap back into the foliage. The recoil flick of the creatures' powerful hind legs against the palm of his opened hand was a sensation that rather amused Richard.

While he was engaged in this sport, an elderly gentleman approached him. Without looking up, Richard moved closer to the edge of the walk in order to allow more room for the man to pass, but instead the man stopped alongside as if to observe what Richard was doing. After a moment Richard glanced at the man who smiled assuringly. "How are you today, Richard?" he inquired in a pleasing, baritone voice.

"O.K., I guess," Richard replied in an off-hand way. He privately wondered who the man was, and he studied him rather carefully now trying to remember where he might have seen him before.

The handsome, elderly man was of medium height and appeared to be about sixty years old. His craggy, masculine face was that of a man of forty-five, but Richard judged him older than that because of the white hair visible where it was not covered by his panama hat. The tropical suit he wore was neat and well tailored, and it showed to advantage his broad shoulders and trim waistline. The man seemed to have an unusual vigor for his age. He carried a walking stick which he obviously did not need for assistance in getting about, for he seemed a very jaunty fellow. The crow's feet about his eyes were the only lines in his clean-shaven face, and they made his eyes sparkle with incipient joviality. His eyes were such a peculiar shade of pale blue, which bordered on a violet blue, that one could hardly escape noticing them. But all in all, Richard felt comfortable in the man's presence. The stranger was so genuinely cultured and considerate that the boy was immediately attracted to him. Richard then decided that he must surely have met the man some years previously, perhaps when with his grandfather.

Richard apologized, "I forget your name, sir."

"My name is Dr. White, lad," he said with a smile. "I'm a very old friend." Richard then noticed that the man spoke with a light accent that might have been a combination of New England and Scottish. "Today is your birthday, eh?" Dr. White continued.

"Yes, sir. I'm twelve years old."

"A very important year, too," the man allowed.

The banality of this statement conveyed a condescending attitude, and Richard's offended reaction to it caused Dr. White to affect a more adult manner toward the boy.

"It's but a few short years until you will be a man," Dr. White said, "and there is much of value that a good man can do in the world. Have you made any plans as to what your life's work shall be?"

"I'm going to be a doctor!" Richard said with pride, for people usually admired that ambition.

"I see. Do you feel you have special qualifications along that line?"

No one had ever come back at him with this question before, and for a moment Richard had no reply. "Well, I'm pretty good at science," he bragged.

"What of importance have you contributed to scientific knowledge?"

Dr. White's question was asked in mock blandness, but Richard knew that he was being taken to task for his boast. He quickly sensed that Dr. White was a precise man who listened closely to his answers and to his tone of voice. Richard took up the summons to speak carefully.

"I mean I easily understand the teacher, and I have a chemistry lab of my own, and I do a lot of reading about science," Richard replied meekly.

"The reading is a good sign. But try to remember that few people are *good* at science. Whatever understanding you may have mastered is of material selected by an adult who knows what the average child your age is likely to comprehend. All through high school and college the student is offered courses in knowledge already gained by others, and original work is not usually done by children or even college undergraduates. Don't succumb to the illusion that you are smart just because you get a good mark in school for understanding the course—it was intended for you to understand it."

This simple truth had never occurred to Richard, and it suddenly made him realize his subordinate position in the realm of learning.

Dr. White sensed Richard's re-evaluation when the boy thought for a while without offering a reply. "Do you have any other reasons for wanting to become a physician?" he asked.

The boy mentally searched himself to supply an answer, and he said, "Because they help others and make them well; and people look up to them; and they make lots of money."

"That seems mostly so," the man agreed. "Which of those reasons appeals to you most?"

"Making people well," was the earnest reply.

"Do you know how many years it will take to become a doctor?"

"No."

"Well, from the time you graduate from eighth grade, another thirteen years of study will be required."

"That's a long time!" Richard repled rather wide-eyed.

"And it's expensive; so you had better be certain that you still want to be a doctor when the time comes to start college. You should work in a hospital for a while after you graduate from high school and see if you like it. You could be a lab helper or something of the sort. The competition is tough in college, and you may find other students better suited temperamentally to the profession as it is practiced these days. Your reasons had better be strong enough to maintain the continued sacrifice necessary to achieve your goal."

Richard was impressed by this authoritative information. No one in his family had been to college; so no one could tell him what to expect. "Was it awful hard for you to become a doctor?" he asked with concern.

"I'm not a physician, lad. I'm a Doctor of Philosophy."

"What kind of a doctor is that? I never heard of it."

"When you graduate from college, you get a bachelor's degree. Then to specialize further, you study about two more years to get a master's degree. If you wish to get the very highest degree in your field of study, you attend more classes, do original work, and write about it. If you're lucky, you are awarded a doctoral degree, which is known as a Doctor of Philosophy, or a Ph.D."

"I never knew that," Richard said admiringly. "I think it will be wonderful when I get my doctor degree."

"Frankly, I believe you would be wasting this lifetime if you went into medicine since you've already mastered that art in previous lives."

Richard peered at Dr. White a bit askance. "What do you mean?" he asked warily.

"Essentially this: you have assumed your present body at this time to accomplish a much more important task."

"You're talking kind of funny, mister."

"Do you know what reincarnation means?"

"Sure! Natives in India think that after they die they come back to life as a bug, or a snake, or a cow."

"What you are talking about concerns the doctrine of transmigration. Were it a valid belief, one would have to suppose that a soul passes from one kind of creature to another. But that would mean that a bug's soul could be equal to a human soul, which is absurd. Only human beings have souls."

"I doubt it," Richard said bluntly. "If you were a surgeon, you would know that there is no such thing as a soul."

"Explain that!" Dr. White said with curiosity.

"Wherever you can look in a human being when you are

operating on him, there is no room for a soul. The body is all taken up with insides. And anyway nobody ever saw a soul."

"How do you know all this?"

"My mother told me."

"Do you suppose it possible that your mother could be mistaken?" Dr. White asked kindly.

"I don't think she'd lie to me."

"That's not what I asked."

"I guess she doesn't know everything," the boy conceded.

"I don't mean to say there is anything wrong with your mother, lad, for I'm sure she has told you just what she herself believes about religion; yet there are many other things she has not told you because she feels you are not old enough to properly understand."

"Yes, I suppose so."

"Your mother turned away from the Lutheran religion in her teens because she was such an attractive girl that her pastor couldn't keep his hands to himself. A few such incidences caused her to revolt from what she felt was a mass hypocrisy. Do you know what that word means?"

"Yes, sir."

"Your father was raised Catholic but refuses to go to church because he has seen the good teachings used to mask the corruption of its officials. Neither of your parents understands the greater values in their respective religions, nor do they much understand the history or struggles of the Christian Church. Theirs is the error of judging the beautiful contents of religion by the gross imperfection of the vessel. Your mother says she is an agnostic but isn't even sure what it is she claims not to believe." Dr. White sighed resignedly, "I suppose that you're an agnostic too."

"I don't know what religion that is, but I'm an atheist."

"What's your version of an atheist?"

"A guy who doesn't believe in God."

"Who told you that you didn't believe in God?"

"Nobody; I decided there was none when I was eight."

"That was the same year you first grasped the concept of infinity."

"Could be—about then."

"When you went to Florida last September with your parents, what strange experiences did you have?"

"Well, we were swimming all by ourselves in the ocean when they were expecting a hurricane except that it hit New England instead."

"Not that," Dr. White coached. "What about your feelings that you had been there before?"

"Oh, that? Many of the places we went were familiar to me even though I'd never been there. It seemed as though I had dreamed beforehand of some of the things exactly the way we did them." Richard rather startled himself that he should tell such things to a stranger. Then after a moment's reflection he exclaimed, "Hey! How come you know about that? I never told *anyone!*" Richard shivered, and the hair on his neck stood up.

"Do you think," asked Dr. White with a pleased smile, "you are willing to grant that there are a few things about the world which you do not understand?"

"Sure," said Richard, still amazed.

"The concept of infinity is impossible to convey in words. You took it up from greater minds in order to help you solve other questions you had at the time. You did this by telepathy. Your foreknowledge of events that occurred in Florida is known as prescience. Would you like me to explain these things to you in a scientific way?"

"Oh, yes!" Richard said with enthusiasm.

"Come then. Let's walk over the corner of Austin and Irving, and I'll buy you a rainbow ice cream cone for your birthday. We can talk as we go."

Despite Dr. White's mention of such objectionably alien topics as reincarnation and souls, his claim to be able to reasonably answer questions which had long intrigued Richard aroused the boy's keen curiosity. Richard's usual wariness of strangers was overridden by his not wanting to be rude to a man who might be a friend of his grandfather; and, moreover, he intuitively sensed that in Dr. White he had a protective mentor.

CHAPTER 2

The Nature of Existence

Dr. White and Richard began to walk toward the candy store which was about a half mile away. The elderly gentleman mused to himself where he should begin; and as they walked, Richard looked up at him with admiration. That this man should take such an interest in him was flattering, and that the doctor should speak to him without a patronizing mien or over-simplified language was even more gratifying. Dr. White was firmly precise but extremely kindly and considerate. An atmosphere of security seemed to emanate from the man.

"Do you know how an atom is constructed?" Dr. White began.

"Sort of," Richard shrugged.

"Tell me what you know."

"Well, it's got a positive center and electrons that are negative and go in circles around the center."

Dr. White asked, "What are the electrons?"

"Bits of matter."

"What does that really mean?" he persisted.

"I'm not sure."

"Do you suppose they can be likened to tiny balls flying in an orbit like planets around the sun?" Dr. White suggested.

That's a good explanation," Richard said thoughtfully.

"Actually, electrons and other sub-atomic particles aren't in the least bit solid; they are 'bundles' of energy. The charges of electricity they are represented to possess are merely a convenience to explain certain attractions and repulsions relative to charged and magnetic fields. You are probably aware that every particle within an atom moves in an orbit. Even the proton in the atom's nucleus travels a very tight orbit which determines its apparent diameter. In addition to orbiting there is another important motion of all sub-atomic particles, and this motion is called nutation. It is valuable for you to understand nutational motion *because it is the very key to the secrets of the universe.* Every sub-atomic particle spins about its own internal axis, and nutation refers to a wobble of the axis of rotation. Each particle in the physical universe experiences a nutation period of precisely the same rate."

"What does that mean?" interrupted Richard.

"It means that each sub-atomic particle of matter and each quantum-particle of electromagnetic energy spins upon its own axis just the way our planet Earth turns on its poles,[1] and that all these axes wobble at one constant rate regardless of the energy or mass of the particle. It is important that you distinguish between spinning and orbiting. Although all particles spin, those particles which also travel in closed orbits comprise matter whereas energy particles travel in straight lines. Energy can be converted into matter and vice versa, but the nutational rate of these particles never varies; nor is there any physical power in the universe which can alter the nutational rate one whit.

"Incidentally, gravity and magnetism, which are different manifestations of the same force, are inherent in the axial spin of etheric particles. One day men will derive more power for motors directly from this source than they shall ever achieve from fuels, electricity, or nuclear disintegration."

"How could that be?" Richard challenged rather scornfully.

The doctor smiled indulgently and said, "You were an engineer and manufacturer during many of your incarnations in the Poseid Empire. The device for taking motive power directly from the atmosphere was perfected about twenty thousand years ago, and you were among the many who understood its workings. Perhaps you may be instrumental in its rediscovery."

"But twenty thousand years ago was before the stone age," Richard protested.

"More exactly *between* stone ages."

"I've never heard of anything like *that* before!"

"Much exists in this universe which would be wholly impossi-

---

[1]Particles are not spheroids but toroids described by eddies in space analogous to the motion of air that forms a smoke ring. Particles also spin on an internal axis.

ble within the framework of your present philosophy. Fortunately, these things do not require your knowledge or belief in order to exist. If you will but listen, have patience, and maintain scientific openmindedness, you will profit immeasurably. All things will eventually yield to full understanding, but you must devote your life to that end.

"Now back to our discussion. As you will see, 'matter' is essentially a concept of our sense perceptors which themselves are of the same 'matter.' Our world and everything in it is composed of atoms, but atoms are only packages of energy whose seeming solidity and integrity are due to the circular motions of their components. An atom is almost entirely empty space consisting of a central blob of whirling energy sheathed by the orbits of electrons. The orbiting electrons describe a more-or-less spherical shell of energy; but don't imagine that this shell makes the atom a hollow ball of some concreteness. The emptiness in which the sub-atomic particles exist can be visualized by the supposition that if the nucleus of an atom were enlarged to the size of our sun, then the shell described by its electrons would be twelve times greater than the diameter of our solar system. A pound of iron, which seems quite solid and ponderable to us, is merely an aggregation of swirls of energy separated by comparatively vast reaches of emptiness. This illustration also applies to our own bodies. The cells which comprise our tissues, nerves, and blood are of the same intangible swirls.

"Do you have these concepts pretty well in mind now, Richard?"

"I think so," the boy said. "Except that I've never really understood what a quantum is."

"Electromagnetic energy—such as radio, heat, light, and X-rays—can be envisioned as traversing the ether in the form of bullets, or packages, called quantum particles."

"I've heard of the radio waves traveling on the ether," Richard said, "but what *is* ether?"

"The entire universe is permeated with a 'basic energy' which is, you might say, of a rarified concentration compared to the energy bundles which comprise atoms and quantum particles. It's hard to conceive of 'basic energy' with the same understanding associated with energy, for the 'basic' type has no motion and cannot impart force. It is quiescent, passive, and imperceptible. It is the mother of energy and matter. It is that from which all things are created. Yet, despite its all-pervasive nature, about the only evidence we have of its existence is the wave phenomena of the propagation of light.

"This 'basic energy,' or ether, imposes a limit on the speed of light. Otherwise we might expect a quantum of light to achieve *any* speed depending upon the amount of energy that could be exerted upon it. If the space were truly empty nothingness, then radiated energy would be able to travel at any rate in an infinite range of speeds instead of having an upper limit which we have named *the speed of light*. All electromagnetic radiations travel at exactly the same maximum speed through space whether it be low-energy radiation or high-energy radiation.

"Analogous to the way that air is the carrier of sound vibrations, the 'basic energy' permeating space is the 'fluid' carrier of quantum particles. Particles of radiated energy must buck the speed-barrier inherent in 'basic energy.' As particles comprising electromagnetic radiation proceed through space, a chattering effect with wave-like pulses results. The more energy a particle has, the greater is the frequency of its chatter.[1]

"Are you following my explanation?"

"Very clearly!" Richard exclaimed. The boy was surprised that words he had never heard before seemed to convey their meanings with acute clarity. It was not until a later year that he realized his understanding was probably induced by Dr. White.

"Fine! But let's not forget that I want to explain reincarnation, prescience, and telepathy. I went into detail concerning atoms and energy so you would have a basis of understanding for more transcendent concepts. What we will discuss next is also basic; and although it will be entirely new to you, kindly remember that many brilliant men and women base their philosophy of life upon these facts. You too will one day embrace these beliefs because only they sustain the test of all experiences and rationality.

"Now that you have a fair knowledge of the inanimate physi-

---

[1] The toroidal particle annihilates into electric and magnetic wave forms which collapse back into a particle again. This cycle repeats endlessly.

cal world, we shall discuss the phenomena of living things in relatively simple terms. To begin, *there are seven planes of existence in the universe*. The Physical Plane is the lowest of the seven, and it consists of atoms of matter and quanta of energy ordered by time. The Physical Plane is referred to as the lowest plane because the nutational rate of its constituent atoms and quanta has the slowest frequency of the seven planes. Our planet, the stars, and the light we see are all of this lowest nutational rate.

"Each of the seven planes of existence consists of atoms and quanta, and each plane is differentiated from the others by the nutational rate of the matter and energy composing it. Therefore, there are seven nutational rates—one for each plane of existence. No scientific instrument on the physical plane of existence can detect or measure the presence of the higher, more refined planes of existence. Atoms and energy of one nutational rate are not *en rapport*, as it were, with those of a different nutational rate. Inasmuch as the nerves composing man's five physical senses are of atoms of the same nutational rate as those of any other physical instrument, these senses are also unable to perceive the higher planes. However, certain powers inherent in Mind can provide the means whereby the upper planes may be 'seen.'

"Intelligent beings exist upon all seven planes, and the bodies of the persons who function upon any given plane are composed of atoms of that respective nutational rate. A being living upon one of the upper planes enjoys the inherent *mental* ability to naturally discern all the planes which are of lower nutational rate than the plane upon which he happens to function.

"Every man alive consists of four bodies—all interpenetrating and coexistent. All atoms, regardless of the seven variant nutational rates, are constructed in generally the same way. And because atoms are almost entirely empty space and are separated from one another by relatively large distances, the four bodies of a man simultaneously coincide in space. The component atoms respective to each body commingle without interference with one another.

"Man's body of lowest nutational rate, which is his physical body, is the one of which we are commonly aware. This body is subject to time, temperature, and the chemical equilibria unique to the lowest nutational rate. Only the Physical Plane is subject to time. As Albert Einstein has shown, time is a function of matter and vice versa. Without matter there can be no time; and without time there can be no matter.[1]

"The next highest body of man functions on the second plane of existence which is known as the Etheric Plane. This body of man, called the Vital Body, coalesces the physical body and determines its shape. Because the physical Body is constantly breaking down and renewing itself with the chemicals provided in our food, the Vital Body maintains the pattern so that we are recognizable from month to month. On the Etheric Plane is also the energy which sustains the vegetable 'Spark of Life.' The Vital Body is within the seed of every growing thing, and as the Vital Body grows, so does the physical body—be it plant, animal, or man. The Vital Body is responsible for many of the phenomena presently ascribed to the genes. Among other things, the Vital Body regulates the healing process after wounds and disease.

"The body of man which is next above the Vital Body is known as the Astral Body. The nutational frequency of its component atoms is of the third plane of existence. This is the plane and body man uses after the death of the physical body. The Astral Body corresponds to the common concept of what is called the 'soul' or 'spirit' of man and the plane of existence is often called the plane of light. Persons of clairvoyant abilities who have gained glimpses of the transcendent and radiant beauty of this plane of existence have given rise to the beautiful concepts of 'heaven' and the 'place of after-life.' The Astral Body, or 'soul,' is composed of atoms just as is the physical body—the difference lies in the nutational frequency.

"The fourth and highest body of man is called the Mental Body. This body is not very well defined in a man until he has developed it consciously from its rather nebulous, immature state into a body through which he may actively function on the Mental Plane of existence. This is the highest estate of man.

---

[1] Einstein assumed that the gravity-time continuum derived from physical particles; whereas gravity is a binding force originating on the Etheric Plane in etheric particles to which the physical universe conforms exactly.

When a person by means of intellect has advanced himself to the extent that he has fully developed his Mental Body, he has then also achieved freedom from re-birth. Forever after he is immortal."

"Wait a minute, Dr. White," Richard said somewhat in agitation. "I have lots of questions."

"What do you want explained?" Dr. White asked patiently.

"First of all," Richard began, "you are talking about freedom from re-birth, and I get the idea that you mean a man can become immortal just by being very smart."

"I used the term in the sense that a man is immortal when he no longer needs to occupy a *physical* body which is subject to pain, old age, and death. When a person earns immortality, he may enjoy continuity of learning upon higher planes without the interruptions inherent in re-birth, childhood, and human error on the Physical Plane."

"But people *do* die!" Richard maintained.

"People *do not* die! Only physical bodies die! Man is man. His realm is upon the fourth plane of existence—the Mental Plane. He occupies a physical body on the Physical Plane in order to learn. Your body is your horse, your vehicle—it provides a means of locomotion and tools in the form of hands and muscles so that you may deal effectively with the world.

"All the human beings occupying this planet came into existence at the same time—somewhat more than a million years ago. Collectively, all of these persons are known as the 'human life-wave.' The term 'life-wave' is derived from the fact that the life-energy for a human being is of the fourth nutational frequency, and nutation can be expressed mathematically as a wave motion. There are seven life-waves—one for each plane. You and I are of the human life-wave of the planet Earth; individually we are known as Egos. The word *Ego* in this usage is always capitalized.

"At any given time, approximately one-sixth of the human Egos assigned to this planet are incarnated into physical bodies or vehicles. To date, you, Richard, have incarnated almost three thousand times."

"But why?"

"Because when our human life-wave was brought into existence, every Ego among us was absolutely ignorant. We knew nothing, but we had certain unique gifts which were designed to make us learn. Inherent in all Egos is Mind—a power of the fourth plane of existence. In this respect we are created in the image of God. The qualities of Mind are memory, desire, will, curiosity, consciousness, conscience, creativeness, intuition, emotion, and reason. Granted these mental endowments, our task is to learn everything there is to be known about the four lowest planes of existence. Naturally, one cannot be expected to start at the top when one is totally ignorant; so the first task of each Ego is to master the most elementary plane of existence— the Physical Plane. This involves learning trades and arts, the science of the physical universe, and most important, how to get along with other Egos socially, morally, politically, and economically. Obviously, this cannot be learned in just one lifetime.

"Is it not logical and just that a man be allowed many, many lifetimes to build knowledge and morality into his Ego's experience? Whatever a man is unable to accomplish in one life he can take up again in the next until he has mastered his problem. Step-by-step, life-by-life, he builds his Egoic experience until, at last, he has mastered every problem offered by the Physical Plane of existence. When an Ego has evolved his mental ability so that he enjoys a perfect body in a personal environment exactly to his liking and has learned to perceive the higher planes of existence while still occupying a physical vehicle, then it can be said of him that he has mastered the Physical Plane. Thereafter, he need no longer take on a physical body and suffer the limitations of being earth-bound. When this stage of freedom from reincarnation has been attained, the Ego is known as an Adept. He may now advance more rapidly in understanding of the higher planes until He has mastered everything there is to be known of the Physical, Etheric, Astral, and Mental Planes. When an Ego has added all this knowledge unto himself, He is known as a Master."

"Such a system seems like so much work," Richard sighed. "What's the purpose of it?"

"Ultimate advancement to the pinnacle of existence—to be

one with God! You cannot become one with God until you are His equal in knowledge of everything. God has provided the means and the intermediate steps to do so. It is the very meaning of our presence here. God created us in order to glorify Him in the greatest way imaginable, which is to elevate ourselves to His very level. This concept must not be thought sacrilegious. It is a long, difficult road for us, but it is rich in the satisfaction it provides all along the way. The higher we progress, the more work we do for others. Our tasks become more difficult the farther we advance; yet the rewards become correspondingly more worthwhile.

"God has His being upon the seventh plane of existence which is known as the Celestial Plane. Just because an Ego has reached the state of perfection where He has become a Master functioning on the Mental Plane of existence does not mean that He is nearly a God. To the average man, the magnificence which is a Master is truly beyond comprehension; yet the Master has accomplished but a comparatively elementary course along the path to becoming one of the Celestial Host. When an Ego becomes a Master, He is ready to progress to the fifth plane of existence. However, his progression must be held in abeyance until the rest of the Egos of the world have also attained Mastership, whereupon They all advance simultaneously. Several millions[1] of the Egos assigned to this planet, who were created at the same time as you and I, have already achieved the status of Master. They devote most of Their efforts now to aiding the rest of humanity along the path towards Mastership so that progression to the fifth plane of existence can be realized as soon as possible.

"The fifth plane is called the Angelic Plane. No man from this planet has ever reached the Angelic Plane of existence."

Richard interrupted Dr. White by raising his arm in the manner of a school child in a classroom. "When I was in second and third grades," Richard began, "I used to go to Bible school. The teacher there told us that people became angels when they die, and then they go to Heaven to fly around playing harps forever."

---

[1]Somewhat more than one hundred million Egos have achieved Mastership on Earth ($7/10$ of 1% of the Egos assigned to this planet).

"That's what many Christians believe, Richard."

"I know. But forever is billions and billions of years. I would go nuts doing nothing for that long. It seemed so silly to me I quit going to church. Your idea sounds more logical, but I can't decide if it's true or not."

"I don't expect you to be converted by my discussion even though the things I'm telling you were well known to you before you took on your present body. Your later reflection upon this information will reopen the way to you, but it will necessarily take many years. It is important that you now be exposed to these facts so you don't stray too far from the truth. And the future questions that will be posed by your ever-expanding philosophy can be answered by dredging up from your brain the information I'm giving you. You will later be able to prove for yourself the verity of what I have to say."

"If, as you said, Dr. White, these things were well known to me before, why don't I remember them now without your having to tell me?"

"You really do remember them because knowledge is carried with you forever as part of your Egoic Mind. However, you must transfer the information to your present brain in order for you to use it consciously and rationally."

"Isn't the Mind and the brain the same thing?"

"Not at all! The Mind is a power—an energy of the fourth plane of existence; it is part of the Egoic equipment. The brain, on the other hand, is a physical organ of the physical body. The brain is a marvelously constructed electro-chemical switchboard and calculating machine. Most of its practical use is as a large automatic control center for body functions like breathing, walking, and digesting food. The frontal part of the brain is capable of what is called conditioned-reflex. This involves the forming of relations between cause and effect and forming memory responses. Such things you will understand much better after you've had more schooling. But right now let it suffice to say that the brain and Mind are intricately interrelated so that each functions to the purpose of increasing Egoic knowledge.

"When you were born into your present physical vehicle, its brain was completely blank. The experiences you have had so far in this life are recorded on it. The ability to break through the barrier between the events remembered by one's brain for this lifetime and the Mind's Egoic memory of all past lives is built into man, but one is not likely to accomplish this feat until trained by someone who has already done it himself. When an Ego incarnates, he brings his character with him. That is why no educational system will ever mold all persons into one type.

"The vast majority of people go through life without trying to penetrate their own Minds. They are like so many paupers carrying with them a vast fortune in rubies tied in a sack but living and dying in poverty because they don't know how to untie the knot. You are fortunate in that you will later be shown the way to untie the knot and perceive your real self. Then you will know that man is deathless. It is lack of knowledge that continues to bind men to the pain and uncertainties of physical incarnation. Once a man finally understands that his every effort toward the acquisition of knowledge furthers his eventual freedom from the cycle of rebirth, then his life takes on an invigorating purpose and a sustaining drive to pursue truth. But the information needed to make men free has been long forgotten by traditional Christianity even though Christ taught it and it was known to the inner circle of the original followers."

Richard considered this for a while and then returned to a previous thought. "Where do people go after their bodies die? Is there really a Heaven?"

"When the physical vehicle dies, the Ego occupying it is said to undergo transition. The Ego then uses his Astral Body and resides on the third, or Astral, plane of existence. The Astral Plane is the resting place of each and every decarnate Ego. Here he may study his strengths and weaknesses in order to plan his next incarnation so that it will afford the situations and surroundings most likely to advance his personality development and his ability to control his environment.

"We have the right to choose our parents, our time of birth, and the circumstances in which we shall be reared. Every one of us alive today purposefully and consciously chose the parents to whom he was born. The race, creed, nationality, body type, and economic status we chose were designed to forward the tasks that will best hasten our advancement.

"It is important that knowledge of our tasks be closed to us after we have reincarnated in order that we may truly master them. If we were aware of our self-assigned problems, we would be all to inclined to feign their solution in hypocrisy and not really have solved the problems at all. For this reason our past lives and experiences are purposely shut from us. However, the *essence* of what has been learned during previous lifetimes comes with us into a new incarnation.

"Despite outward appearance, all mankind is striving for perfection, but very often the tasks of a lifetime are so difficult that we lose ground instead of advancing. The Ego acquires knowledge through actual practice, for all information must be actually tested to become knowledge. Thereby, he builds his soul. Soul, then, is *knowledge* which becomes the means by which the Ego may accelerate his progress and deal effectively with the problems of life until all such problems have been solved.

"It is God's Justice that we shall not be tested beyond our ability. However, we may be required to strive to our utmost to pass our tests. We should seek adversity, for through adversity we grow. At every turn mankind has the kindly offer of assistance from Those who have already risen to the rank of Mastership, which we could just as well have gained had we applied ourselves as They had. They were just as blank as new Egos as we. Our habits of scepticism have for many lifetimes closed the door to wisdom; yet the blame is wholly ours that we do not experience the security, immortality, wisdom, and power it is our inheritance to enjoy. Indeed, we have added to the burdens of those seeking spiritual advancement by our condemnation and persecution of them."

"You said before that we all go to the Astral Plane when our bodies die," Richard said. "Does that mean there is no Hell?"

"The Christian concept of a beautiful after-life for righteous souls is called *Heaven*, and it can be correctly identified with the upper Astral Plane. When I make the distinction of *upper* Astral Plane, I do not mean to imply a greater altitude but rather a higher degree of spiritual attainment. Everyone resides on the Astral Plane between incarnations, and that includes evil men as well as good men. Good men gravitate to the upper level of the Astral Plane where they experience a beautiful, bright, and serene existence; but depraved Egos descend to the lower reaches of the Astral Plane where darkness, hatred, and misery abound in hellish, wild confusion."

"Where are heaven and hell?"

"Right here, all around us. Egos like you and me who are in physical bodies, and those occupying their Astral Bodies, and Masters occupying Mental Bodies are all co-existent here on the surface of the Earth."

"Do you mean spirits could be walking alongside of me right now?" Richard asked with a shiver.

"Yes. As a matter of fact, there is quite a following of especially interested Egos who are accompanying us at the moment."

Richard stopped in his tracks. "That's quite a thought!" the boy exclaimed. "How do you know?"

"Because I'm able to see them," Dr. White assured him.

For more than a minute Richard stood quietly savoring the thought of unseen, intelligent beings standing within his reach. "It's funny," he said slowly, "I can't see anyone or hear anyone, but I've often had the strangest feeling about someone being around me. I never considered it seriously though. I'm sure glad the sun is shining!"

"You see, lad, no matter what a person may do, there is someone observing his every action. Even our private thoughts are automatically recorded for all eternity."

Richard's eyebrows raised in wonderment as he glanced at Dr. White.

"Remember that the Mind is a radiant power of the fourth nutational rate. Mind exerts a special power on the second plane of existence known as the Etheric Plane. Every thought and deed of every human being since our creation is impressed upon the Etheric Plane by vibrational means. This record can be transcribed by Minds capable of attuning to the recorded vibrations. The way it is done is similar to a radio picking up only one desired wave-length out of all the different frequencies being broadcast by many stations. The phenomenon is a matter of sympathetic attunement. The Etheric record is known as the Book of God's Remembrances or as the Akashic Record. Now you can see how I was able to know about your prescient experiences during your trip to Florida and about your comprehension of infinity.

"Come, let's continue on our way to the candy store. I see we are almost there."

Richard's mind was preoccupied with all the things he had just learned; so he resumed his stroll beside Dr. White in an automatic way. They had walked about a half a block when the boy broke the silence. "You mentioned prescience again. How could I have known something was going to happen before it happened?"

"You dreamed it during the twilight phase of sleep. Sometimes the Ego stretches forth his consciousness into the Astral Plane during sleep in order to receive advice on some particular problem or to learn certain things of current concern. Usually we have no conscious remembrance of these astral contacts, but certain persons seem able to retain partial awareness of their experience there. If you recall, I said that time is a function of the Physical Plane. No other plane of existence experiences the rigid sequencing of events as does the physical. This means that Egos functioning above the Physical Plane, including persons temporarily contacting the Astral Plane during their sleep, enjoy a mental perceptiveness which affords projection into the past and future."

"I have another question, Dr. White."

"What is it?"

"You said that when people's bodies die, their spirits go to the upper Astral Plane which is like Heaven. But if, as you also said, no man has ever reached the Angelic Plane, aren't churches wrong when they claim we become Angels after death?"

"That's a Christian folk legend, Richard. Nowhere in the Bible does it state that man becomes an Angel after death. This idea probably got its start from a misinterpretation of Christ's answer to His questioners concerning marriage in Heaven. He replied that those who have earned resurrection are *like* the Angels since they do not die again nor do they marry (*Mark 12:18–25 and Luke 20:34–36*).[1] It was the Angels who created the Earth and evolved man's physical vehicle. The Angel in charge of the Angelic Host and Their great work of creation was Jehovah, who is so great in comparison to man that He is as God

---

[1]Italicized Biblical references inserted into the text are for the reader's convenience and are not part of the conversations reported in this book.

to us. So how could a man become equal to his creator merely by the death of his physical vehicle?

"Before you ask, Angels do not have wings. This idea persists from the days of the ancient sculptors who devised the idea of portraying Angels and gods with wings to differentiate Them from statues of mortal heroes and kings. Since the gods of the ancients were of the 'upper world,' wings seem to have been a reasonable symbol. Actually, Angels have bodies composed of atoms of the fifth nutational rate, and They function on the fifth plane of existence where there is nothing comparable to our atmosphere to sustain winged flight.

"Even though Jehovah and the other Angels are very high upon the evolutionary path, there is still another plane of existence between Them and God. It is the sixth or Archangelic Plane. The Archangelic Host of our Solar System is presided over by Melchizedek. It was He who took on the physical vehicle of a man and was known to us as Christ.

"And now you have learned the names of the seven planes of existence which, in ascending order, are the Physical, Etheric, Astral, Mental, Angelic, Archangelic, and Celestial."

Richard looked perplexed; so Dr. White asked him, "What is it that bothers you?"

"You say that the Angels were our creators. That just doesn't agree with science. How do you account for dinosaurs living hundreds of millions of years ago; and what about Darwin?" The boy had never doubted the scientific version of evolution, but now he could not easily choose between Dr. White's statements and the school texts. The growing admiration he felt for Dr. White caused him to respect the man's opinions even when they were in conflict with his own ideas.

"I shall tell you the truth about creation, and you will see that no facts are left unaccounted for. But first I'm going to buy that ice cream cone I promised you."

Richard had not noticed that they had arrived at the candy shop. They went inside, but the boy's anticipation of an explanation of creation supplanted his usual eagerness toward the rare treat of his favorite confection.

CHAPTER 3

Consecration

Dr. White and the boy emerged from the store each with an ice cream cone. "Shall we return down Austin Avenue the way we came?" Dr. White asked as he began to turn in that direction.

"Sure, it's quieter," Richard agreed.

"Before I talk about the history of creation, I'd first like to explain the method by which creation is accomplished."

"O.K."

"Do you recall that I mentioned that every thought is permanently impressed on the Etheric Plane to form the Akashic Record?"

The boy nodded as he licked an impending drip from the side of his cone.

"The Etheric Plane is so designed that Mind has a special effect upon it. Every casual and passing thought leaves its mark upon the Etheric Plane; therefore, just think what an impression is made upon it by a Mind concentrating all its power upon a particular problem or upon an inventive effort!

"I also told you that one's physical body is coalesced by an etheric pattern known as the Vital Body and that this Vital Body is in the seed of every growing thing. As a matter of fact, every single item in the Physical Plane—including atoms, living cells, rocks, planets, and stars—is formed upon an etheric pattern to which physical manifestation corresponds in precise detail. One might say that the etheric pattern is a framework for physical substance.

"A Mind trained to intense concentration can form etheric patterns mentally. All Egos have the mental equipment to perform this feat; however, it takes much effort to learn how to fix one's attention upon an idea to the total exclusion of all else for, say, five minutes. Usually only Adepts and higher Egos have achieved this extent of concentration. A Master can visualize a chair, for example, and in a matter of several minutes of intense concentration He will have formed an Etheric Pattern of His visualization which He then Mentally clothes with appropriate physical atoms already present in the surrounding area. Thus from His visualization has proceeded a complete chair by wholly mental means. The chair can be serviceable and as well constructed as if built by a craftsman using the best methods and the finest wood. The phenomenon is known as *precipitation from the ethers* or just as *precipitation.*"

"If people can do this," Richard said, "why go through all the bother of manufacturing things? Wouldn't people just go around precipitating things instead of buying them?"

"Were a person to attain the skill whereby he could create his needs directly, he would be a Master. It is characteristic of a Master that He has total control over His environment. But it is not likely that you will find a Master precipitating wealth for Himself, for He functions upon the fourth plane of existence where He has no need whatever for physical articles.

"To be quite exact, however, any person who can develop the power of intense concentration is able to precipitate. But as a rule, only a balanced personality such as is found in Adepts and Masters is likely to achieve the overall knowledge and self-discipline prerequisite to direct control over the physical plane. Try to imagine the knowledge involved in visualizing every minute cell-structure comprising the wood of which our chair example would be made. Few scientists of our day could hope to explain what ingredients would be required to achieve the graining, color, texture, density, and structural strength in a given wood.

"But Masters have gained all the knowledge possible to be known on the lowest four planes of existence. Such knowledge encompasses everything in the realms of chemistry, physics, mathematics, and all the sciences. This does not include such fields of knowledge as history and geography which constantly change; or of philosophy, which is but mortal man's groping explanation of himself; or of the fields of poetry, literature, and music; but rather the true and unalterable essence of reality involved in these experiences of mankind. Most of the books in the libraries here on Earth contain a pitifully small amount of ultimate truth. Certain observations can be said to be correct, but for the most part, our books are but lies and bias arranged into history, and the rest is but repetitive philosophizing. Even the sciences are usually in error when they enter into theory and hypothesis. Such 'human knowledge' isn't worth considering when it comes to building our soul knowledge."

Richard sighed, "It's all pretty much out of my reach anyhow."

"Not necessarily, lad. There is practical value for all human beings in the method of mental creation. Even if an individual stands far below Adeptship, he uses the visualization and concentration sequence to bring a thing into physical reality. Everything fabricated by man had its beginning in an idea. A machine has to be visualized mentally and formulated into a plan before it can be built.

"When an ordinary man seeks to build a new home for himself, he has first to dream of all the things he wants to incorporate into his home; then he must plan it, obtain the money for materials and land, and gather together the talent and resources in proper order. Unwittingly, that man is using precipitation to a great extent, but it occurs in a natural, commonplace way.

"By using the mental means of creation granted him by God, a man can bring into his environment any condition or material possession he sincerely and avidly desires. The ability to precipitate directly from the ethers comes only with great spiritual advancement; but one usually draws wealth, or whatever else he seeks, into his possession through use of the laws of mental attraction. When a man thinks about an idea, he sets up vibrational patterns in the ether. Other men who concern themselves with similar ideas are subconsciously attracted by these broadcasted thoughts. In strange 'coincidental' ways, two or more such individuals who can mutually benefit one another are drawn together. Exceptionally successful partnerships have arisen between 'strangers' who each had some essential ability to bring into complementary union with the ability of the other."

"I don't quite get the idea, Dr. White," Richard exclaimed in exasperation.

"Don't worry about that now, Richard. When you grow older and more able to understand, this information will be explained to you in detail. For the present, I want to give you a general concept of mental creativity."

By this time the boy was near mental exhaustion from concentrating on new information which was coming at him in heavy dosage. His desire to comprehend Dr. White's ideas was sincere, for the boy sensed the value of the lecture.

Dr. White remained silent for a while and then digressed to other topics so Richard could have a change of pace.

"Let's turn down Berteau Avenue and walk to the park," Dr. White said.

Richard silently acquiesced.

"How are you doing in school now?"

"Oh, I don't know!" Richard shrugged.

"Are you getting excited about starting eighth grade next month?"

"Well, I'm not going to be here long."

"What do you mean?"

"We're moving to Elmwood Park at the end of next month; so I'll be starting a new school soon."

"It's odd that your folks would take you out of school so near to graduation."

"I asked them if we could move soon," Richard confessed.

"I see. But why to Elmwood Park?"

"Because my parents are building a new house there."

"Do you think you will be happier in a new place?"

"I suppose so."

"I know you haven't been getting along as well as you used to with the other children, but don't you think you can overcome this difficulty without running away from it?"

The boy was again reminded that Dr. White was able to see through him with amazing clarity.

"It's too late now," Richard said. "The home is bought, and we'll be moving into it."

"I'm aware of that, but the same difficulty may arise again. You see, Richard, whenever a person doesn't enjoy the approval of his group, he should look within *himself* to seek the answer to his problem. You've always been one of the gang because you were in no way different from the average. Now you suffer the penalty of being unique because you wear glasses and are small in height. To be different is to suffer at the hands of the normal.

This is a valuable lesson to learn. Yet sometimes it is better to so suffer if it causes you to seek explanation of why some persons have to undergo such distress. Those who find ready acceptance wherever they go rarely ponder the whys and wherefores of existence.

"During the next year you will cease to be a good-looking child. You will have to learn how to compensate for this loss by the exercise of reason. You must come to learn that you can achieve acceptance through other, more noble attributes. At the same time you must learn that it is but vanity to seek social acceptance of the world.

"During a previous life you took on a rather ugly body, considered grotesque by your erstwhile contemporaries, in order that the suffering brought about by their snubs would help to awaken in you the ability to perceive your environment for what it was. This was done because you were born as a Pharaoh's son and might have otherwise become either power-mad or dissipated by luxury and surfeit. At that time you incarnated in order to achieve a very worthwhile advance for mankind. When you became Pharaoh, you wrought many changes in Egypt's science, art, religion, and government.

"You were not universally loved by your subjects any more than any reformer is loved. All political personages must endure hatefulness and misunderstanding; but if they could not bear disapproval, they would be obliged to do nothing lest someone take offense at an action. Unfortunately, history has a garbled version of your magnificent work as Pharaoh because your biographer was of the opposition group. Nevertheless, your consolation lies in the knowledge that the Masters who award vitally important tasks to Egos of proven ability are perfectly aware of the true facts.

"When you incarnated this time, you came to earth out of your proper time and place. Do not expect to fit into this world as it is today, for you cannot. If you succumb to the world you will have lost much. You have a task to perform, and every possible help will be offered to assure the achievement of that task."

"But why should I have tasks unloaded on me?" Richard wailed.

"Because you have earned the right to work hard as a reward

for hard work well performed in the past."

"Am I supposed to be a king again or something?"

"No, Richard, you will never rule again. But you will *lead* men! You will lead the kind of men who do not require a ruler in order to bring potential human greatness into reality. And lest you believe yourself exalted in any way, most of the great men with whom you will associate in later life will be those who have been wise rulers and administrators in past incarnations. Together you will enthrone enlightenment and end forever the age of rulers on Earth.

"I must make it quite clear at this point that whatever I tell you must be kept absolutely secret until such time as you are permitted to reveal it. You must not seem wise lest people fear you. When the prudence of humility is firm within you, you will find no desire to seem wise. Learn to play the fool. People are less on guard against the man who deals lightly and easily with life, and this makes it easier for him to learn more about human beings than the person who appears capable and astute. People are wary of evident wisdom and cautiously conceal their real natures from those who seem knowing and intense. Therefore, be the least of men, and so learn how in truth we are all very small. The know-it-all is universally despised—especially if he proves to be right all the time. Pride is the foremost personality attribute of the child. So long as you sense pride in yourself, you will know that you are not fully mature. But self-respect must be differentiated from pride. Pride is folly, but self-respect is the mature attitude of a person who enjoys a sense of personal worthiness and healthy emotions."

"But how shall I do all these things?" Richard quailed.

"One at a time! You will not be deserted at any moment. Whatever is needed shall be provided. First, however, you must undergo the requisite training. Situations most likely to make you grow will be presented to you from time to time until your solutions to the problems placed in your path are satisfactory."

"Why me? Why don't you get a man to do what you want?"

"Because God's works are done by tiny babies who are carefully drawn to adult stature and developed to accomplish important advancement for mankind."

"How did God get into this?" Richard retorted.

"It's a phrase, Richard."

The boy frowned as he sought to relate the wide range of topics covered by Dr. White. They walked silently for a block or so as Richard finished the last of his ice cream cone. He looked down at his hand to find that it was rather sticky, whereupon Dr. White offered the boy his handkerchief. The cloth was so white and neatly pressed that Richard demurred, but the elderly gentleman persisted in the offer. Richard accepted the cloth with a sheepish grin, and Dr. White smiled compassionately. The boy suddenly sensed the fatherly concern in Dr. White's demeanor, and it surprised and pleased him.

"Shall we talk about the Creation?" Dr. White inquired as he pocketed the grimy handkerchief.

The boy nodded and said, "That sounds like a good idea."

"Well, then," Dr. White began, "the universe is ordered by intellect in its every phase; and without Angelic and Archangelic thought to sustain it, the Physical Plane would not exist. It is reasonable to suspect, then, that man is not a product of chance but of order."

Richard interrupted. "But science has proven man is the end result of chance mutations and that life began as an accidental compounding of chemicals."

"That theory is but a reasonable assumption, Richard. No scientist even pretends that it will ever be provable by scientific standards. If one believes the theory of chance evolution, one must also accept the idea that our thoughts are the manifestations of a brain which is merely a physical organ evolved through the ages. But since the brain and the cells which compose it are made up of atoms, one is faced with the absurd deduction that, by chance, atoms have been arranged in a human brain in such a way as to perceive themselves. Only Mind can perceive sub-atomic structure; and Mind is a power created solely by God and made part of the human Ego.

"In order to make it easier for you to understand the Creation, I'm going to start quite far back. The information I will relate to you was learned directly from our Angelic Host by Masters of our life-wave who then passed it down to Adepts and certain other Egos.

"To begin, we'll go back about seven billion years to another

39

planet which we shall call Klarian. On that planet the civilization of men had reached such heights that they were nearing the point where their vast technology was barely needed. The majority of these human beings were past the need of rebirth, and most of them were Masters upon the mental plane of existence. The necessity for physical instrumentation was becoming obsolete because of the ability of the planet's inhabitants to precipitate their needs from the ethers. After a few thousand more years, except for those Egos of the planet who lagged too far behind to attain Mastership, the billions of Masters from the planet Klarian advanced in one moment with all the other Masters of all the other planets of the universe to the Angelic Plane of existence. Those lagging human Egos who had to remain behind were deprived of every iota of soul knowledge that they had gained and then were returned to the Celestial Host to be held in abeyance.

"The Angels of the fifth plane, who had originally created Klarian, advanced at that same moment to the Archangelic Plane; and the planet Klarian, which They had created, They dissolved into nothingness. Their Archangels moved up to the Celestial Plane, and They disintegrated the star about which the planet Klarian had revolved. The same was done throughout the universe so that all the stars and their attendant planets ceased to exist. Time, because it is a function of matter on the Physical Plane, came to an end.

"This great event, which occurs every several billion years, is known as the 'Progression of the Life-Waves.' All was still and void on the Physical Plane because it had ceased to exist. But upon the Angelic, Archangelic, and Celestial Planes of existence there was much activity. There was what might be likened to training and subsequent organization of Angelic and Archangelic Egos into groups with elections of the fittest to preside as regents. This was followed by further planning and co-ordinating of the great work of the future. When all was in readiness, creation began!

"First, the Archangels created the stars—and time began anew. Around each star in the universe the Angelic Hosts precipitated attendant planets from great gaseous clouds; and upon each and every one of the myriad planets whirling in their orbits about countless suns man has been evolved.

"The Christ, who was Angelic when Klarian was created, is now Regent of the Archangelic Host which created our Sun. This is why He is sometimes referred to as the 'Day Star on High.' Jehovah, who was human upon the planet Klarian, was elected Regent by His fellow Angels who created our planet Earth. Each of the planets of our solar system has its own Angelic Host, and human life currently flourishes upon each of our sister planets. The physical forms of the men upon the planets of our system are recognizably human by our standards. However, the temperature and gravitation differences between the planets necessitate widely variant body chemistries and muscular apportionments. But moral and intellectual aims are identical throughout the universe. Kindliness, love, and faith are everywhere the same.

"As our planet slowly cooled, the surface rock crystallized into land. At last all was cool enough for the dense mantle of steam clouds to condense into rain and make oceans of the depressions in our Earth's surface. One day, light shone through clear skies upon the land and sea, and the stage was set for the Angels to create life. They began with one-celled plants and one-celled animals.

"These They consciously evolved into complex organisms. All the animal bodies that They experimented with were devised in order to incorporate certain specific structures and metabolic processes into a self-perpetuating genetic pattern which would eventually be developed into a perfect human physical vehicle.

"It was on a certain island-continent that the most promising human form was developed and subsequently chosen to be endowed with Mind. Mind—that great creative power of the fourth plane of existence—was individualized into Egos by God and intricately linked to the human physical vehicle by Angels. Other tentative human prototypes, which anthropologists shall uncover throughout the world, were made extinct at the time the selected strain was being further perfected.

"When man was endowed with Mind, he was on his own. After that, man's further evolution was forbidden to be manipulated by Angelic Thought. This explains the strange mystery of why man's body has remained essentially the same for the past million years whereas other mammalian forms have been evolved radically since then. The Angels still develop lower animal forms for our future advantage. Man too has learned how to hybridize races within a species—plant and animal—and therefore outdoes natural selection. But only Angels can evolve new species."

Dr. White paused to let Richard think over his explanation of creation. After a prolonged silence which neither the man nor boy felt to be awkward, the elderly gentleman asked, "What thoughts come to mind that you would like amplified, Richard?"

"Well, for one thing, how long ago did the animal developed for man's vehicle first get Mind?"

"About one million ten thousand years ago."

"Then it takes a long time to become a Master, doesn't it?"

"Yes, it does, lad; but it shouldn't be taking as long as it has. The Earth is the furthest behind in the development of Masters."

"You mean that other planets are better than ours?"

"Yes, by far, I'm sorry to say."

"But why should that be?" Richard complained with a note of distress.

"For many reasons," Dr. White said tersely. Richard noted that the man seemed pained by some inner contemplation that brought a look of sorrow to the otherwise serene, strong features of his face.

"But we'll finally get there, won't we?" Richard asked hopefully.

"Yes. Many wonderful, deserving Egos will fulfill the purpose of this planet's creation and thereby repay the efforts of the loving Higher Beings who have labored so in our behalf. But there is not much time left before the deadline will be upon us."

"You said the rest of us must become Masters before those who are already Masters can go on to be Angels; so how can there be a deadline?"

"Just as on Klarian, Richard. Those Egos who cannot make the grade within a reasonable length of time must be abandoned. More than a million years has proven ample elsewhere.

Our planet cannot hold back the Masters of other solar systems who are long since ready for progression to the fifth plane."

"How much longer do we have, Dr. White?" Richard asked as a chilling fear began to take hold of him.

Dr. White could sense the boy's acceptance of him as an authority. He knew that Richard felt quite keenly about the wondrous phenomena of human existence, and so he hesitated to answer this direct question lest the truth crush the new enthusiasm.

"You have asked a question which I did not expect to be called upon to answer, but I shall answer it man-to-man." He paused for a moment to gauge his listener and said, "We have about seven thousand years left."

Richard came close to tears as he explained to Dr. White, "I always figured that when I would one day die, that would be it. No afterlife; no thoughts; just blank. That I could stand, but what made me really feel bad was when I read that the sun would burn out after billions of years and all life on Earth would die. I couldn't stand the thought that people would no longer be. If chance had given rise to life which evolved into people on this planet only, what a terrible loss our end would be. I wondered if ever before or if ever again a creature with a mind able to consider the stars and the beauties of life would exist.

"You have made me happy with your explanation, Dr. White. But now I'm scared I won't become a Master."

"I wish I could reassure you, laddie, but only *you* will determine whether you will indeed achieve that glorious goal."

"It's just that seven thousand years is so little time compared to a million," the boy complained.

"Once on the right track, an Ego can make the grade in just a few lifetimes; but the world today is not conducive to starting on the path. Our present civilization ranks low compared to others of the Earth's past."

"How about this country though?"

"This country together with the others that comprise what is called Western Civilization may be regarded as the fifth greatest in the list of civilizations. The four greater ones, which precede the current knowledge of history, were superior as regards their likelihood of evolving Masters.

"The only real purpose of a civilization should be to promote the development of advanced Egos. Peace, prosperity, freedom, and happiness are important because these conditions enhance spiritual advancement. But without the proper philosophy to guide men there is no progress. Truth is the *seed* of advancement; a sound, serene civilization is the *climate;* and man's Mind is the *fertile soil*—together they give rise to human perfection."

"I wish that we could have such a civilization again."

"It is essential, lad. The Masters have been making preparation toward that end for thousands of years. The civilization they are helping to recreate will be the most perfect of all. It is to be called the 'Kingdom of God.' In that nation men will enjoy a form of government perfected long ago by highly advanced Egos. All the great inventions long lost to man will be made available to that nation. When the 'climate' of enlightened government has been developed, the 'seed' of truth will come in magnificent glory. The Archangel, Melchizedek, the Christ, will come again in human form to guide mankind. At an accelerated pace we will see human beings advance toward Mastership."

"Will I live long enough to see that nation?" the boy asked meekly.

Dr. White smiled and began to laugh in a very happy way. "It's you, Richard, who have been appointed to begin that nation."

Richard was stunned.

Dr. White's eyes twinkled as he viewed the boy's consternation. He further explained, "A nation such as the Kingdom of God cannot achieve the beginning of its intended grandeur in less than five centuries; but even the beginning will so greatly surpass anything within man's present knowledge, that it will be hailed as an achievement in itself. Understandably, establishing a new nation is a project of considerable magnitude and complexity. Many persons will be needed who have special talents to contribute.

"Your specialty will be the co-ordinating of an advanced community and subsequently a new nation colonized from it. Your inborn ability to perceive the character and motives of people is an essential aptitude. But again let me caution you. Don't verbalize your analyses of people. This is offensive and deleterious to co-operative effort. Judge wisely but kindly. Change your judgments as you perceive another's character growth. Encourage advancement, and forget and forgive shortcomings that have been outgrown.

"Among other things, you are to be known as 'Judge of Israel.' With God's help, let us pray that you are worthy of the title."

"Israel has something to do with the Jews, doesn't it?"

"Not in its greater meaning! Israel is a very ancient term used long before the day of Abraham. On the great island where man had his beginning, the land was composed of many valleys each approximately the size of the Mississippi River Valley. Over a period of a half-million years the people occupying each of the twelve more-or-less isolated areas developed racial characteristics peculiar to the respective valley. Different skin color, physical size, and special adaptations relating to variant climate arose. Each race also took on strongly developed personality traits.

"When the first civilized nation began, it was a consolidation of the twelve primitive tribes. The consolidation was termed 'Israel'; and inasmuch as every man belonged to one of the tribes, all Mankind was referred to as the 'Twelve Tribes of Israel.' Therefore, the meaning I intend when I say 'Israel' is all Mankind."

"But what is meant by judging Israel?"

"Equal representation of the twelve original tribes must be fairly apportioned among the inhabitants of the Kingdom of God. This is important in order that a balanced civilization be recapitulated. Twelve thousand representatives of each tribe will be selected from the first community you found in order to populate the forerunner-nation of the great, final civilization. A Universal Race will generate from these hundred forty-four thousand selected persons. The selection will be the Judgment, and it will occur during your jurisdiction.[1]

"The future inhabitants of the Kingdom of God are incarnating now. For the most part they are persons who have not incarnated for twelve to fifteen thousand years—not since the last great civilization was extant. They have avoided incarnating into the turbulent millennia between then and now because the times were not conducive to soul advancement. They have had to wait

---

This selection will be made by the Brotherhoods from among Brothers everywhere in the world as well as from the community founded by Richard.

a long time to resume their way along the path to Mastership. Fortunately, there has always been a sprinkling of higher Egos within every generation to prepare the way toward the realization of the Kingdom of God. Western Civilization has acquired its concepts of humane ideals by way of a grand conspiracy by Masters and Adepts."

"But why hadn't this sort of thing been done before we have only seven thousand years left?"

"Because man must raise himself by his own effort. If Christ, the Angels, or Masters did it for him, he would be as a puppet. There are, however, reasons beyond man's control which delayed our advancement.

"Man on this planet did not progress as was to be normally expected during the first 400,000 years after he began incarnating. Jehovah, having been responsible for our creation, was loathe to bring us to the trials that would make us grow through adversity. Instead, He provided man with a superabundance of readily gathered food in a subtropical climate. That was Eden which was located somewhat north and west of the present Hawaiian Islands. There man lived, bred, ate, and slept. He did not begin upon the path to greatness because he had no need or incentive. In effect, man as a race vegetated. Instead of advancing from innocence to virtue, he remained a clod.

"This state of affairs gave rise to two factions in our Angelic Host. On one side were those who believed, as did Jehovah, that man would attain his destiny more readily in a serene environment free from the distractions of strife. The other faction believed that only through hardship and struggle would men actively seek the better way and thus strive for perfection. The latter belief was more in keeping with the history of man's rise elsewhere in the universe. It is a hard way, but the quickest and most effective. Even though the passing millennia demonstrated that man was not learning and was indeed lagging far behind human life on the other planets, Jehovah and his followers clung to Their altruistic experiment. Those other Angels who differed with Jehovah finally took matters into Their own hands and set about to destroy Eden. This was done under the leadership of the great Angel, Lucifer, to whom we owe the advantages of our present advancement.

"Earthquakes and the first glacial period of the pleistocene epoch destroyed Eden, and man had to struggle to remain alive. He had to hunt, contend with wild beasts, learn how to protect himself, work to provide for his needs, and co-operate with others to defend what small lands he needed for the cattle he later learned to domesticate. Man began on the road to advancement.

"Unfortunately, man became very learned in the arts of war. In times of famine and over-population he resorted to killing in order to take the land he needed for his own sustenance. If he had learned co-operation instead of war, his history might have been far different.

"The world is again on the brink of war because fools in power really believe war is the surest way to settle disputes. But those who accept the inevitability of war are destined to be destroyed by it. Armageddon," he sighed, "will finally put an end to war."

"What's Armageddon?"

"It is a series of wars, or more exactly one war with pauses, which began in 1914 and will grow more destructive and vicious as this century draws to its close. Armageddon's violent culmination will take place about a year before the turn of the century. It is a major instrument of the Judgment."

"Can't the Masters stop it?"

"They could; but may not! To interfere with the natural outworkings of human self-determination is forbidden to advanced Egos. Man has forged the means of his own destruction. But you Richard, will sound the call to unite those Egos who are now incarnating to build the new nation. Those souls who are inclined toward peace will hear and respond."

"You mean I'm supposed to start a new religion?"

"No! Mankind has had enough of that! *Truth* is what man needs. True, the religions of the world are somewhat based on universal truth but only smatterings of it. Yet churches have done a wonderful job with the little information with which they have had to work. The *whole* truth must be incorporated into a grand philosophy which, incidentally, will enrich all presently established religions. Christ didn't reveal all of His message nineteen centuries ago—just part of it. The Masters, in conjunction with Christ, have prepared the way for unveiling all of the

47

secrets of God which are within the ken of men's minds. This information will be made available to those persons who will act upon such information properly. Just three years ago the facilities to disseminate that information were established on Earth."

Richard shook his head doubtfully. "The whole thing begins to sound like you're fooling me. How could I do all those things? I'm not even interested in such matters."

Dr. White grew sternly serious and replied, "What I'm telling you is no joke! A great deal depends upon you. Before you incarnated into your present body, you made arrangements with the Masters to allow Them to interfere in your life to the extent that They might guide you along the right road and train you properly. You have a specialized body which, with proper care, will maintain its youth and vigor for an exceptionally long time. However, you still enjoy free will; and if you are determined to do so, you can throw away this opportunity. If you *do* demur, other arrangements will be made to substitute for you.

"Because you're a child, I cannot expect you to understand the great tasks and responsibilities I've outlined. It takes a lot of living to make a life, and no one becomes a man overnight. Maturity comes to us piecemeal. Have faith and belief in what you are taught until you grow to the point where you can fully understand and *know* that what you have been told is truth. Much information must be accepted blindly until such time as you can test it and prove it to yourself. Experience is the test of truth. As a student, you are obliged to regard everything you are taught as being true. For instance, you could not possibly know firsthand all the scientific principles you have been persuaded to believe.

"Religion is at a disadvantage now that the Bible has often been contradicted by scientific findings. But religion and science have their major purpose in common: both seek the why, whither, and whence of human existence. Science purports to demonstrate our beginning and has considerable physical evidence to support its conclusions. Religion is primarily concerned with our purpose on Earth and our destiny. Both these fields of philosophy will continually merge into a unified area of truth.

"Cultism and fanaticism have given religion an unsavory taint which has turned away many persons who could benefit from religion. However, science fanatics are as bigoted as religious fanatics. Fanaticism is a trait of the immature mind, and those who exhibit it are to be avoided.

"Be wary of fanatics and the merely curious who delight in esoteric knowledge so they may appear knowing of hidden mysteries. You will know the sincere persons! They unobtrusively practice higher morality and use advanced information for practical advancement of themselves and others.

"Live the Golden Rule, Richard. Empathy and kindly consideration implement it. Be conscientious in all things, but take care that you don't appear goody-goody. Be natural; a man among men; enjoy human beings; don't affect superiority just because you come to possess great information. You must make your way through life without leaving ripples in your wake, for this is the skill of living.

"Be courageous to teach that which must be taught. To be persecuted for one's convictions seems inevitable. Yet, to allow yourself to assume a persecution complex or a martyr complex is self-defeating. Trust others, for it is better to be fooled occasionally than to be suspicious. Weigh your actions carefully before you act. After you've made a decision, don't be afraid of failure. Failure is an impostor; and when, like Lincoln, you have learned this thoroughly, you may pursue righteousness with confidence. Your greatest opposition will come from those closest to you. They will be the ones most ambitious for you to be successful by the standards of the times. If you are too much influenced by your family and friends, you will belong to the world instead of to Christ.

"All these admonitions will be proven to you during your early life so that you will be ready to begin in earnest your tasks for mankind's uplift when you have reached your middle thirties. Wait patiently, learn, observe, and grow ready. Remain obscure, and don't be blatant in your beliefs. Don't attract attention before we can prepare you thoroughly. Your life will certainly be an eventful one; so don't go looking for trouble—you will be presented with just the right amount of it."

At this point, the man and boy arrived at Central Avenue where they waited for a break in the stream of cars so they could cross. After a hurried crossing, the boy was surprised to note that he had taken the elderly gentleman's hand in the process.

The comfortable feeling induced by Dr. White's presence was a puzzle to Richard. The man was a stranger but not at all *like* a stranger. The penetrating gaze of the man's violet eyes was sometimes disconcerting but always wonderfully warm. A unique atmosphere of peace enveloped the boy while Dr. White was near.

They strolled along the path in Portage Park for a short distance to where the shrubbery veiled them from general view. Dr. White stopped and asked the boy, "Will you take on such tasks as are appointed you by the Masters, Richard?"

"I'm sort of mixed up right now to be certain."

"What do you really *want* to do about it?"

"I'd like to do what I'm able."

Dr. White removed from his pocket a tiny silver flask with blue porcelain designs. "Kneel before me Richard!" he requested.

"But someone might come," Richard blurted in fear of embarrassment.

"No one will come," Dr. White insisted.

Richard somehow knew that Dr. White's assurance was in itself a shield. Rather awkwardly, the boy got down on both knees. Dr. White put one hand on Richard's head so that the boy had to look straight down at the ground.

"Now hear the offices and titles by which you shall be known! For thou art the Harbinger of Aquarius, the Judge of Israel, the Builder of Lemuria, and the Fountainhead of Christ, which is the translation of the new name I give you now. In the presence of this assembly, you are herewith consecrated to God for the benefit of man." And with the pronouncement of the new name, Dr. White emptied the contents of the vial upon Richard's head.

"Hold this name sacred and reveal it to no man. With blood and pain it shall soon be made part of you so that you may not escape your identity. Now close your eyes and give silent thanks to God!"

As the boy closed his eyes, he felt Dr. White remove his hand from his head; and this caused him to look up. To Richard's utter astonishment there was no one there. He hurriedly rose from his knees and peered in every direction. He was completely alone! Sudden panic overcame him, and the boy wanted to run, but there was nothing to run from or toward. After a moment, that feeling of peace returned, and he looked around fully expecting to see Dr. White nearby. The strange conviction that the elderly gentleman was close persisted even though there was nobody to be seen.

Richard thought perhaps the whole thing was an hallucination, except that the sweet-smelling oil oozing down his face decided him against that explanation. Slowly, the boy turned and walked back home. His mind was awhirl with the events of the day which he reviewed as best he could as he went.

When he arrived home, his mother took him to task for getting "all that junk" in his hair. He didn't offer an explanation nor was he much disturbed by his mother's irritation with him. He declined a regular lunch and spent the afternoon in a reverie. The philosophical upheaval which began on this day marked for Richard the onset of adolescence.

CHAPTER 4

The Brotherhoods

Three weeks after Richard's birthday, the outbreak of World War II was headlined in the Sunday newspapers. France and England had declared war against Germany in defense of Poland, and Richard was aghast that large and seemingly stable nations would resort to wholesale destruction and killing in an attempt to solve their differences. But he was not politically sophisticated enough to appreciate the circumstances leading to the war; and the boy was too much impressed by the butchery and insanity of the recent Ethiopian and Spanish wars to accept any justifications for the major powers of Europe indulging in even greater violence. His respect for the dignified-looking adults in charge of running the nations of the world was severely shaken.

A heavy sadness burdened the boy whenever he thought of war. His innate empathy obliged him to feel the hurts of everyone suffering at the hands of man's most stupid convention. To Richard, mankind was a precious, marvelous, soaring concept of greatness. The ignorant, the foolish, the thoughtless, the hateful, and the corrupt individuals to be found among mankind were intolerable to him. They spoiled the picture of what he felt men were supposed to be or at least could be. But these ideas, as he found out when he tried to talk to other children or adults about them, were alien to the minds of those with whom he sought to commiserate.

He had the strange feeling that he was a lonely island in a great sea of indifference. He came up against the wall people erect to protect themselves from serious discussion of anything important. He rather sensed that his elders felt him to be pretty small game for philosophic or political argument; but some people just refused to speak in anything other than platitudes or jests concerning serious matters, and young people apparently never had a philosophic question cross their minds. Such charges against people in general would appear justified, but Richard believed that these persons were exhibiting variations of a protective device. No one wants to stand for any particular idea for fear of being considered queer. Almost everyone's deepest and most profoundly exhilarating flights of imagination are destined to be withheld from other people's approbation for fear of misunderstanding or laughter. People seem intrinsically abashed by their own greatness; perhaps because when one was a child, one's innermost thoughts were vulnerable targets for jeering ego-deflation when verbalized. Richard would often see much wisdom within people bursting to be told; but youth will not listen, and the chronic preacher is an irksome bore. As a consequence, much beauty is never transmitted.

Richard and his parents moved into their new home about two months after the school year began, and the boy's transfer into a different school allowed him to start anew among classmates who had no cause for preconceptions about him. He made friends and maintained casual good relations with everyone in the class. These small social successes engendered his old self-confidence, and he unfolded his personality to the world-at-large. His interest in school work revived; and although his scholastic achievement at John Mills School was far from spectacular, he began to learn how to study. In short, Richard began to enjoy a happy frame of mind.

It was on the 27th of November, 1939, that his new friends invited Richard to go along with them to the Elm Theater to see a moving picture which their teacher had suggested would be particularly interesting. Richard asked his parents if he could walk to the show with the others, and he employed all the best arguments he could think of. Much to his amazement he was given permission to go. There were many admonitions and warnings included by his mother and father, but he was to be allowed for the first time to see an evening movie without the accompaniment of his parents.

Richard got a somewhat late start from home; so he walked alone directly to the theater. As he hurried past the school building through the dark November chill, he heard a man call his name from the direction of the school. Richard thought the man probably was calling someone else named Richard, but he stopped to peer at the caller to be sure. The man stood in the open front-door of the school, and Richard could see by the light from the hallway behind the man that he was dressed in janitor's garb. However, he was nobody the boy had ever seen before. The man beckoned him to come closer, but Richard was afraid to get involved with a strange man on a dark night.

The janitor held the door open lest it close and lock him out, and with his free hand he motioned again for the boy to come near. "Don't be afraid, Richard!" he said. The voice had the same unique gentleness as Dr. White's, but it certainly was not he. Richard's curiosity was aroused; so with his adrenals ready to send him into a dead run if needed, he cautiously approached the stranger.

The man was heavy-set with a smooth face that was pleasantly full but not fat. Although he was elderly, he stood straight and strong. It seemed to Richard as if he could have been a wrestler in his younger days. The voice was clear and strong—seeming to emanate from a large barrel—and he spoke with an English gentleman's precise, clipped accent.

"Good evening," he smiled down at Richard. "My name is Berkeley. I believe we have a mutual friend called Dr. White."

That strange flooding of peaceful warmth seemed to enfold the boy when he heard the name, and all apprehension departed as he mounted the step to shake the man's outstretched hand.

Berkeley held the door open for Richard and said, "Please come inside where we can talk. I have special news for you."

Richard eagerly entered the familiar building.

"Why don't we go up to your classroom, Richard? We can sit down there and talk more at ease."

Richard nodded approval, and they proceeded together. The halls were dimly lit and looked strange by night. The boy was used to the hurry and bustle of children in the building; now the familiar seemed eerily unfamiliar. They made their way to Richard's home classroom in which all the lights were on. The man opened the door at the rear and motioned the boy to enter. When Richard saw what was in the room, he stopped short.

Never in his life had he seen such a sight as he now beheld!

There in the front of the room sat seven men on chairs arranged in a semicircle. To the boy's eyes they were a strange looking group because he had never before seen a gathering of so many races at one time. Although the surprise at seeing the men might otherwise have been frightening, a deeply pervading feeling of well-being and safety enfolded him. The men didn't smile or frown or, for that matter, indicate any thought or convey any intent. They all looked at the boy steadfastly, searchingly. For a full minute everyone was virtually motionless.

Seated at the far left was a tall, blond Nordic man; next to him sat a Mediterranean—dark-haired, square-jawed, and broadly built; the next man appeared to be a Greek of medium build with a handsome, curly, black beard; in the center sat a gracefully proportioned Chinese of slight build; a broad-shouldered Semitic was just right of center, and the man next to him was also a Semitic whose face was narrow and dark in color; a well-fed looking Hindu completed the group. They all wore the same kind of white, loose-fitting monk's robe and were bare headed.

The feeling of friendly acceptance that emanated from the group put Richard totally at ease. However, the boy had the very strong impression that these men were something more wondrously special than he had ever imagined of human beings. He wanted to bow or kneel before them in acknowledgment of his unexplainable spontaneous respect. But not knowing how to properly express this peculiar desire, he looked up at Berkeley for some sign of further instruction. At that point, the Chinese seated in the center spoke.

"Won't you please come in and stand closer that we may more easily see you?" His tone had qualities of gentleness and consideration that were unprecedented in Richard's experience. The pitch of his voice was high for a man, but his motions and manner were strikingly masculine and sweeping.

Richard stood in the midst of the seven men for their inspection. The Chinese spoke again with a pleased smile, "You have devised a body very apropos to your tasks in this lifetime. Congratulations!"

The boy was embarrassed by reason of his inability to understand. He shuffled his feet uncomfortably.

"Would you care to sit down?" the Chinese spokesman asked.

Richard looked back at the students' desks behind him, and while doing so caught a glimpse of Berkeley who subtly signaled against sitting down. The boy turned again and replied, "No, sir, I think I'll stand."

The entire group smiled in approval, and their spokesman continued, "You know you have serious and important tasks assigned to you!" he said with deep concern.

"Dr. White spoke to me about it," Richard replied. "Yet I still don't see why you pick me."

"Don't concern yourself at present, Richard. We know well the man who now functions in the child's body. We have no doubts; why, then, should you be fearful of your ability to fulfill your goal?"

The boy stood without reply. He could think of many reasons to doubt his ability, but it was apparent that to pursue this doubt was out of place at the moment.

"We have met here for a specific purpose, Richard," the Chinese said in a reverent tone. "These, my Brothers in Christ, have come from distant places to officiate at the ceremony for which you have been summoned."

"What ceremony?" Richard asked quickly.

"The one concerning the name which has been given you; for did not our Brother, Dr. White, tell you that soon it would be made part of your body?"

A sinking fear took hold of the boy which not even the sweet sense of Love filling the room could ameliorate. He blanched and felt a little faint.

"Why do you tremble, Richard?" the Chinese asked sympathetically.

"Dr. White said 'in blood and pain' it would be made part of me," the boy answered with closed eyes. He thought he might cry.

"Most fears are engendered of those things which we imagine but do not know. Do you think that we shall harm you?"

"No!"

"These things must be endured because they are essential. Most certainly we will not cripple you! You can bear a dentist's ministrations because you know his work is for your benefit;

furthermore, you realize the pain he causes is unavoidable and is of short duration, and so it is more easily withstood."

"Yes. I know," the boy agreed.

"The ceremony you face at the moment is parallel to the example I have just given. We would not, however, ask you to submit yourself blindly. The name the Lord has ordained unto you will be cut into your skin where it will be hidden by clothing, and the scar tissues will be pigmented so that it will be brightly legible for the rest of your life."

"Do you give me gas or something?" Richard asked hopefully.

"No anesthesia," the Chinese said softly.

The boy clenched his fists tightly. The sweat in the palms of his hands seemed cold and deathly. "Then let's do it as soon as we can. I don't want to have to think about it too long."

The men smiled cheerily which made Richard feel somewhat better; and having made the decision, his anxiety was lessened.

With a slight motion of his hand the spokesman instructed, "Berkeley, prepare whatever is needed!"

Berkeley quickly produced the necessary equipment, and requested that the boy lie on his side upon the teacher's desk which had been moved aside to make room for the semicircle. Richard was required to lower his trousers whereupon Berkeley cleaned the skin and began to cut without delay. The boy held perfectly still without being instructed to do so even as he felt the knife cutting into him. He perspired profusely from the muscular exertion of maintaining silence and immobility. The pain was unexpectedly intense, and the boy was made all the more squeamish as he felt his blood running down the side of his leg.

After about a minute he focused his eyes upon the men who sat quietly intent on the proceedings. Simultaneously they all seemed to turn their attention to the boy's grim face, and at that moment all physical awareness departed from the boy. From the corner of his eye Richard could see that Berkeley was still operating, but now he felt strangely remote from reality as if disembodied.

"Why did you do that?" the boy asked pleasantly.

The Chinese replied, "There was no need of suffering. You have done your part."

They turned their attention again to Berkeley's work which

took another fifteen minutes. Finally he announced, "It's done!"

The Chinese stood up and the other six did likewise. "Now those things have come to pass which were required of this date according to prophecy. Praise the Lord who fulfills His promise that your kingdom and throne are established forever. You, Richard, possess the Key of David by which your continued works are given authority. Now, to the extent that you are with Us, We are with you. Give thanks to Christ who guides us all!"

The spokesman smiled broadly, bowed slightly and vanished into thin air. In a twinkling only seven empty chairs stood before the dumbfounded boy. He rolled over to see that Berkeley was still standing there. "Don't go away!" Richard pleaded.

"I won't," Berkeley assured him. "We have much to talk about tonight."

"I don't think I can stand to have people disappear ever again."

"I can understand that," Berkeley said with a wry smile of sympathy. "Come on, you can get up now."

Richard got to his feet and buckled his belt. "I still don't have any feeling where you cut me."

"You probably won't for many hours to come."

"I feel normal all over now except that where you were working is still numb. Did they do that or did you?"

"They did."

"How?"

Berkeley looked thoughtful for a moment and said, "I thought for a moment that it was by telepathically imposed hypnosis that you were anesthetized, but I perceive now that the etheric pattern for that nerve path has been altered so that the nerve must regenerate for a short distance. It will afford prolonged painlessness."

"What do you mean, you 'perceive now'?" Richard asked shrewdly.

Berkeley sighed as though with tiredness and stepped over to one of the chairs and sat down. He seemed troubled as to whether he should evade the question or answer it. After a moment he explained, "There are many persons who can perceive the Vital and Astral Bodies of living creatures. In order to heal sick physical bodies, it is very advantageous to be able to look within the Vital Body to see where deficiencies really are. I merely looked within you to see what means had been effected to relieve your pain."

"Is it a fairly common ability among adults to see the invisible bodies of the higher planes?"

"Not at all," Berkeley exclaimed with eyebrows raised in astonishment. "What makes you ask such a thing?"

"It's just that adults don't talk much about what they seriously believe. I just had wondered if most people were clairvoyant but just didn't mention it."

"Well, I'll grant you that more people have the ability than are willing to admit it," Berkeley said. "As a rule it is a rare ability, but most people can be trained in it."

"While you're in an answering mood, perhaps you can tell me how Dr. White and the gentlemen here tonight can just evaporate."

Berkeley chuckled. "I can see that really bothers you. Dr. White merely imposed a hypnotic suggestion that you could not see him even though he was present. The Masters who seemed present here tonight worked it just the opposite—They were here Egoically but not physically."

"Masters?" Richard started. "But why didn't someone tell me?"

"Because They were aware that were you to have known, you would have behaved differently in a way that would have interfered with your decision tonight. You will never have a chance to thank Them, or worship Them, or truly acknowledge Their greatness, for They anticipate your every thought. Some way or another They will divert your attention from Themselves to the purpose They have in mind."

Richard stood in contemplation and tried to savor the emotion of having been so close to not only one, but seven Masters. He hated himself for not having been aware of Their greatness at the time.

Berkeley broke into the boy's musings and said, "Sit down and be comfortable."

Richard complied in an automatic way; and as he sat down, a thought suddenly occurred to him. "Say, isn't the light in here likely to attract attention?"

"Don't give it a second thought. Our presence here is veiled, as it were. No one will know or suspect anything out of the ordinary. By the time I leave later tonight everything will be in order."

"You mean that you use telepathic hypnosis to veil us?"

Berkeley winced. "As a matter of fact, that device is rarely used by persons seeking to achieve spiritual purity. Hypnosis may *never* be used for self-aggrandizement, for control over others, for display of 'magic,' or for evoking awe or worship from others."

"Didn't Dr. White use it though?"

"But only because it was necessary to impress upon you the authority with which he spoke. Had he merely walked away or boarded a bus and rode away, you might have decided he was just a crackpot. He saw that it was essential to perform a 'miracle' to penetrate any last defenses against your wholly believing him. Perhaps only once in a century does a Brother use hypnosis in a way that adds to his own prestige. But great things are at hand, and you have seen more than any man since those who witnessed the mighty Christ walk the Earth. Incidentally, Christ used the same device for disappearing when He was in danger or was beset by crowds. The High Adept, Moses, used telepathic hypnosis when He made His rod turn into a snake before the pharaoh. The Egyptian priests were also able to perform the feat with ease; but because He was an Adept, Moses was able to verify the superiority of His power by causing His 'snake' to devour those of the priests. The priests and pharaoh were thus imbued with a proper awe of Moses' personal power.

"However, these are rare occasions of the use of hypnosis; and whenever used by a Brother, it is not for the purpose of gaining hold over the hapless subject of the hypnosis."

"What do you mean by the term *brother*? You seem to place a special meaning on the word when you use it."

"Ah! That is the main subject of our discussion for tonight, Richard. I'm glad you brought it up." Berkeley leaned back and smiled. The large, powerfully built man displayed a ready joviality. Richard found the man's manner reminiscent of Santa Claus. The unruly shock of thick white hair that emerged from beneath the old gentleman's cap when he removed it further enhanced the boy's impression.

Berkeley continued, "You have already learned of Masters and Adepts; but another important bit of information for you to know is that all Masters and Adepts work within the framework of an organized association known as a Brotherhood. There are twelve Brotherhoods throughout the world. Five of the Brotherhoods are composed of only Masters who function exclusively upon the Mental Plane of existence. These five are known as the Greater Brotherhoods. Their members engage in highly transcendent philosophical pursuits of great importance to the increasing uplift of mankind. The remaining seven Brotherhoods are composed of Masters and Adepts plus other advanced human Egos whom They have selected from among mankind for special attention and instruction in order that they too can be elevated to Adeptship.

"All the Brotherhoods were personally organized by Melchizedek, The Christ, and each was established to perform some major task in looking after mankind. The oldest and most important of the seven Lesser Brotherhoods was established about twenty thousand years ago. The most recent was established about five thousand years ago. The principle reasons for the organization of the Brotherhoods are: to provide facilities for instruction of worthy candidates aspiring to human perfection; to garner all knowledge of the truths of existence; to preserve a continuous history of mankind; to relate and analyze the causes for the successes and failures of civilizations developed by man; to prepare the way for the perfect Kingdom of God; to implement Christ's plans; and to protect and guide the entire population of the world.

"The Brotherhoods are composed of the finest men and women of every race, and for thousands of years these individuals have functioned in *perfect* harmony and close co-operation."

"There are women in the Brotherhoods?" Richard asked with great surprise.

"Certainly!"

"I guess the thought just never occurred to me."

"As a matter of fact, every degree of advancement attained by an Ego, male or female, takes place only under the supervision of a Brotherhood and in accordance with a Natural Law established by God. This law prevents the advancement of an Ego until there is another Ego of the opposite polarity, or sex, to act as a balancing complement. For every male Master, there is a female Master. Through every degree of Adeptship the number of male and female is precisely the same. For every human being on Earth there is a member of the opposite sex somewhere in the world to balance exactly his advancement—however high or however base. How and why this balance is maintained so scrupulously is a Celestial Mystery, but it probably is associated with the fact that Egos were created either male or female in the beginning and cannot be altered."[1]

"Do male Egos always incarnate into male bodies, and do female Egos always incarnate into female bodies?" the boy asked.

"Always! Typically masculine and feminine traits are part of the Ego's soul characteristics and manifest even in infants at a very early age.

"Getting back to my discussion of the Brotherhoods, Richard, Their close world-wide co-operation has been maintained by instantaneous intercommunication by telepathy which is taught Them."

Richard interrupted Berkeley. "You say I've been hypnotized telephatically; yet science says that there is no such thing as telepathy. How come?"

"Probably because telepathic thought-transference is just so much nonsense to a person not trained in its use; but to one who uses it daily, it is a fact from which, obviously, nobody can dissuade him. What is more, Adepts of the Brotherhoods have long since mastered time, space, energy, and the atom; but this is presumed impossible by those whose minds have not yet grown aware of all of nature's secrets.

"Six of the seven Lesser Brotherhoods have been actively engaged in disseminating the great truths entrusted to Them for mankind's advancement. Because there are basic personality types in the world, each of the Brotherhoods has developed and perfected a mode of appeal to the group of people assigned to

---

[1]This statement is correct so far as it goes; however, approximately seven percent of human Egos are able to change back and forth from one sexual polarity to the other. This in no way accounts for homosexuality.

its jurisdiction. Strictly speaking, the Brotherhoods and Their members do not in any way control the activities of human beings or their institutions. *Never* will the Brotherhoods interfere in the affairs of a nation. Neither will They operate in the environment of any individual without expressed invitation to do so, and even then They help only if the person who has invited Them has done his very best to help himself and can go no further without aid.

"The Brotherhoods often show mankind the way by arranging for a philosopher to expound 'new' ideas for men either to accept or reject as they will. Each man must elevate himself! No one can do it for him! A great many historical personages were spokesmen developed by the Brotherhoods. For instance: Moses and Socrates were trained by the Hermetic Brotherhood; Jesus and John the Baptist and Their respective parents by the Essene Brotherhood; Buddha by the Brahmic Brotherhood; and George Washington and Benjamin Franklin by the Luciferian Brotherhood.

"Such training is begun through mundane preparatory schools; and as the individual advances in character and mental abilities, he is later contacted directly by the Brotherhoods. All the Lesser Brotherhoods now have preparatory schools in the United States of America which is the only country in the world so graced. The most ancient of the seven Lesser Brotherhoods opened its first and only school just three years ago. The inauguration of this school on September 16, 1936, is one of the most important signals planned by Christ and the Great White Brotherhood. On that date was celebrated the Feast of Trumpets as the Seventh 'Angel' sounded the Seventh Trumpet, thus heralding the revelation of God's mysteries to men. That day was prophesied in the Great Pyramid of Gizeh and in the Book of Revelation (*10:7*).

"Until 1936, each Lesser Brotherhood concentrated on the promotion of its appointed 'mystery,' which means a *profound truth*. Because of this term, the mundane schools operated by the Brotherhoods are often called Mystery Schools. Regardless of nationality or race, a person may be specifically in need of solving a major personality problem essential to his advancement. Practicality, for instance, may be deficient in a man's character so that it precludes a satisfactory adjustment to the earning of a livelihood; or it may be lack of efficiency, precision, balance, love, devotion, or brotherhood. The Brotherhoods know which person will benefit most from a particular mystery or lesson, and They will expose him to situations conducive to developing his own successful solutions. If the man is of sufficient intellect and seems amenable to secret instruction, he is unknowingly guided to contact the appropriate mundane school.

"Since 1936, all the Lesser Brotherhoods have come under the direction of the oldest of the seven. The whole program of developing a civilization worthy of the Kingdom of God is now co-ordinated by a council of seven representative Masters, one from each Brotherhood."

The boy asked, "Is that who was here this evening?"

"That is a discerning observation. Unfortunately, I may not answer that question to your satisfaction."

"It's strange that a Chinese man seemed to be the one in charge," Richard observed.

"He is a Master, not a Chinese."

"What do you mean by that?"

"Until He chose the body you visualized here this evening, He had incarnated into practically every race and nationality. He doesn't have an oriental mind or an occidental mind but rather the Universal Mind of Mastership. Just before attaining Mastership, an Ego sometimes incarnates again to develop a perfect, immortal, physical vehicle to use whenever his appearance among mortals is necessary. For His final, glorified body the spokesman of tonight's group chose a body of the oriental race because His most famous incarnation as a beloved Lemurian Emperor of all humankind occurred when He was using an oriental body."

"You were talking about the Brotherhoods' mundane schools," Richard said. "Can you tell me what religion they teach?"

"The Brotherhoods have developed and trained virtually every true spiritual leader after whom has arisen a great religion; but the Brotherhoods Themselves are in no way whatever connected with any religion. Mankind has institutionalized and corrupted the truths of every great religious leader's teachings to the point where the religion as practiced today has little resemblance to the philosophy of the man who inspired it. For this reason the Brotherhoods promote no religion among men. They preserve Their knowledge in unprofaned perfection by entrusting truth only to those Egos who have achieved the deeper understanding necessary to fully appreciate it. As each degree of advancement is earned by a man, he is granted information appropriate to his increased awareness. He is expected to use and test the information to further advance himself spiritually.

"The Brotherhoods build no temples, but each maintains a physical headquarters hidden within a mountain retreat. They remain far removed from the interference of men and the machinations of civilization. In short, there is no way to identify Them or to find Them. However, by Their own means They contact the worthy seeker of truth who has made the effort to seek a teacher; for when the student is ready, the teacher appears. The Brothers are always on the alert for those who can contribute to the uplifting of mankind. But even if a direct contact is made, the candidate is not likely to realize the Brother with whom he is dealing is anything other than an ordinary man.

"Whoever makes himself known as a Brother, whether by so declaring or by acting and talking in such a way as to convey the impression, is surely an impostor. A Brother may under no circumstances reveal His identity as such to anyone but another Brother. The outstanding characteristics of a Brother are his boundless patience, love of mankind, all-pervading kindliness, unassuming nature, and His humble, almost self-effacing demeanor. He is efficient while giving the appearance of unhurried calm, and He brings an air of serenity wherever He goes. He does not affect piousness or superiority or a grand manner. He cannot be discerned from the majority of mankind except by long observation, for Brothers remain unobtrusive.

"Were They to display Their amazing abilities, the Brothers would be persecuted because of man's basic fear of the unusual. Those courageous Brothers whose work for mankind has required Their revealing superior powers have universally been persecuted and often killed. Were all Brothers to function openly in the world as it is today, They would be so occupied with overcoming the enmity, distrust, and vicious scorn of the

65

general populace that They would have little time to concentrate on Their great work. The one worthwhile leaven of hope for mankind would thereby be seriously hampered."

"You talk about degrees of advancement," Richard mused. "Does that mean there is instruction which entitles a person to another degree when he has finished the course? You know— like Bachelor's degree and Doctoral degree?"

"No, this is quite different," Berkeley stated. "The degrees of advancement recognized and conferred by the Brotherhoods are rigidly established. The degrees are distinct measures of true advancement toward human perfection. They aren't academic. There are twelve degrees of advancement. The highest—the twelfth degree—is the mark of Mastership. After an Ego has passed the seventh degree, He is known as an Adept and needs no longer function upon the physical plane in physical incarnation. The tenth degree entitles one to be known as a High Adept. The first through seventh degrees are indications of control over one's self and one's environment among those Brothers still bound to physical existence.

"To attain the first degree of Brotherhood, an Ego must possess: spiritual and emotional balance, control over his body to the extent that he has superlative health and stamina, controlled clairvoyant ability, a cheerful and willing personality, a long record of good works which compensate for any sinful errors of past incarnations, and a high level of skill in at least one trade or profession. Perhaps the most important qualification of all is the burning desire to be a Brother and work untiringly for the advancement of mankind."

"No wonder it takes three thousand incarnations to become a Brother," Richard sighed.

"True! But once the first degree has been earned, the advancement toward the attainment of the twelfth degree becomes more and more accelerated. Even so, it is no easy task to achieve Mastership, for a Master must know everything possible to be known on the first four planes of existence and be highly proficient in at least one-hundred-forty-four trades, arts and professions."

"It hardly seems possible for one person to know so much," Richard gasped.

"Unfortunately, to say that a Master has all knowledge of the first four planes doesn't convey anywhere near the magnificent greatness of Mastership, for *you* can't *begin* to visualize the powers available to man on the higher planes. Even the unlimited Goodness and Love of the Masters is beyond your comprehension. The charity, patience, forbearance, and humility of these Egos laboring for the good of all those persons below Them are not qualities we are likely to encounter in our relationships with men on earth—at least not to the extent to which Masters have refined and intensified them. The Masters are perfectly free from hate, fear, envy, lust, and pride. They are the Perfect Ones! They are above evil forevermore!"

Richard was carried along by the reverent awe in Berkeley's tone whenever he spoke of Masters. A hint of Their greatness was beginning to dawn in him. After a moment the boy said, "A while back, you mentioned the names of some men whom you said were trained by the Brotherhoods. Were they Masters?"

"Buddha and Jesus were each an eleventh degree Brother who had incarnated in order to have a perfect physical body for His Mastership. Buddha's philosophy of brotherly love and tolerance was His mission. Jesus developed what was perhaps the finest physical vehicle ever possessed by a human Ego on Earth for the specific purpose of providing a human body for the Archangel, Melchizedek, to occupy during His ministry as the Christ.

"Moses and John the Baptist were both High Adepts who incarnated for important work. John's and Jesus' parents were Adepts, all of whom came into incarnation expressly in order to bear and rear Their eminent sons. Socrates was granted the first degree just before his transition; and Washington and Franklin were highly advanced students of the mundane school of a Brotherhood. They had not received their first degree, but they were nearing completion of the requirements."

"That was the Luciferian School, right?" Richard asked in order to impress the name on his mind.

"Not exactly," Berkeley corrected. "They were under the guidance of the Masonic inner court. The inner court is the core of Masonry of which almost no present-day Masons have understanding. The Masons grant degrees, too, but their degrees are academic at best. Except for the symbolism associated with a degree, a Masonic degree has come to be virtually meaningless. Freemasonry at the time of King Solomon had a real value toward preparing Egos for the first degree of Brotherhood. There was a resurgence of its original purpose about the time of the American and French Revolutions, but now it has been degraded by the shallowness of its members into little more than a social club. A conscientious student of symbolic lore can still learn there if he is determined to do so, but conscientiousness is rapidly becoming passé in America. Other mundane preparatory schools, like the Rosicrucian and Theosophist, are suffering acutely from the general downgrading of student caliber and the tendency toward cultism and profiteering. The truly capable student, however, can penetrate this growing external apathy and gain the attention of the inner court of his chosen school. Ultimately, he may be contacted by the Brotherhood itself which is pure and incorruptible.

"The Brotherhoods haven't kept Their mundane schools under rigid control because the schools are institutions of men. If men choose to cast aside a golden opportunity through laxity, it is within their free will to do so. Men have minds to discriminate between laxity and virtue and the end result of each alternative. It is not the purpose of the Brotherhoods to push men's noses to the grindstone, but They make every effort to provide the means and the voices of guidance."

"Why is it that there were so many Prophets in Biblical times but none now?" Richard inquired earnestly.

"Because advanced Egos who have direct contact with the Brotherhoods and have the mental power to see future events are hesitant to run the risks of exposing themselves to public attention these days. Also, the morals of the society into which an Ego incarnates have a strong effect upon his early attitudes as a child. If negative and vile attitudes cannot be overcome by the Ego during adulthood, then the Ego may backslide instead of accomplishing his mission. For example, King David fell prey to the morals of his times when he was a young adult. He collected a harem as did the other Eastern Potentates, he took delight in winning battles, he succumbed to the charms of Bathsheba and connived to have her husband killed, and in many other ways he lived as did the people of his day. But David incarnated among the Jews in order to uplift and unite them. As a child his advancement was apparent to the trained eye. Fortunately, David *more* than redeemed himself in later life. Bathsheba became his only wife in practice, and his wisdom became truly great. Nathan the Prophet, David's minister, had set him on the path again.

"Such is the danger of incarnating into barbarous societies such as ours. Only a few hundred advanced Egos have been willing to risk the likelihood of losing some of their hard-won soul development by incarnating to help floundering mankind. Often they have fallen terribly and have lost advancement which required perhaps a hundred lifetimes to attain. However, the courageous ones who have come through successfully have proven indispensable to the program of human uplift planned by Christ and the Brotherhoods. Most Egos of advancement have understandably not seen fit to volunteer during the perilous, black millennia since the destruction of the last great civilization twelve thousand years ago. A Brother who incarnates now is obliged to choose a physical vehicle born to average parents, and therefore He must forego the invaluable childhood training which only parents of advancement can provide. When a Brother takes on the body of an infant, His advancement is of no value to Him until He elevates His brain and emotions to the point where He can break through the physical limitations of the vehicle.

"During Biblical times the risks of retrograding were lessened for a Brother incarnating in the Holy Land because of the special attention the Brotherhoods were then giving to the Jews. The Brotherhoods had sub-adepts in incarnation there at all times. All the major and minor Prophets of the Old Testament were Brothers, and all the authors in the New Testament were Brothers except Saul of Tarsus, later known as Saint Paul. His doctrines are very fallible; so do not base too much on his epistles.

"Paul managed to unify the church through concessions and compromises made with the self-appointed bishops of the Mediterranean Basin, and the precedents established by their early councils still plague the modern churches with their faulty interpretations. Christianity was thus contaminated by alien beliefs such as the Eastern concept of the triune nature of God. And from the African church in Egypt the idea of granting salvation in a single lifetime was adopted ostensibly to attract the followers of the strongest rival of Christianity in the Roman World—the religion of Isis. To this day, eternal salvation is the most profitable item religions presume to deal in. Paul was undeniably a great organizer, and the Church might not have grown strong without him; but he both knowingly and unwittingly compromised the Uncompromising Christ. Nevertheless, the work of the Church and its Protestant offspring has accomplished much toward humanizing the world. Western Civilization is as advanced as it is today because of Christianity and the continued influence of Christ and the Brotherhoods.

"Western Civilization offers the greatest likelihood for mankind's ultimate perfection because this branch of civilization has been nurtured and advanced for some six thousand years to its present state."

CHAPTER 5

The Divine Conspiracy

Richard was startled by the thought that the Brotherhoods had conspired to guide civilization along a prearranged course. Berkeley paused to let the idea sink into the boy's consciousness; then he explained by saying, "The Brotherhoods' prime concern with Western Civilization has been to foster a mature, humane philosophy of life by which men can govern themselves happily and prosperously without periodic wars and strife. These ideals, however, are continually thwarted by the overwhelming majority of low-grade Egos of which mankind is composed. Therefore, when the Kingdom of God is gathered together in the near future, its Citizens will be limited to men and women who have satisfactorily demonstrated their ability to practice the precepts of human perfection taught by the Brotherhoods. And I might add, it is important that you fully understand that man *can be taught* to be perfect. Every Ego who has already ascended to the rank of Brother is living testament to this.

"No matter how wise a nation's leaders might be, they can never legislate civilization into existence. But if all the individual members of a nation *are* perfect, then the nation they comprise will be perfect! That is why the Brotherhoods are concentrating on the development of individuals. Each responsive and capable Ego is the true building unit of a lasting and purposeful Kingdom of God. Even though the world-at-large cannot now be joined in true civilization, at least those Egos who are ready for the next step forward can be assembled into a nation of their own where they will enjoy the advantages of the Brotherhoods' assistance and counsel.

"The United States of America was designed as an important stepping-stone toward the evolution of the kind of citizens and civilization conducive to a balanced society. During the revolutionary era of the 1770's when the colonists were persuaded to separate from England, there were men of greatness on hand to guide the budding nation. Several students of the Brotherhoods—notably Franklin, Jefferson, Madison, and Washington—managed to establish the political machinery most conducive to a society based on the high ideals of their time. The dominant philosophic atmosphere of the period was based on the doctrines of Reasonable Man, Rationalism, separation of church and state, the fallacy of the divine right of kings, human equality, democracy, John Locke's treatises on property rights, and the mysteries of a resurgent Freemasonry in France. The politicians of Europe thought the political idealism of our country to be naive. Nonetheless, the "radical" trends expressed in the Declaration of Independence, the Constitution of the United States, and the Bill of Rights have now come to be regarded as mileposts of human achievement. Our founding fathers had difficulty in persuading the colonies to remain united and to accept their untried theories, but the continuing success of the United States is evidence their ideas were sound.

"The faith, vision, and fortitude of these founders were the result of their training. They guided the new nation in accordance with instructions and had foreknowledge that they would succeed. As students of the Brotherhoods they knew that the nation they were forming was planned about six thousand years before. The sub rosa influence of the Brotherhoods throughout the world prepared the way for the founding of the United States of America; yet the Brothers worked so inconspicuously and adroitly that nobody sensed the fitting together of a detailed grand design begun six millennia before."

Berkeley dug into a pocket of his overalls and pulled out a dollar bill. He motioned for Richard to come closer, and he held it up so both could look at what Berkeley was pointing to on the back of the bill. "This is the Great Seal of the United States of America," Berkeley began. "It is replete with mystic symbols. The esoteric meanings of these symbols are not for you to know as yet, but I want to point out the Latin inscription on the reverse side of the seal. It states that our country is the *Novus Ordo Seclorum* which is literally translated *New Order of the World*. The most important symbol is pictured on the reverse side of the seal. It is the Great Pyramid of Gizeh which is a significant factor in the Brotherhoods' divine conspiracy for mankind's uplift.

"The pyramid was built under the supervision of the Brotherhoods in order to record in permanent stone the plan for the evolution of a superior society. The dates and events foretold in the pyramid were accurately predicted—usually to the minute—and the Brotherhoods have adhered strictly to this established timetable.

"The pyramid was constructed by the people known as the Hyksos who were foreigners to Egyptian soil but who gained control of the government by infiltration. During a period of about a century, the most capable governmental administrators were predominantly Hyksos. They soon were able to elevate one of their own kind to the highest ruler of Egypt. The Hyksos had been assigned the task of building the pyramid; and with typical patience, the Brotherhoods guided them to a smooth and peaceful integration with the native Egyptians. The Hyksos were a Semitic-White race that came out of Ethiopia.[1] They completed their tasks in Egypt and then departed without disrupting the nation. Most of the Hyksos emigrated to Crete and to Phoenicia in the Holy Land. A large portion of them migrated to the British Isles, and it was these people who built the Stonehenge Circle which incorporates astronomical relationships if measured by the Pyramid Inch—which is the same as the *old* British Inch. This split migration accounts for the fact that only the Hebrews and the British inherited the Pyramid Inch, and this seems to indicate that those two peoples were intended to translate the pyramid's message when the proper time came.

"The pyramid is a masterwork of mathematical precision and engineering excellence, and it is so constructed that its dimensions will reveal certain fundamental mathematic and astronomic relationships. The pyramid rests on a square which is exactly 36,524.2 Pyramid Inches in perimeter. One one-hundredth of this figure is 365.242 which is the precise number of days in a solar year. The projected apex is 5,813 Pyramid Inches

---

[1]They had recently immigrated there from an area east of present-day Turkey.

from the base, and that figure is equal to the radius of a circle 36,524.2 Pyramid Inches in circumference. Other such relationships indicate the exact unit of measure known as the Pyramid Inch which is used throughout the pyramid. The Pyramid Inch, incidentally, is precisely one five-hundred-millionth the diameter of the Earth through its polar axis. These things reveal an intelligence, technology, and science of a superior degree.

"When it was discovered that the old British Inch and the Pyramid Inch were the same, a renewed interest in the pyramid was kindled among British archeologists. Subsequent to the first discoveries, many more such relationships have been determined which establish that the British had the key to the pyramid's secrets. It was not long until the prophetic nature of the pyramid was demonstrated. The language used is mathematics, and the Pyramid Inch is again the key.

"If one considers the thought that must have gone into the preparation and construction of the pyramid, he is amazed at the thoroughness of the work. First, a monument was devised which would endure weather and earthquake so that minute measurements could be taken centuries later. The relationships used for clues were such that not until science became precise— that is, outside of the Brotherhoods—and the proper unit of measure was discerned could man solve the mystery of the pyramid's purpose. The persons who conceived the pyramid used no language in its prophetic portions lest that language be lost or equivocality arise. The builders used a universal language of mathematic symbolism which could be translated by a race sufficiently learned to decipher it. David Davidson, a structural engineer, published his analysis of the 'language' after twenty-five years of intensive work on the subject.

"When the tomb was entered by Egyptologists, it was apparent that the pyramid was never intended to be a pharaoh's last resting place or to hold a mummy. The Great Pyramid of Gizeh is unique in this respect.

"The pyramid was constructed about 4700 B.C. You will probably encounter considerable confusion among authorities as to when and by whom the project was undertaken; there's about a 500,000 year spread between the estimates made by Egyptologists. The ancient Egyptian priest-scribe, Manetho, from whose chronology of dynasties archeologists base their dating, ascribes the pyramid to Cheops; but Cheops is buried in the funeral grounds near the base of the pyramid. The unusual barrenness of the king's chamber and lack of ornamentation are not in keeping with the final resting place of a rich and powerful pharaoh. No, the pyramid had an entirely different function from that of a tomb.

"The Great Pyramid is one of a group of three large pyramids adjoining the Great Sphinx. A small temple which lies between the paws of the Sphinx was used by the Mystery School of the Brotherhood responsible for the construction of this group of magnificent structures. In the underground labyrinths and passages which connect all three pyramids to the Sphinx, the School met in secret in order to escape persecution by the Egyptian priesthood. The School's main function was to keep alive the truths of human existence which the priesthood withheld from the common people.

"The corrupt Priesthood of Isis instituted the belief in resurrection and the use of the body in afterlife in order that the fantastically lucrative embalming business could be foisted upon the populace. This priesthood invented Set, the Master of Evil, in order to terrify the gullible followers of their religion. It was the same priesthood which introduced in Egypt a multiplicity of gods because it provided an infinitely greater income than did the individual's proper mental attunement with the one true God Whom the Osirian antecedents of Egypt had adored.

"One of the most gratifying episodes arising out of the teachings of the Mystery School at the Temple of the Sphinx was the advent of Amenhotep IV, often called Akhnaton, who began his reign as pharaoh about 1375 B.C. Armed with the truth taught him in the Mystery School, he openly fought the Egyptian priesthood when he came into power. Akhnaton was influential in the reawakening of Egyptian art, architecture, science, and religion. He separated the priesthood from state functions, promulgated the concept of one God, and established the religion of Aton wherein Ra was the Creator and Director of the universe. Just as all the arts and sciences blossomed in Egypt, the Mystery Schools flourished in the open for the first and last time in mankind's history. Akhnaton was finally murdered by the priesthood, but his courage and works shall be remembered by the Brotherhoods.

"It was within the framework of Akhnaton's great release of knowledge that Moses, born about 1300 B.C., was educated. He too was taught in the Temple of the Sphinx by the same Mystery School. But Moses was already a high Adept of the Brotherhood and had a mission to perform which was prophesied in the Great Pyramid. The large stone crypt, which can still be seen in the King's Chamber of the pyramid, was the repository of the golden Holy of Holies of the Tabernacle in the Wilderness. This revered relic was placed in the sealed pyramid for safekeeping some 3,400 years prior to Moses' birth. It had previously been secreted in the long-since destroyed Temple of Isis where it had been brought by Osirians from Poseid. It was imperative that the evil Mentalists who had contrived the Egyptian priesthood never seize the Holy of Holies to use it as a rallying point for their religion, for in those days many Egyptians still knew its significance.[1]

"The Ark was intended to be delivered into the custodianship of the 'Israelites' who would hold it safe. It rested in Solomon's Temple until the Kingdom of Judah was established under Rehoboam, Solomon's son. The Ark served as the symbol of the scepter—meaning Salvation through Christ—which was prophesied to come through the tribe of Judah (*Genesis 49:10*). Precariously, but continuously, the Ark remained in Judah's possession until Christ was crucified. At that time the Ark was overturned, and it disappeared. It is now in safekeeping by one of the Brotherhoods.

"It is unfortunate that the period of the pyramid's prophecies will come to a close in August, 1953, because the pyramid has always been correct about the major events of every year since Biblical times. It even predicted the exact time of the 1929 Stock Market crash. Modern interpreters of the Great Pyramid's records are somewhat apprehensive concerning the year 1953, but this is merely the date for the closing of the Piscean Age and the beginning of the Aquarian Age. An age is one-twelfth the period

---

[1]The Ark of the Covenant was built by Moses in order to carry the Holy of Holies out of Egypt.

of time required by our Earth to make a complete circuit of its precessional wobble, which takes about 26,000 years; so 2,100 years is generally assumed the duration of an Age. The Ages are named after the zodiacal sign toward which our polar axis is inclined at the time. The Revelation of St. John the Divine is principally concerned with the events of the Aquarian Age, which includes the last half of this century.

"One of the most significant fulfillments of the Gizeh prophesies was contained in the public revelations made by Isaiah around 700 B.C. The Hebrew prophet disclosed the Brotherhoods' plans for the appearance of the Christ in Galilee. His descriptions of the event to occur 700 years later were very detailed and precise. After Isaiah's disclosure, the Brotherhoods began in earnest the preparations for Christ's coming in the body of a man to work directly among us, Their long and tedious preparations were coming to a climax. The Holy Land was then the crossroads of the two main trade routes of the world, and this location was chosen by the Brotherhoods for Jesus' birthplace because it provided a good means of disseminating Christ's teachings when He would come.

"The century following Isaiah's advent was truly remarkable for the appearance of religious leaders along the whole of the Eastern trade route. All were Adepts of the Brotherhoods, and each of these leaders was successful in reawakening religious understanding among the people to whom He revealed insights into the meaning and conduct of life. The impressive list includes Zoroaster the Iranian, Lao Tzu the Chinese, Mahivira the Jain, Buddha the Indian, and Confucius the Chinese. These are some of the greatest men to have ever appeared in the East; yet all were born within a span of 79 years—between 630 B.C. and 551 B.C. The impact of the teachings of these men upon Their respective peoples was such that each inspired a religion which still flourishes. By A.D. 30 almost the whole known world had been exposed to great truths. However, the people who heard these Teachers obviously were not ready for great truths, for the teachings of all of Them were soon corrupted almost beyond recognition.

"The Zoroastrian philosophy deteriorated into astrology and mysticism. The Jain and Buddhist ideals were diluted by the preposterous beliefs of the Hindus so that now the Jains are mostly a food cult, and the Indian Buddhists believe in the desirability of no desires. Buddha, on the other hand, preached right action and right desire. He dreamed of brotherhood and tolerance, but His ideas never dented the Hindu caste system. Lao Tzu's writings have inspired the Taoistic cult of magic and vain contemplation of obscure interpretations of His cryptic book. The Prince of Peace was called upon to sanctify the Crusades and other wars—all of which are 'holy,' of course. Christ's sacraments have been appropriated by fee-hungry ministers; brotherhood is rigidly defeated by the congregations assembling in His name; and the beautiful, simple truth He taught has been interpreted out of existence by theologians. Only Confucianism has remained near its founder's intent.

"The Brotherhoods take the human element into consideration and allow plenty of time for Their plans, for They know how many years are needed to promote even one small philosophic change. A nation will often go off in the wrong direction according to its collective free will; so the Brotherhoods usually develop several reserve agencies to achieve Their goals in case the primary agents fail or decline.

"One of the Brotherhoods contrived to uplift the Grecian culture to the point of becoming an intellectual springboard for the Christ's deeper teachings, but the perverse character of the Greeks seemed to persist in remaining impractical, frivolous and emotional. Because of their fratricidal wars and moral deviations, they did not benefit from the Brotherhood's program but fell into decline in the third century B.C. Nevertheless, their language *did* become a universal tongue for the spread of the Hebraic and Christian doctrines.

"Alexander the Great was instrumental in establishing the Greek language as a universal tongue by his conquest of virtually the whole civilized world of his time—about 330 B.C. His overwhelming, relatively easy success was not merely a freak of good fortune; the accelerated exchange of learning which followed his consolidation of diverse cultures was much too valuable to Christ's impending arrival.

"The Romans inherited the job of spreading Christianity through Europe by default of the Greeks. As a people, the Romans were very practical, emotionally austere, and enterprising in character. Therefore, the Roman Empire was at its height during Jesus' life. Christ came to uplift the people of the world, but we human beings were not yet ready to receive all He has to offer us. As in the New Testament allusion (*Hebrews 5:12–14*), one must first learn to assimilate milk before one can have the meat. We certainly were barely ready for the milk.

"During Christ's stay two thousand years ago, the world was a horrible place to live. Other than the very small upper class, there was nothing civilized about civilization. Even the patrician and king lived barbarously and brutally. In our vilest imaginings we cannot approach a true concept of life as it was in those days. The average life span was 25 years. Filth, disease, hunger, poverty, unspeakable oppression, hideous punishments for minor misdemeanors, and slavery at its worst were commonplace; and a strolling man or woman or child might commonly become a test for the range of an archer's bow or the soldier's new sword. There was no social legislation, and even children were exploited, maimed and murdered with virtual impunity.

"The establishment of the Roman Church through St. Paul paved the way to law and order in Europe. Before the era of the Church dawned, tribal lords, kings, and chieftains raided, slaughtered, and pillaged without end. With enforced obeisance to the Roman Church came the concept of protected, established, and defined feudal boundaries. Law enforcement eventually became feasible, and written laws were recorded by a learned, literate priesthood and the court scribes. The clerics who formulated the system often created kings and noble families to run it. The Church *was* government. More likely than not, Bishops and Cardinals actually ruled Europe while childish nobles were but pawns. The efficiency and stability of their systems were not effective overnight, but a certain degree of security entered the lives of European tribes for the first time. With security came establishment of an economic system which could be trusted from year to year; and as security grew, leisure could be bought with accumulated wealth. With leisure time came learning, with learning came the university, and thereafter came the rapid exchange of ideas. The foremost task of the Roman Church was completed, and its authoritarian discipline was ready to be challenged. The political and economic security it established in Europe was then firm enough to sustain the Reformation. The resultant intellectual freedom during the Renaissance promoted the phenomenal advances of culture which we now enjoy. But we still stand *far* below our goal.

"We shall soon enter the Aquarian Age—an era of great importance. The concepts Christ expounded two thousand years ago have been slowly taken to heart by many people. They have refined these concepts and have passed along their mental and moral advancement to their children and communities in an ascending spiral so that now a nominal proportion of the world practices mature attitudes of humaneness. At last Christ has some reasonable raw material with which to work—a far cry from the wretched creatures He found two thousand years ago.

"It is obvious that not all of the world aspires to the finer aspects of morality and wisdom exemplified by Christ, and this backward element continually keeps the world in a state of unrest. The desires of the more advanced persons to achieve a serene society free from the threat of destruction seem forever frustrated by the baser Egos. The conscientious citizens of our world strive to attain some measure of decency and progress in an environment seemingly bent on degradation and violence, and their creative efforts are the mark of mature adulthood. The Brotherhoods are now engaged in coalescing this minority of conscientious persons into an impregnable core of right-thinking, right-acting men and women. The Brotherhoods regard this action as essential to the preservation of the advancement that mankind has so painfully gained over the ages."

CHAPTER 6

And Evil Grew

Richard had a question to ask Berkeley which had been nagging him since his encounter with Dr. White. "Dr. White often referred to other, greater civilizations than ours which had once existed long, long ago. You also mention this idea. According to all the books I've looked up, civilization began in Mesopotamia a few thousand years before Christ. Before that the whole world was in the stone age. Can you tell me what really happened?"

"Yes, I may," Berkeley replied. "The human animal was evolved on a continent which no longer exists, for it now lies at the bottom of the Pacific Ocean."

"Is that where the legend of Atlantis comes from?" the boy interrupted.

"No. The land known as Atlantis was in the Atlantic Ocean, and it did not become a continent until after the continent in the Pacific sank. The Pacific continent was called *Mu* by its contemporaries. The present geological name for the continent is *Lemuria*. This huge continent was so very large that all the oceans of the world were drastically lowered when the waters rushed into the newly formed Pacific Basin. The relatively small islands which had existed in the Atlantic during the time of Lemurian civilization were left high and dry by the receding ocean, and the newly emerged land joined the Poseid Archipelago of the Atlantic Ocean into a large continent.

"Lemuria was an island which embraced all of present-day Australia, New Zealand, the Philippines, Oceania, western North America, and everything between. It was destroyed by earthquakes and then submerged about 26,000 years ago. Man's first civilization arose on the continent of Lemuria 78,000 years ago. This civilization lasted in the form of an empire for 52,000 years and reached heights so great that our present civilization can barely be considered a civilization when compared to it. Government, religion, and science achieved such perfection as to be far beyond our present comprehension. Western Civilization is only about 2,500 years old and has narrowly survived its power-seeking rulers and priests. Our science and technology are but in their infancy and as yet consist of but relatively few rediscoveries. The religion of Lemuria was established upon the laws of the universe by Christ Himself when He ruled Lemuria under His true name, Melchizedek.

"The advantage of 52,000 years of continuity cannot be matched by any other civilization, and the great majority of the Masters of the Brotherhoods achieved Their status within the duration of the Lemurian Civilization. It is present man's Egoic memory of these glorious days of human greatness which spurs him to strive for better government and fuller knowledge of the truths of existence. The gnawing but undefined subconscious desire to achieve our former greatness leaves us discontent with the immense shortcomings of our present way of life. Fortunately, the Brotherhoods have complete records of what we shall recreate, and every invention of mankind is being held in safekeeping toward the day when a civilization of merit has been re-established by man.

"In the Lemurian Empire there was one language and one government. Education was the keynote of the empire's success; and because every citizen was versed in the laws of the universe and was given thorough training in a profession or trade, magnificent prosperity resulted. A child's education was compulsory to the age of twenty-one in order for him to be eligible to attend citizenship school. Training for citizenship required seven years; so the earliest age at which a person could become a Citizen of the empire was twenty-eight years. In order to be eligible for election to public office, all the terms of which were for life, a man had to complete seven additional years of specialized training which also earned him the right to cast two ballots. Therefore, no one under thirty-five years of age could hold office."

Richard asked in wonderment, "But if it was so wonderful, why did it end?"

"It was in the formative years of the Lemurian Empire that the seeds for its destruction were sown. The nation's early growth was much more rapid than its mechanical and scientific development; and the persons who had earned Citizenship felt such a pressing need for manual laborers, that others who were not trained in Universal Law and the high precepts of citizenship were allowed within the nation. With typical magnanimity, the Citizens allowed these laborers to share equally in the abundance of the economy. Eventually noncitizens lived on a scale exceeding that available to present-day millionaires. The Citizens' original expectation that the noncitizens would soon aspire to Citizenship never materialized. The laborers wouldn't bother with the effort of schooling since they could expect nothing more in the way of physical comfort. Only Citizens could vote; but the laborers seemed to like this arrangement, for then they didn't have to share in the responsibility or administration of the nation.

"Before long there were more noncitizens than Citizens in the empire; but because the Citizens were those striving on the path to immortal perfection, the power inherent in their aggregate advancement far outweighed the lower masses. From the Citizens arose the Egos who have already earned Mastership.

"The laborer class could not comprehend the religious philosophy of the Citizenry and therefore was not attracted to it. In hopes that the laborers could be enticed to study Universal Law and come to an understanding of the vast advantages of striving for perfection, the Citizens set up 'churches' for the laborers. Breathtakingly beautiful buildings were provided, rituals employing fascinating symbolism were instituted, and the church leaders were provided with magnificent robes and other trappings. The laborers eventually were attracted in droves for much the same motivation that people go to a parade or a circus. The plan was to arouse the curiosity of the laborers and then unobtrusively implant the desire and incentive toward concerted soul uplift.

"The plan was a miserable failure; for not only didn't the laborers seek to understand and advance, but with the passing of centuries the 'church' leaders succumbed to the delight of being literally worshipped by the laborers. The nation was so abundantly prosperous that profit was not the motive of those who later became known as priests; it was public adulation and the delicious control over others that made these priests seek ever greater power for themselves. Noncitizen laborers were attracted to the priests' promise that they would return the Empire to Edenic paradise if the priests could achieve control over the government. Not all the laborers, however, were taken in by the priests' claims, but these exceptions were in the minority. The priests promised that no one need ever again work if Eden could be re-established. All that men would have to do is to pick food from the nearest tree and have all day free to play or rest. The unthinking, impractical believers of this vision of paradise were told by the priests not to try to reason out how this return to Eden would be accomplished but merely to put themselves into the hands of the church and have faith that it would work. The highest motives of spiritual good were mouthed by the priests, and for generations their followers clung fanatically to this dream of endless bliss. Every effort by the government to stamp out the perverted lies by which the priests enthralled their followers only made martyrs of the priests and drove them underground. The priests promoted sedition, and their followers were eager to die in defense of their priests and lofty ideals. These impractical laborers gave themselves the name *Katholi* and believed themselves to be highly spiritual and idealistic.

"On the other hand, the practical-minded noncitizen laborers realized that a return to Edenic conditions would put an end to civilization and all its advantages. The Lemurian Empire enjoyed an abundance of labor-saving appliances and luxuries which are beyond your present understanding, Richard; yet the Katholis had been duped into wanting to trade civilization for a labor-free paradise. The priests had freely implied that none of the material comforts would be given up in paradise and that their God would provide everything for the Katholi believer in return for his true worship. Because the great Angel, Lucifer, had been responsible for the abolishment of Eden in order that men could begin on the road to spiritual advancement, the Katholi were led to believe that this Angel was the most loathsome Ego ever associated with the Earth.

"Those laborers who couldn't swallow the idea of a paradise replete with endless luxuries and civilized conveniences without anyone working to manufacture these commodities or to provide public services gravitated to an alliance with the Citizenry of Lemuria. The noncitizen laborers who could not tolerate the priests of the Katholi churches banded together and called themselves the *Pfree*. They were usually craftsmen and highly skilled metalworkers who enjoyed their skill in building things. These practical laborers even adopted Lucifer as their patron in order to strongly differentiate themselves from the Katholis. Their natural ability to become foremen and leaders in their crafts brought them into close contact with engineers and administrators who had the education entitling them to Citizenship. This contact provided a natural opportunity for the Pfrees to learn the advantages and philosophy of the Citizenry.

"The idea that men might enjoy a paradise of plenty without effort is absurd. The Angels provided every possible raw material which man can use to further his understanding of the physical plane, but not until man expends effort upon raw material can it serve him. In this world there is no such thing as something for nothing! Man has a built-in desire to visualize and to achieve goals. To achieve anything necessitates the expenditure of human thought and energy. When a man is working toward a goal, he is happy; when he has no goal, he becomes dissipated and feels cast adrift. To build and to create are the bases of man's joy. To build is to bring wealth into existence.

"The Katholis and Pfrees came to be poles apart in their philosophies, and yet both were wrong. Each faction of laborers lacked the Citizens' proper balance between blind faith and scepticism; the Katholis prized idealism and the Pfrees practicality. The obstinate onesidedness of each group of laborers inevitably led to open conflict between them, which was much to the distress of the Citizens and to the detriment of the Empire. Finally, the Citizens began a movement to encourage the emigration of the Katholis to hitherto unpopulated continents by offering extraordinary inducements, and hundreds of millions of laborers became enthusiastic enough to colonize other lands. The thought of being able to found their own nation according to their religious beliefs strongly appealed to the Katholis. The principal Katholi colony was India where the Katholis' priests established a hierarchical rule over the settlers and readily enslaved them. Meanwhile, multitudes of Pfree laborers set up their own nation on the Poseid group of large islands in the Atlantic Ocean. Because of their long friendship with the Citizenry, the Pfrees invited Citizens to administer their new country and establish industries. To this plea many adventurous Citizens responded.

"The Lemurian Empire continued to be slowly undermined by the organized priesthood until civil war became openly manifest. The Citizenry abandoned the Lemurian Continent, and it was rent by earthquakes and subterranean explosions until one night the continental arch collapsed and the continent sank beneath the waters of the Pacific Ocean. Hundreds of millions of lives were lost on the continent alone, and many millions more were drowned in the resultant tidal waves that swept the heavily populated coasts of surrounding continents.

"I think you can see, Richard, that in view of the perverted Egoic attitudes instilled in both factions of the laborer class during their many incarnations of wrong thinking, the Brotherhoods must insist that only trained Citizens be allowed in the Kingdom of God now gathering here on Earth. The world today is populated wholly by the Egoic types still designated as Pfrees and Katholis just as it has been for the past ten thousand years. For the first time in many millennia, however, the ancient Citizenry are now beginning to come into incarnation in order to form the Kingdom."

"If the Lemurian Continent was so huge and the civilization was so great," Richard began, "why is it that nobody knows anything about it?"

"Oh, but people do know about it!" Berkeley replied. "In your libraries are books which discuss Mu. Many geologists argue in favor of a former continent in the Pacific because it is a logical deduction to account for observable rock formations ringing the Pacific basin. Moreover, there are still remnants of the Lemurian civilization visible in Oceania.

"On the southeastern shore of Ponape Island lies an immense ruined city called Metalanim which could have conceivably housed two million persons. The city is constructed of gigantic blocks of stone weighing up to fifteen tons apiece. Artificial waterways capable of passing a modern battleship intersect the city. Metalanim is remarkable for its architectural and engineering excellence and is not at all like the primitive works one associates with the natives of Oceania. The stone used is not found on Ponape, nor does the population for a thousand miles around exceed 50,000 total. This city was apparently built by the people of Lemuria of rock hewn from now submerged lands.

"On barren Malden Island stand the remnants of forty stone temples of the same architecture as on Ponape 3,400 miles away. Roads of basalt blocks extend from these temples in every direction only to disappear into the Pacific Ocean. On Rarotonga Island is another section of the same road. In fact, on almost any of the mountainous Pacific islands such remnants of evidently similar architecture can be found, which are regarded as sacred by the native inhabitants. Therefore, it may be logically concluded that many Pacific islands are mountain tops of what was once a single continent.

"The Pacific Basin is ringed by mountain ranges, often volcanic, which were raised when Lemuria sank. Near the prehistoric city of Tiahuanaco, which is on the shore of Lake Titicaca in the Andes Mountains of Peru, are the remains of stone-lined canals which served as a connection between the Pacific Ocean and the geologic Amazonian Sea which was formerly part of the Atlantic Ocean. The canal is now about two-and-a-half miles above sea level. Tiahuanaco is built along the same lines as Metalanim on Ponape and is also intersected by canals.

"Excavations south of Mexico City revealed a former ocean port which is now far inland at an elevation of 7,000 feet. When this ancient buried city was unearthed by William Niven, it had a total of thirty-one feet of debris above it consisting almost entirely of boulders, gravel, and sand. The only way so much material of this type could have been deposited is by a tidal wave of colossal magnitude. If nothing else, these archeological findings indicate that man was well civilized during the last era of mountain raising and that he experienced floods of appalling destructiveness. The tale about Noah's Ark finds its inspiration in these events.

"After the destruction of Lemuria, Atlantis grew to be a great nation which subsequently proved to be the world's second-ranking civilization. It flourished for some 14,000 years until its submersion about 10,500 years ago. The name of this nation was

Poseid, and it was the offspring of the colony which the Pfrees had originally established.

"The nation of Poseid was inventive far beyond the wildest imaginings of modern scientists. Their fantastically advanced technology afforded consummate leisure, comfort, and a vast abundance of material things. Unfortunately, the people were much too preoccupied with the pursuit of physical pleasures and with the accumulation of luxurious possessions to take advantage of the opportunity to attain Citizenship, and this shortcoming ultimately resulted in their downfall. Internal conflict arose when large numbers of Katholis deserted their cities in South and Central America and migrated to Poseid in order to escape their savagely war-like neighbors. The Katholi priests set about to bring Poseid under their sway, but they only succeeded in destroying the governmental and economic system which produced the wealth and luxuries they sought to usurp. Civil and religious warfare vexed the land until it submerged beneath the ocean waves.

"Many conscientious adherents to the philosophy that had made Lemuria and Poseid great in their beginnings abandoned Poseid several centuries before it submerged. They fled to what is now North Africa and there evolved a nation which eventually became the world's third-ranking civilization. These people adopted the name of a martyred High Ruler of Poseid who had been murdered by the Katholis. He was a High Adept known as Osiris, and He had incarnated specifically to help preserve Poseid. The Osirians were the ones who took from Poseid the revered relic of the Holy of Holies, later carried in the Ark of the Covenant. The Osirians' religion was based on Melchizedek's Universal Laws, and they became a devout and practical nation. A singular characteristic of these people was their proficient use of Mind Power.

"Later, when Poseid sank, the great fertile valley of the Osirian nation became flooded to form the Mediterranean Sea. The Osirian survivors of the cataclysm migrated to the Nile Valley where they later joined with descendants of original colonists who had come to northeastern Africa from Lemuria by traveling westward. After they recovered from the desolation wrought by the submergence of Poseid, they became the forebearers of the ancient Egyptian culture.

AND EVIL GREW

"In Egypt the priesthoods again arose to smite civilization. They learned all too well the techniques of great mental power from the predynastic Egyptians and used them to subjugate the people. Fear was their weapon of rule. The priests never needed to worry who was Pharaoh, for even the nobles and kings were terrified of Set—the early Egyptian god of death, evil, and hell. Only the priests could provide 'protection' against 'evil,' and how could Egypt be better guided than when 'seers' and priests be sole counsel to its rulers? The priests reaped benefits for themselves at every turn as they laughingly made slaves of the people and puppets of the Pharaohs. A ruler's frightening dream, if properly interpreted, could send Egypt rattling off to war and conquest. Priests didn't go to war; what then had they to fear? If famine struck the land, priests grew all the fatter from the frantic sacrifices of the populace to the gods, who, after all, only priests knew how to propitiate. If men grew restive under the smarting demands of the priesthood, the priests could bring them back into line through the judicious selection of 'dangerous thinkers' for human sacrifice to Egypt's multitude of gods. The priests thus held men by the throat for their self-aggrandizement.

"The ancient Rama Empire in India—which became the fourth-ranking civilization under a dynasty of enlightened leaders who for a period of several centuries suppressed the priesthood—and predynastic Egypt had both managed to salvage some of their culture after the fall of Atlantis, but the rest of the world was reduced to a condition of brutal struggle for survival. The colonies of the world were irretrievably shut off from the technology of Atlantis, and in a few generations they reverted to a stone-age existence. The few manufacturing facilities not destroyed by world-wide earthquakes and tidal waves soon deteriorated from lack of raw materials to feed them. Stone replaced smelted metals for tools, and all too soon subsequent generations couldn't believe anything other than stone had ever been used. Egypt and India were precariously spared from the far-reaching upheaval, and their weakened governments gradually succumbed to evil priests and war lords.

"The seekers after power have almost destroyed mankind!"

"Couldn't the Brotherhoods do something against the priests?" Richard asked.

Berkeley sighed wearily and said, "The Brotherhoods cannot take men by the hand and enforce observance of Universal Law. No one may rightly interfere with the free will of another Ego. Nonetheless, the priests always sought total control over the will of their victims even though the priests knew that they must eventually suffer severe penalties for their violation of the Laws of God. It is man's negative view of life that gives the dark forces of the world their power. When a man is joyful, loving, and confident, he is naturally attuned to the Lord of Joy, Love, and Confidence—the Christ. Then Christ functions through that Ego by sympathetic attraction. But when a man is fearful, hateful, and without hope, then he is naturally attuned to the evil forces of Fear, Hate, and Despair. Evil functions through that Ego by sympathetic attraction. Because men are subject primarily to negative emotions engendered by thousands of incarnations of blind, stumbling ignorance of God's redeeming truth, they become natural prey to evil men's nefarious devices. The truly happy Egos are those who have room in their hearts for only beautiful, clean thoughts. Wherever they look they see only the good, and they find delight in their alliance with the Christ. Such are the Brothers—bright, radiant, joyous, always moving forward toward perfection." Berkeley's eyes twinkled now as he beamed at the boy.

After a moment Berkeley became more somber again and resumed his discourse. "Five of the seven Lesser Brotherhoods were established on Egyptian soil in order to combat the fierce onslaught of the priests and their evil. But the common people were so lost to the priests that little could be done to save them. Many deserving Egos were drawn to the Brotherhoods but far too few to have much influence over the affairs of the nation. Finally, all but one of the Brotherhoods removed Their headquarters from Egypt.

"The priests in Egypt consisted of perhaps the shrewdest and cleverest men history has ever seen in conspiracy. Fortunately, their lust for individual power has since kept them from maintaining a disciplined organization, for each would have himself to be ruler of the world. These priests learned the mental process of maintaining their bodies in vigor for hundreds of years; however, they were unable to achieve the immortality inherent in the true spiritual advancement of those who struggle upon the path to perfection and achieve Adeptship in the Brotherhoods. Nevertheless, the priests of Egypt learned well the powers of the Mind, and they perfected Black Mentalism.

"Egypt's priests mastered the mental ability to impose their will upon others telepathically. They also learned how to 'tune in' on the thoughts of others and thus maintain surveillance on their enemies telepathically. Adepts and Masters of the Brotherhoods also have these abilities, but They will not, under any circumstances, impose Their will upon another or in any way operate in the environment of a person without that person's expressed request to do so.

"Priests have used telepathic mass-hypnosis to dominate whole nations in Africa and the Orient. Today they still function on a world-wide scale by mental means. Their evil operates through human instruments who are unwittingly made to conform to the telepathic bidding of the Mentalists. These instruments are readily recruited from among those persons who are inclined to fear, to hate, to lust for power, and to seek privilege over others. The people who fall into the grip of the insidious, unbelievably clever Mentalists are characteristically arrogant in their belief that they are especially qualified to rule over others and often believe themselves to be divinely inspired and unable to do wrong.

"The major evils in the world today can be ultimately attributed to the Black Mentalists and their dupes. Evil is totally of human origin. There is no such thing as the Devil or a fallen angel leading the forces of evil. Man alone is responsible for the present discord in the world—for disease, insanity, war, poverty, and oppression.

"Man can raise himself from this sort of environment by acquiring truth and putting it into practice in every phase of his life, but he seems grossly unaware of the inherent Mental power for good that resides within him. One day, man's practical knowledge of truth will gain him freedom from the troubles of the world. Whole nations can rise above the world's shortcomings; but, for the most part, only isolated individuals have achieved control over their environment and have created their own oases of serenity in a hectic, overwhelming world.

"When a man sets his feet upon the path to perfection, he immediately becomes a target of the Black Mentalists. They will do everything in their power to dissuade or destroy each such aspirant. They will cause trying temptations to manifest in the aspirant's life which are designed to delay and distract. Evil is so subtle that it usually disguises itself as good. The Black Mentalists can cause prosperity or security to enter one's life if the lack of these things had prompted the search for a better way. Opportunities for fame and power are provided by the Black Mentalists to ensnare those upon the difficult road to spiritual greatness. These tactics are changed to suit the situation, and the weakest aspect of every man's character is exploited by the Mentalists to prevent his advancement.

"For the most part, the Black Mentalists could destroy any man starting out on the path to perfection. Except for Christ's protection, we would be unable to rise. Christ, through the Brotherhoods, holds the Black Mentalists in check so that we may advance. When we attune ourselves to Christ by proper desire and right living, we are assured special help from the Greater Beings of Divine Love on our own human life-wave. One's constant, conscious aspiration to emulate Christ's philosophy and one's sincere prayer for guidance from Christ will *always* bring the needed protection for one's fight against evil.

"The Black Mentalists are aware that when enough human beings have attained spiritual powers and when men shall have established a perfect nation on Earth, their evil power over man will come to an end. That is the reason for the Mentalists' bitter struggle against each and every person striving toward greatness. Our need for Christ is imperative, for only through Him and His mantle of protection shall we come safely into the fold of the Brotherhoods on our way to ultimately becoming one with the Father God.

"The greater part of humanity does not suffer direct control by the Black Mentalists; however, we are all immersed in their influence. To be essentially neutral in the battle for good over evil results in being ignored by the Mentalists. If one does not constitute a threat to the Black Mentalists, then one does not warrant their concern. So long as one merely lives and dies without advancing upon the path of perfection, the Mentalists are pleased. It would appear safer for an individual to remain obscure and to endure the dictators and tyrants elevated to power through the schemes of the Black Mentalists than to overthrow them, but in the long run this usually proves disastrous. It is as evil to submit to slavery as it is to be a slave master!

"The Black Mentalists concentrate their efforts against bright children and young adults. The current spread of perverting entertainment, literature, pornography, and narcotics is a determined effort to destroy the moral strength of civilization. Promising young men and women are all too often stricken by loss of mental contact with reality, called schizophrenia, which is the struggle between the incarnate Ego belonging to the body and a vile decarnate entity who seeks to take over the rightful Ego's physical vehicle. Lack of *proper* religious and moral guidance from the parents, whether through ignorance or ineptness, is indicated when a child is left unprepared to ward off these dangers."

"How can I stay out of trouble with the Black Mentalists?" the boy asked with alarm.

"It's easy to avoid difficulty with them merely by making use of the fact that the Mentalists' sheer, black hatred of mankind is overridden by Christ's love. When a person is troubled by unnatural thoughts, disturbing compulsions, strong desires that are counter to his conscience, and by the fear that he might be losing his mind, then he is a victim of the telepathic influences of the Black Mentalists. In order to dispel the evil of their implanted thoughts instantly, one needs to *earnestly* and *frequently* pray, 'Dear Christ, by Your divine power I humbly ask that You deliver me from the influences of evil and keep me from temptation.'

"In effect, each man is a battleground between good and evil; and it is the individual Ego who, blindly or knowingly, determines which force will prevail in his personal environment. Evil actively seeks domination over an Ego, but the Brotherhoods are dedicated to free will and therefore can overcome evil's inroads in a man only at his invitation. Until an Ego achieves a considerable degree of advancement, he is no match individually against the power of the Black Mentalists; so he needs to actively enlist the willing protection afforded by Christ through the Brotherhoods.

"The relentless struggle between mankind and the Black Mentalists is especially difficult for man because not only is he largely unaware of the existence of his prime antagonist, but he doesn't even sense the nature of evil's methods. The great majority of people try to do their best in the world and manfully resist immorality; but lacking the simple knowledge of how to render evil ineffectual, they are unable to resolve the battle. Thus they grope through a neurotic life of discontent and confusion. Those who seek relief from the exhausting conflict by surrendering to base influences are soon lost in despair, decay, insanity, and death. But he who has prudently allied the forces of good on his side enjoys serene freedom from evil. Then a man knows the thrilling happiness of being master of his fate: free at last to forward his uplift.

"In connection with this, Richard, you won't be subjected to the sordid side of life until you are able to view such aspects of the world without being adversely influenced by them. But have pity on those children who, when exposed to moral corruption, are persuaded that their knowledge of the perversions of mankind is a romantic sophistication. Many young people mistakenly suppose that the obscene activities in which some notorious segments of society indulge is typical of the behavior of all adults, and this is all the more unfortunate since young people's discovery of the panoply of adult vices usually coincides with their desire to become adult and to do what they *believe* adults do.

"You, however, have earned Our specific protection through the attitudes and good works of your former lives. Moreover, like many other people, you simply are not attracted to the type of activities which warp and coarsen the Mind. It may seem grossly unfair that persons who should have protection when they need it most are not saved from developing a degrading and crippling philosophy, but men must rise by their own volition and learn the advantages of the higher way. If they must suffer the dejection, fear, and unhappiness brought about by the wrong way of life in order to seek the comparatively joyous way outlined by Christ, then needs be they must grovel before they can rise.

"The Ten Commandments and the Sermon in the Mount are not intended to be blindly obeyed without understanding but should be analyzed from the standpoint of one's own advantages when they are complied with. God offers us His Love not His dictatorship. The rules given to mankind in the Bible are for the greatest good of every man. Following the law will eliminate all threats to ultimate happiness! Sadly enough, men rarely profit by the experience of others and instead choose their own way. They seek to belie the wisdom of the Bible but succeed only in doing themselves harm. After enough lifetimes of self-inflicted abuse, men finally are driven to find a more peaceful and beneficial way.

"That is why it is not in God's plan that we have a guardian Angel to direct our every step and avert dangers for us at every turn. Men must learn to control their words and actions, for everything we say and do brings a response from other men. To curse a man is likely to bring his fist justly into our nose; to steal is likely to earn us a noose; but to praise men will net us the courtesy of others. To love one another will engender more love. If we do not use discrimination in the use of words or if we are improvident of our needs, should we not suffer? The consequences of error force us consciously to seek the cause of our failures and thus take account of cause and effect. Men must have the freedom of will to test and evolve wisdom; otherwise we would be letting others do our thinking for us. As long as there are those who are willing to let others think for them, there will be Black Mentalists happy to oblige them.

"The Brotherhoods have vast power compared to the Black Mentalists, but how would it aid man's acquisition of wisdom if all evil were arbitrarily obliterated? Men must not be so paternalistically controlled that they cannot experience the negative emotions that each man must overcome because it is the greater way. If war and its causes were negated by the Brotherhoods, and if the nations were ruled by Masters, and if the inventions of all time were handed to us, we would have no challenge to pit our God-given Minds against. We must learn to solve our own problems before we can hope to create and direct a planet yet to be. Our present Adepts and Masters overcame all; there is not one excuse for our not equalling Their achievement especially since Christ has removed so many stumbling blocks to human advancement."

"What do you mean?" Richard asked in puzzlement.

"When the Archangel, Melchizedek, came to Earth as the Christ nineteen centuries ago, He did so not only to be an example to us and to guide us toward the future but also to place limitations upon the powers of the Black Mentalists who then held mankind in abject subjugation. During the first forty days of Christ's ministry among us He established permanent barriers between the lower Astral Plane and the Physical Plane in order to prevent the ready contact this open avenue had afforded evil Egos. Just how this was accomplished is information reserved for the Brotherhoods; the important point is that henceforth men have been free to choose between good and evil of their own accord instead of being inescapably influenced by the Mentalists. Moreover, it was during that same forty day period that Christ removed the vast karmic indebtedness of the entire world so that men could be freed of that crushing burden which very nearly destroyed mankind."

"What is karmic indebtedness?"

"It's another way of saying *unatoned sins.*"

"I'd like to find out something here," Richard interrupted. "Can you tell me what sin is? People I've asked all seem to agree that it's something you're not to do, but they don't seem very clear in their own ideas about it."

"That which is sin is very easily defined, Richard. *Sin is any human thought or action the eventual result of which is not for the good of all the persons affected.* Thoughts must be included in the definition because of the power of Mental activity to influence other Minds and because thoughts are the forerunners of action. As you think further about this definition, you will begin to understand that every act of your life demands considerable attention to the ultimate details of eventual outcome. In the skill of this, more than in anything else, are sages divided from fools."

"I guess I understand your definition of sin all right, but I still don't know what karmic indebtedness is all about."

"My use of the term karmic indebtedness refers to a kind of *karma*. Karma is the principal device of God's justice—the word itself comes from the Sanskrit language and means *carry-over*.

"When we observe a person who has prospered even though his wealth has been gathered through trickery, dishonesty, and violence, his life seems to belie the moral teaching of the Bible and the Golden Rule. It naturally offends our sense of fairness when the person who unjustly seizes power enjoys the unearned fruits of others' labor. But be assured that in all of Nature there is no such thing as something for nothing! Every man, corporation, and nation must compensate fully for accrued profits and benefits. If one acquires more than he has rightfully earned, he assumes a karmic debt. If one is cheated or robbed of that which is rightfully his, he receives a corresponding karmic credit. If a man's karmic debits and credits have not been balanced out by the time of his transition, that is, death of the physical vehicle, they are carried over until the next incarnation. Absolute justice is maintained through all the universe in this way, and karmic accountancy is recorded automatically on the Etheric Plane of existence as set up by the Celestial Host. This record is part of the Akashic Record.

"Between incarnations, while we function upon the Astral Plane of existence, we can have our personal Akashic Record reviewed for us in order that we can better plan the tasks we shall assign to ourselves in our next incarnation. Karmic debits, however, impose certain conditions upon our choice of parents, environment, and body; for if we have carried-over debts to be balanced, we can't be allowed to incarnate into luxurious circumstances.

"Karmic justice extends beyond mere economic considerations. If a man has murdered another and has not suffered the same fate during his present lifetime, then he will be struck down by a murderer during the prime of his next incarnation. In the same way, cruel tyrants may subsequently be born into slavery; oppressors of human rights may be born to the oppressed; the father who deserts his children may be orphaned in his next incarnation; he who crippled or dismembered another may later suffer the same fate as did his victim; a disseminator of racial bias may be born again into the race he debased only to suffer the cruel fate he himself instituted in the former lifetime. God takes no part in these man-created hardships. He established the Universal Law that governs such things, and it is up to man to discern God's Law and guide himself accordingly to avoid future suffering. Every action instituted by an Ego puts into motion a reaction of equal value which will return to that Ego. Good returns as good; evil returns as evil. God and His Law exist whether man believes in them or not, and the wise man enjoys the serenity inherent in conscious conformance with them.

"Karmic debits can be offset by karmic credits so that a person can atone for his crimes by good works. Essentially, atonement is a matter of restitution, repentance, and determination to do works that are designed to equalize the indebtedness one seeks to offset. The workings of karma do not always wait until subsequent incarnations but can be almost instantaneous.

"If a man has done good works all his life and has never sought to gain where he has not earned but then cheats a customer or accidentally destroys a neighbor's property, he may conceivably have no *net* karmic debt for his crime if he had previously accumulated sufficient karmic credits which could be used to equalize the account. In all instances intent has important bearing on the case. The automatic equalizing of karmic accountancy without further punishment demands that the crime be without premeditation. Still, all hurts and damages must be accounted for karmically even if the original intent was to be helpful or if they occurred as a result of ignorance or foolishness.

"The art of doing good works requires a fine knowledge of ultimate ramifications, for what may seem a good deed may actually not be for the greatest good of the person for whom it was intended to be. To give money to a panhandler increases his karmic indebtedness because he has received something for nothing. The giver of the money in this case has contributed to the karmic indebtedness of another Ego and so must suffer an equivalent karmic debt for his act. Charity given to one who won't make his own way in the world, even though he is able, only compounds the loafer's indebtedness. Charity to those truly in need is blessed. Yet, all recipients of alms have the karmic debt to repay when they recover from their trouble. If charitable cases hadn't had an accumulation of karmic debts in the first place, misfortune beyond their control would never have befallen them.

"Since most of us cannot know the exact status of his own long-range karmic account, it is wise to use utmost discrimination in every word and act. No one can afford a karmic debt.

"For a person to do nothing other than good during his lifetime will certainly earn him comfortable circumstances for the outset of his next incarnation. But there is an infinite combination of factors involved in the environment of one's rebirth. A person's karma may be all good, but the Ego might still choose a body of a despised race in order to help uplift that people, or he might choose a crippled body to learn, perhaps, humility. It is not always correct to assume that an individual's hardships are due to karmic indebtedness; just the opposite is not altogether unlikely.

"There are times when an Ego has earned so much karmic indebtedness that hundreds of incarnations of suffering will be required to fulfill justice. The Brotherhoods have made a merciful provision to distribute large karmic debt over many lifetimes so that retribution will not crush the atoning Ego with too great a burden for one incarnation. This cushioning provision, however, is gradually being diminished in order to coincide with certain plans for the end of this century. Mankind will soon suffer or enjoy the effects of its actions almost immediately.

"It should be clearly understood that nations as a whole each have a karmic account. The sins committed by one nation against another nation or by the government against its populace are karmic debts which must be balanced. The balancing usually takes the form of invasion and attack from another nation, pestilence, economic collapse, drought, earthquakes, and the like. National karmic indebtedness resulting from the sinful actions of a whole generation are the sins that fathers visit upon the children of later generations. It was such national karmic indebtedness that Christ removed nineteen centuries ago. In effect, all the nations of the world were allowed to carry on with a clean slate from which was erased the just retribution due them for the wars, enslavements, political knavery, and false economic systems in which they had engaged. The removal of this crushing burden from the world was absolutely essential if mankind was to become civilized again.

"The people of the world had become hopelessly enmeshed in the vicious circle of a progressively worsening karmic situation, and the resultant, unrelenting hardships and cruel oppressions provoked despairing mankind into committing even worse evils. Eventually, retribution lagged so far behind the rate at which new sin was being committed that only wholesale destruction of the human race could have evened the account. As it was, Christ would have arrived too late to save us if the Archangelic Host had not already been cushioning us for generations from retribution. Christ not only saved the world from the direct influence of evil, but also from the rightful destruction we deserved as the result of our own sins.[1] This saving action by Christ was analogous to the rescinding of a national debt—each citizen thus enjoying a proportional relief from the karmic indebtedness into which he had been born. The vast legacy of unrequited sin left by generations of ancestors was lifted from the individual's shoulders, but Christ could not absolve *Egoic* karma even in the slightest. He took away the sins of the nations of the world *but not of any individual!*

"When, during Christ's ministry, He would tell a person that his sins were forgiven, He did not mean that person's karmic indebtedness was blotted out but rather that he was not in a state of condemnation. Here was the beginning of hope after long generations of despair. Christ's Divine Love for all men and His boundless compassion for everyone He encountered attracted people to Him wherever He went. For all His humility, He was nevertheless the most powerful Ego ever to tread the Earth. He has the power to kill all alive on Earth by Mental means, and He can even personally dissolve the planet into basic substance. Since these powers reside in all who are Angelic and above, it becomes apparent that only *perfect* Egos may be granted Angelic Life.

---

[1] There is no way by which Christ and the Archangelic Host can Themselves dissipate this vast karmic indebtedness of ours. They can only hold the account in abeyance, for it must eventually be returned to our Human Life-Wave where we must deal with it ourselves. It is planned that this will be released upon the world at the end of this century.

"When a person has led a life wherein he renders greater service to his employer, patrons, and neighbors than anyone has the right to expect, he accumulates karmic credits. When one receives a salary for services properly performed, there are no excess karmic credits gained because the salary is full compensation. The loafer who does not give his employer a full day's work is over-compensated by his wages and thus he acquires karmic debits. Conversely, the employer who underpays his workers nets karmic debits. But if the worker performs tasks in excess of those agreed upon for his wages, he gains credits over and above his wages. Karmic credits are the 'treasures in Heaven' to which Christ referred (*Matt. 6:20*). He who has a backlog of karmic credits has security, for he can draw upon these credits to fulfill his mundane needs. These credits also can be expended to afford protection from enemies and exemption from disasters.

"The status of a man's karmic 'account' has a strong bearing on his success at bringing his desires into physical reality. If one does not have the accumulated karmic credits sufficient to compensate for the benefit obtained through mental attraction or precipitation, that benefit will soon be forfeited. However, Egos of powerful will can often retain a precipitated acquisition even without the credits to secure it, but this results in the accrual of karmic indebtedness because he is enjoying the possession of a thing for which he has not sufficiently compensated. Precipitation through mental attraction is a marvelous, God-given ability which should not be abused. To employ the laws of precipitation without taking into proper consideration the laws of karma can be disappointing."

"Precipitation is something that really interests me," Richard said with enthusiasm. "Just how is it done?"

Berkeley shook his head and smiled. "That will have to wait until you are formally a student in a school of a Brotherhood," he said apologetically.

"Really? I'll be a student?" the boy said with much excitement. "How soon?"

"Slow down!" Berkeley cautioned. "You must have patience, Richard. Not until you're a man will you be able to profit fully from detailed instructions and examinations. But there are preliminaries which you must begin immediately."

CHAPTER 7

A Lesson in Morality

Richard was eager to undertake whatever action Berkeley might prescribe; but when he was advised what he should do, he was deeply disappointed.

"You should become confirmed in a church," was Berkeley's admonition.

"But that's going backward," Richard complained. "Isn't there something more interesting that I can study?"

"You have to study preliminaries first, Richard. In your eagerness you want to fly to great heights, but you don't even have your feathers yet. I know how you feel," Berkeley added sympathetically, "but try to realize that you are still a child. There are so many things that you must learn, it will literally take a lifetime to acquire the knowledge and proficiency demanded of you."

Richard wasn't convinced. He merely looked dourly at Berkeley. The boy exhibited a response akin to the hurt a child feels when rain has cancelled a happily anticipated picnic.

Berkeley rose from his chair and went to the blackboard. "Are you good at mathematics?" Berkeley asked.

"Pretty good," was the casual reply.

"Here, solve this problem!" Berkeley said as he wrote on the blackboard.

"Jeepers!" the boy exclaimed. "I don't know anything about that kind of stuff."

"That's a relatively simple equation in integral calculus," the elderly man chided.

"But we haven't studied anything like that yet."

"Perhaps this will illustrate my point, Richard. You are good at mathematics and are being prepared for algebra. Yet in order to solve the equation I've written here, you must also understand

trigonometry and analytical geometry. To come to that understanding will require four or five years of further study. It will
be so arranged by the school system that you will advance step by
step from the simple to the complex. Years of background training will be necessary before you can solve this equation. It can't
be taken in one jump. Proficiency in math leads to proficiency in
algebra which in turn leads to proficiency in each subsequent
study.

"So it is in all of life. Perform each assignment with enthusiasm and master it to the best of your ability. Your life's work is of
utmost importance to the world. The Brotherhoods will see to it
that each step comes your way at the proper time. You must
learn before you can function wisely and efficiently. For the next
twenty years you must learn, learn, and then learn some more. It
won't all be by formal schooling because you must learn of men,
business, politics, and religion. The challenges and problems
that will make you stretch and grow toward maturity will be
unfolded before you all through your life.

"Do you imagine that the Brotherhoods would leave you unprepared for anything that will be needed in the building of the
Kingdom of God? Do you believe yourself qualified to organize
a nation next year or the year after? You will have had to live a
full life of energetic proficiency before you can begin to lead
men toward the greatness proposed for the future. Only with
experience as a man living in the world of men will you come to
know what you are to lead mankind from, and then you will also
see why the world you shall create is such a desperately needed
relief from what it is now. There are many corners to turn and
bridges to cross before you will be a fully rounded and balanced
adult. You can't just point the road to greatness—a sign post
could do the same. You must lead the way by being up in front!
And it is the possession of knowledge and wisdom that will entitle you to be the leader.

"Your preparation for this life's work goes far back into history. In your past lives you have been faithful over comparatively
few things so that now you are to be given control over many
things in this incarnation. Continue by doing that which will
prepare you for even greater things in later incarnations."

"I understand," Richard said, and he smiled in gratitude.

103

Berkeley smiled in return. He erased the blackboard and sat down again. "You will take confirmation instruction in a Lutheran church nearby. We will see to it that your parents so desire it."

"Is that the best religion?" the boy asked earnestly.

"No. Overall, it's no worse or better than any other denomination. All of them are so lost in error that it is hopeless. However, all churches can inspire faith; and despite their stumbling, they have brought Christ into the spirit of Western Civilization. They serve Christ in typically human fashion; but since they are the best expression of which the majority of mankind is presently capable, they must, perforce, be the principal institution for preaching good. The hypocrisy of Christian leaders and their flocks is monstrous, but it is better to suffer churches than to abandon the world to an existence without any knowledge of Christ and the Bible.

"The reasons for choosing the Lutheran faith lie in the future. However, do not join any church or work for the expansion of any church. If you do, people may take it as your endorsement of a particular denomination. Leave churches alone! You may attend services if you experience satisfaction or inspiration by so doing, but the churches of the world will work out their own destruction without any help or hindrance from you."

"What do you mean by that?" the boy asked in surprise.

"All the churches in the world are part of the antichrist. By means of religion the Black Mentalists hold the faithful in bondage to misleading doctrines. The rest of the people are disposed toward atheism; so the Black Mentalists thereby block spiritual advancement for both the faithful and the cynical. Only truth will free men from the Black Mentalists, but evil's wily propaganda has predisposed the great majority of men to find the truths of existence unpalatable.

"The love and patience which Christ has toward mankind is truly magnificent. Despite the prevalent rejection of His Truth and its teachers, He endures the exasperating ignorance, perverseness, and hatefulness of men in order to bring even one deserving Ego to Mastership."

"Are all priests Black Mentalists?" Richard asked.

"Certainly not! There are many truly fine Egos working within the established churches in order to help mankind in whatever way they may. Some priests, ministers, pastors, and rabbis are doing a worthwhile job. These men are dedicated to a loving vision of God and seek to emulate His love of humanity. Unfortunately, such men are few. They are really *men of God*, and you will have no trouble recognizing them. Their work, unfortunately, is limited by their lack of true knowledge, and in this respect they are bound by the Black Mentalists. Those pastors who somehow acquire true knowledge are forbidden to teach or profess concepts over and above the doctrines of the denomination they vowed to preserve. As enlightenment comes to sincere pastors, they sometimes quit in accordance with their conscience and integrity. Others often remain within the facilities of their organization in order to have a continued opportunity to do the work they love even though they must not teach beyond the prescribed beliefs of their respective church.

"Unfortunately, the greater part of the priests and ministers of the Christian sects, as well as those of the other major religions of the world, are what is known as *grey occults*. These men are the unwitting servants of the Black Mentalists. They have the type of personalities which have caused them to gravitate to positions as religious leaders. The foremost characteristic common to these grey occults is their desire for control over others which is more vicious than a plutocrat's or dictator's ambitions to establish control over men, for the grey occult enters the realm of the soul. They seek to control an Ego's very thoughts and philosophy of life, to dominate his soul, to set limits on his free spirit, and to exact his obeisance. The highest and most noble of human aspirations of spirit are perverted by the grey occults into the very tools for shackling the spirit. The driving incentive of these grey occults is the exultant sense of power they experience as they make men tremble under the lash of offensive sermons oozing with hypocritical piousness. These are *never* happy men. They preach hellfire, damnation, death, guilt, and fear instead of preaching the joy of receiving Christ into one's life.

"The grey occults twist clean souls. They convince young people that everyone was born full of original sin which damns us to hell. But do not despair, for theologians then come to the rescue! They assert that the agonizing eternity of hell-fire can be avoided by merely confessing faith in Christ so that He may grant redemption. Thereafter one needs only belong to His Church and support it generously with money!

"No wonder the religion business is booming. Faith saves! Jesus saves! These traps for fools have been twisted in meaning to attract membership of the sinner who doesn't want to earn his salvation but feels more comfortable believing that mere faith in Christ will snatch him from the clutches of devils.

"The pagan magic which infiltrated the Christian doctrines early in the Church's history still besets us. Not only do people expect God to fill their needs without practical compensation, but they childishly seek a mystic mumbo-jumbo which will give them salvation without earning it. They look for spiritual enlightenment and omniscience as an outright gift from a Holy Ghost. How grossly unjust God would have to be to permit such travesties on Egoic self-responsibility.

"Men are lazy when it comes to exercising their Minds, but exercise them they *must* if they hope to achieve immortality. Man's body is but a chemical machine. His *glory* is Mind. Man *is* Mind! Man is even more man *without* his body than with it, but death has been made such a bugaboo by the Church that man is terrified of losing his body. He wants it back so bad that Christians have been promised that their physical bodies will be returned to them after Judgment Day. Moreover, it is to be a *special* body that will be returned to him—it will never die! They're right back to the Eden concept again. An eternity of heavenly pleasure without work but all the advantages of the delightful desires of the body. They are children who want to have their cake and to eat it too. The grey occults are happy to promise it to them. Why not? It provides them with a good living and high social status."

"Why do you want me to expose myself to this sort of thing if it is so bad?" Richard asked pleadingly.

"You must come to understand the atmosphere in which the spirit of Christ struggles. You will see the good in people seeking expression of greatness yet having to be content as best they can with church charities, mission work, and congregational comradeship. The people seek to create something greater than themselves and tend to express this innate human drive by building a magnificent edifice to house their God. They build together, and plunge into sacrificial debts together. All too often a congregation is held together solely by a mortgage in common. Their identification with an impressive structure gives them a sense of pride and security, and the pastor of the flock encourages ever-greater expansion of his church. The bigger the building and the more members in his congregation, the greater are his prestige and comforts. Instead of building souls, the pastor builds his monument to pride.

"The sincere church-goer seeks the Word of God, spiritual inspiration, communion with the Higher Beings, and a sense of doing right in the eyes of God. But then there are those who attend for fear of social ostracism or fear of God's wrath. Least of all are the members who seek social status by belonging to the *right* church and who tend to become influential in the church so they can exercise control over others. The latter type try to make a private club out of the church, and they frown upon visitors and new members who present a vague threat to the balance of power within the membership.

"The most hapless of church-goers are the children. They are indoctrinated from the beginning with the ideas that God cannot be understood, that the mysteries of the universe are beyond man's Mind, that one cannot know ultimate truth and so must be content with blind faith, that religion is the antithesis of science and logic, and that we are at the mercy of a powerful and incomprehensible Lord whose moral laws we must obey without question. Man has a Mind in order that he may understand. Morality isn't a matter of unthinking compliance to rules; morality can withstand the most rigorous logical examination. Man's very survival and his happiness result from intellectual moral integrity and not from cowering obedience to rules set up by an external agent. Any carefully observant person with a logical mind will arrive at generally the same code of proper human behavior as concluded by the wise men whose writings are represented in the Bible.

"Every rule, commandment, and admonition in the Bible outlines the path of the most serene and satisfying way of life. The Bible contains marvelous wisdom presented in palatable story forms. No wonder the Bible is still the greatest book ever written. The methods by which one can gain and maintain communion with the Lord are written for the wise to discern, and the full panoply of karmic pitfalls are warned against and entertainingly dramatized. The warnings and rules proffered in the Bible are designed to minimize one's accumulation of karmic indebtedness with its attendant sorrow and misfortune."

"And the ten commandments tell us how to treat other people right," Richard interjected brightly. He intended to show Berkeley that he was at least aware of the commandments and their content.

"Yes. Very true, Richard. But treating others right is only a by-product of following the law. The commandments are directed primarily to the individual for his own Egoic uplift. We aren't on Earth for others; we are here to glorify God by elevating ourselves to His level of perfection. Positive karma is very essential to Egoic advancement, which is why the Higher Beings who are assigned to helping us advance have made such an issue of the dangers of sin in the Bible. To lead the good life is divinely selfish, for one gains for himself in every way.

"Helping people along the path to advancement is generally considered a high expression of excess service to others; but while giving help, one's own mundane responsibilities must not be neglected nor should one give so much of his time and energy that his personal advancement is hampered. Nobody can advance another Ego. Each individual is strictly responsible for himself. One can try to provide the proper environment and information conducive to another's advancement, but not even Christ may intercede for an Ego nor may He elevate anyone."

"Why should there be so much confusion in religion?" the boy exclaimed in general exasperation.

"Because the Black Mentalists have done everything in their power to withhold and distort truth. Moreover, they have actively fostered the rise in power of every political, spiritual and intellectual tyrant ever known in order to quash men's freedom to acquire truth and broadcast it. Nobody hates freedom for mankind as much as the Black Mentalists do. Freedom is precious but easily lost because everywhere there are those who wish to impose their power, privilege, and ideas upon others.

These persons are the least to be trusted with rulership, but they are the very ones who seek power over others. It is far better to be an able public servant elected by equals to work for the general welfare at a just salary than to seek to be king over clod-like, dull-eyed serfs. In the first instance, the man is a man-among-men chosen by reason of his excellence. In the latter instance, there is no compliment to the ruler. The herder of sheep is not exalted for his position—neither by the sheep nor by other shepherds.

"Religious and intellectual despots seek power by concealing truth and by imposing their views rather than by persuading logically. Inquisition and secret arrest are their rebuttal to the wise man's logic. They cannot bear to permit another man his own convictions, and they are reduced to childish rage when others do not believe their self-proclamations. The bigots, the fanatics, and the shrill claimants to revealed mysteries are of such small spirit that they will smash bodies and defame greatness in order to bring everyone to their ridiculous level.

"The man of broad intellect knows that truth alone can keep men free. If men permit themselves to be ruled by evil, they must suffer national karma for the evil acts of their rulers. Witness the German people who have not revolted against Hitler and who now must suffer the karmic consequences of a war to which they have given their tacit consent. Had they used their wisdom and summoned up righteous courage to fight the evil spreading through their land, the world would still be at peace. Men *must* revolt against monstrous doctrines and evil rulers or else suffer the tragic consequences. But, on the other hand, men are wisely cautious not to revolt if the government can be bettered through the gradual evolution of wise legislation.

"England is politically stable because she used legislation to correct abuses of power. France is fractured because she chose civil war. It is better to sustain order and build upon established government than to try to rebuild in the chaotic aftermath of revolution. Strong men rise to dictatorship out of the ruins of revolution and provoke further revolution.

"Even the founders of the United States recognized the right of our citizens to revolt should unforeseen abuses arise against the populace. The provision that our citizens shall always be allowed to maintain arms in their homes guarantees their right to self-protection against a dictator. When a nation is deprived of this internal defense against corrupt police or a punitive military, it is delivered into bondage. Men must use every means at their disposal if it becomes necessary to defend their lives and their political and intellectual freedom. To fail to do so is to surrender to the forces of evil.

"Another major field of confusion induced by the Black Mentalists involves the relationship between men and women. Love is not the problem, for there never shall be too much love in the world! God himself is pure Love, and Christ is that Divine Love made manifest to men. The love that a man feels toward his God, his parents, his wife, his child, and his neighbors is all the same thing. However, toward his mate man demonstrates yet another facet of human nature—sex. The churches will tell you that love is pure because it arises from the Mind but that sex is vile because it arises from the body. Because sexual desire can cause so much mischief, it has been maliciously labeled a cesspool of filth by our near-sighted society in hopes that man could be persuaded to disown and obliterate it. Sex in itself is not filthy. All animals have the mating urge, but no one can say that a bird or a horse is obscene because of it. Without the sexual drive the world would be uninhabited. The Angels lovingly created human bodies to experience deep emotional fulfillment during the sex act and designed sex to be a unifying expression of love and mutual tenderness between a man and his wife. A marriage without sexual expression is hollow.

"Unfortunately, sex has been made into a very effectual tool of the Black Mentalists for disillusioning and debasing souls by promoting sex as being most romantic and exciting when it is forbidden and dirty. The practice of sex is a two-edged sword: if it becomes a guilty act of sniggering smuttiness, it can lead one to depths of despair, depravity, and morbid psychological fears which can preclude happiness for a lifetime; or in its Angelic dignity it can elevate one to heights of love and marital bliss. How you will use sex may well determine your whole outlook on life, and the converse is equally valid. A man's sexual morality is a reliable barometer of his overall morality. The effective power of his intellect to control the powerful sex drive so it will be wholly beneficial is an indication—by extension—of his ability to command his other ambitions and appetites.

"Intellect must command man's emotional nature if his desires are to serve him and be beneficial to him in an ordered, self-disciplined way. His self-esteem and spiritual strength arise from his sense of control over external nature and over his own human nature.

"Social conscience is a personal battlefield of adult intelligence versus childish desire. Morality is the wisdom to perceive that those desires which adversely affect the common good must be checked in order that other men will be encouraged to hold their like desires in check. The security of civilization depends upon this cooperation and mutual consent. Unfortunately, these days we still need legislation to limit the inherent freedom of all men just because of those who are too weak, stupid, selfish, or arrogant to employ self-discipline. Self-discipline is the means to soul growth. Stupidity requires legislative coercion from which no Egoic growth arises.

"Morality and karma are closely interrelated, and it should be evident that virtuous morality averts karmic debits. Immoral actions generally arise from one's lack of personal wisdom and strength of character, for immoral actions are those which are not for the eventual good of all persons concerned. Note that this is also the definition I gave you for sin. Sinfulness can be avoided by observing the inescapable laws of karma."

"How do I learn the laws of karma?" Richard asked.

"Primarily by observation and logic. However, you will be aided in this respect when you become a student of a Brotherhood."

The boy was still reluctant to undertake confirmation; and in view of the promise of eventual instruction from a higher source, he hoped to talk his way out of it. "I've already read the Bible, I don't see that I'll learn much more by being confirmed."

"If you were to read the Bible a hundred times, you would get more out of it every time."

"Sure, but am I supposed to believe things like Adam and Eve and Noah's ark?"

"These stories have their roots in truth even though they've been handed down to us in fanciful form. You will eventually come to know which stories are allegory and which are literal fact."

"Not very easily from what I can see," the boy complained.

"Nevertheless, you must become acquainted with what others believe; and furthermore, confirmation is necessary to fulfill future needs of which you are yet unaware. It won't hurt you. The church won't teach you to commit crimes."

Richard shrugged his resigned acquiescence.

"Since the discrepancies in the Bible disturb you, Richard, let me give you a few examples that may help guide you. Don't fret about Adam and Eve, for in the fifth chapter of Genesis the second verse explains that *Adam* and *Eve* are symbolic names applied to the first race of human beings. Cain, symbolic of the farmer, overcame the herdsman, Abel, as a way of explaining that man ceased his nomadic way and settled down to till the soil. His stability on the land gave rise to civilization. Noah's Ark dramatizes the submersion of Mu, and the tower of Babel symbolizes the colonization of the far-flung world. Abram is likely wholly symbolic, for his name means *Father God of Mu*. Even St. Paul refers to some of this episode as an allegory (*Galatians 4:24*). That Melchizedek was brought into the story of Abram and was referred to as the King of Salem only increases the likelihood that Genesis is allegory, for in Timothy's epistle to Hebrews (*7:2*) it is explained that Melchizedek is the King of Peace—Salem meaning *peace* in the language of Mu. It is therefore possible that Abram signifies Jehovah, for Timothy brings out the point that even the chief of Angels is less than Melchizedek. Incidentally, Jerusalem was originally *Harasalem* which in ancient terms means *city of the god of peace*. Further allegory is seen in Jacob's being called Israel and his twelve sons being prophesied each to give rise to a tribe, the futures of which are later foretold by Jacob. All of Genesis is an esoteric, allegoric parable in which only one real historic personality of note is recorded—Joseph, counsel to Pharaoh—whose tale is deeply symbolic of Christ's advent and forgiveness of man.

"The great confusion in the early books of the Bible arose at the hands of Ezra—the priest who translated the writings of Moses from Egyptian into Hebrew about six hundred years after Moses withdrew from His people. Moses wrote His books in highcaste Egyptian. Ezra and other learned priests of the Jews sought to translate the sacred papyri, but they were unaware that the Egyptian hieroglyphs each carried two meanings: a priestly, secret meaning and a common meaning conveying spoken language. The Jewish scholars were doomed at the start. Had they been Brothers, we would now have the true story of creation in our Bible; but Ezra's scholars were power-seeking priests subject to the Black Mentalists. They altered what they did not understand and made up what they couldn't fill in. The begats and the ancient lineages were fabrications of Ezra's priests. These fraudulent devices were intended to establish a divine right of the Levites to enjoy hereditary priesthood and the highest rank in the society—the same kind of sham as was manipulated centuries later in Europe to establish divine rights of rule for kings and popes by interpretation of scripture. The net result of Ezra's perfidy was to withhold from mankind the last great gift of true knowledge and history handed down to us from the archives of the Brotherhoods through Moses. The same archives had been drawn upon by Pharaoh Akhnaton to enable him to bring about a renaissance in Egypt just prior to Moses' birth. I often wonder how far Western Civilization might have come with that information."

"Couldn't Christ have given us that information when He was here?" Richard asked.

"He did, but only to His apostles in secret. The Sermon in the Mount as recorded by Matthew and Luke was only a small part of His special instruction to the twelve. Much sacred information was divulged to them which is ordinarily disseminated only through the Brotherhoods. They were taught by Christ along with members of an Essene retreat built inside a mountain on the shores of the Dead Sea. Isaiah founded this Judean branch of the Essene Brotherhood which had its main headquarters in Zoan, Egypt. The information received by the apostles was intended for their Egoic advancement and for their several ministries after Christ was crucified. We have no public record of the greater teachings of Christ because the writers of the Gospels were quite guarded in all their statements. They refrained from writing anything which would conflict with Christ's claims during His ministry on Earth.

"Christ couldn't preach counter to the Bible, or otherwise the devout Jews who became the first Christians would have rejected Him. Christ taught the general populace that He had come in fulfillment of the Law and the Prophets. Indeed He *had* come in fulfillment—and *more!*"

"Did He tell His apostles about reincarnation?" Richard inquired. "I don't recall seeing anything about it in the Bible."

"Christ most certainly taught His disciples the fact of reincarnation. Did He not state quite clearly that John the Baptist was Elijah, the Prophet of old? (*Matt. 11:7–15 and 17:10–13*) It is apparent that the disciples had been taught the doctrine of reincarnation, for in the Gospel of St. John (*9:2*) a disciple inquired of Christ saying, 'Master, who did sin, this man, or his parents, that he was born blind?' Obviously a fetus cannot commit sin before it is born. The disciple was inquiring whether this man was a practical example of karmic blindness carried over from a previous incarnation's misdeed. Christ was able to quickly perceive that this particular blind man had chosen blindness specifically to experience the works of Christ upon his person. There were many Egos who incarnated at that time primarily to enjoy the earthly manifestation of Christ as it personally applied to them. Christ answered His disciple saying that this man was such a one. The answer in itself is further indicative of reincarnation, for the incarnating Ego would have had to choose the time and circumstances before his birth as a blind babe."

"Are there any books of the Bible which are especially valuable to read more than others?" the boy inquired.

"All of them are valuable, of course. But I would say that three books are particularly meaty: the prophesy of Isaiah, the Gospel of St. John, and the epistle to Hebrews from Timothy."

"What about the writings of St. Paul? You don't seem to think much of his epistles," Richard observed.

"Not as a source of valid Christian doctrine, I don't! Paul was a practical Pharisee and a stickler for details of observance. His calls for discipline and practical Christian behavior are well taken. Let him go at that."

Berkeley dug out his pocket watch and said, "I think that we had better call it a night. It's getting late." The man stood up and started for the door whereupon Richard followed him. As they walked down the stairway to the first floor of the school building, Berkeley reached into his overalls and presented the boy with a small jar.

"What's this?" Richard asked.

"It's a pigmented collodion to cover the name we wrote on you tonight. It's not likely that you'll need it very often, but there will be times when it will come in handy. It's tinted to the exact shade of your skin."

"Who'd see it anyway?" the boy asked in surprise.

"You are to conceal that writing until the first boy is born in your household—absolutely not before!"

"Why not?"

"Because you have just been instructed not to. Furthermore, you are never to reveal the full meaning of that which is written upon you to anyone as long as you live. If a person can tell *you* what it means, you will know he's a Brother authorized to give further instruction. Now, memorize this sign and countersign!"

Berkeley made sure that Richard understood the details of his new name and of certain identifying codes. Then he briefly outlined the movies the boy was supposed to have seen that evening in case anyone should question him about them. Berkeley then opened the front door, and Richard slipped outside. He walked a few steps and suddenly returned as Berkeley was closing the door. When the man saw him coming back, he opened the door again and waited with curiosity.

Richard extended his hand, and Berkeley took it. The man and the boy shook hands solemnly, and then the boy smiled broadly. "I like you very much, Mr. Berkeley."

Berkeley grinned and chuckled with pleasure. As they parted the old man waved and softly called, "May God go with you always, my boy!"

CHAPTER 8

Intervening Years

The morning following his meeting with Berkeley and the Seven, Richard was awakened about dawn by a burning pain at the site of his operation. If his adventure had seemed only a dream, the reality of the pain now dispelled it. Unable to sleep any longer, he lay awake reviewing the marvelous happenings of the previous day which, as it turned out, had not been entirely unblemished; for he had incurred the displeasure of his father and was to be in a state of parental discipline for the next month. Because of the late hour, his father had thoughtfully driven to the Elm Theater to give him a ride home; and when Richard failed to emerge from the theater at the end of the last show, his father became deeply concerned. Fortunately, the boy had returned home just before his father telephoned his mother. Richard underwent a rather close questioning when his father came home, and the boy's nervousness made his father suspicious even though his excuses were plausible. As Richard lay thinking in bed, he concluded that the advantages of the evening had nonetheless outweighted the disadvantages. He only wished that he could share with someone the experiences he had enjoyed.

During the next several years, Richard came to realize that there was no one to whom he could speak or from whom he could obtain corroborative information. His sense of aloneness was heightened throughout his early teens, but at the same time his ability to perceive the nature of life and the foibles and struggles of human beings was sharply increased. The unique information bestowed upon him provided a rare insight into the ways of the world. The vantage point from which he was able to view the actions around him was as from a great height which left the troubles of the world peculiarly remote and untroubling to him; but the greater horizons afforded him were from an altitude which was necessarily cold and lonely.

The boy, however, seemed to create two separate worlds for himself. In one sphere, he was an analyst and philosopher on an adult level; in the other he was a gregarious, normal child. The two worlds were unable to intermix. His deeper perceptions were exceptionally mature, but his personal reactions to every-day living were common to a boy his age. He held his mind aloof, but his personality expressed eagerness to please others and to enjoy the company of friends.

The remainder of his last year in elementary school was un-distinguished. He graduated in June, 1940, from the John Mills Public School, and in early spring of the same year he was con-firmed in the Westwood Lutheran Church.

The following September Richard entered C. P. Steinmetz Senior High School in Chicago. Most of his schoolmates from elementary school went to their local township high school, but Richard lived in a section of Elmwood Park which allowed him to attend the Chicago school. For all practical purposes Richard had to make new friends again.

His freshman year was devoted to the struggle of learning how to study effectively and efficiently. He did exceptionally well in the course of General Science where he became closely acquainted with Dr. Daniels, a teacher who was to have an important influence on the boy's early life. Mathematics was also well liked by Richard, but Latin and English did not spark his interest. During the first semester in school he enrolled in the required physical education course, but during the second se-mester he transferred to the band which was nominally associ-ated with the Reserve Officers Training Corps program of the United States Army. He joined the R.O.T.C. Band primarily to avoid having to undress in the shower rooms after gymnasium. He was using up the jar of pigmented collodion at a rapid rate in order to conceal the name written upon his body. Having to wear an R.O.T.C. cadet's uniform didn't particularly appeal to Richard, but it was his only alternative to physical education classes.

The band proved to be the boy's key to school activities. The band was required at school functions, assemblies, rallies, and sports events; and tickets were not needed by band members where they performed. In Richard's sophomore year he was promoted to corporal in the band which obliged him to attend the non-commissioned officers' school of the regular R.O.T.C. Despite his strong objections to war and armies, he discovered that he enjoyed the precision of close-order-drill and the clear-cut status afforded by the observance of rank and precedence. Perhaps because he was living in a world torn by war and uncertainty, the orderliness he discovered among the cadets in the non-commissioned officers' school appealed to him. In the band, on the other hand, military observances were regarded with a fine disdain not uncommon to musicians. The band's lack of discipline and conscientiousness became a sore point to Richard, and therefore in his junior year he transferred from the band to the R.O.T.C. cadet regiment. Within a year-and-a-half he was a captain in charge of training the recruit company. He earned the position by developing a new training program, but the Brothers assisted by arranging a series of unusual opportunities to allow Richard to display his talents where they could be appreciated. He declined an offer to become Regimental Adjutant at the rank of Major in order to be able to implement his training plan as an officer of the line. In the R.O.T.C. he learned many valuable lessons: how to achieve recognition, how to guide subordinates, and how to earn the comradeship of buddies. He formed life-long active friendships with about a dozen fellow officers of the high school's R.O.T.C.

Richard's scholastic abilities improved appreciably from his sophomore year; and by the time he graduated from high school, he was in the upper five percent of his class. He usually had enough interest in his studies to go well beyond the requirements of the course, and he did his best to fulfill Berkeley's admonition to learn, learn, and learn some more. The sciences were his forte. He squeezed five science courses into four years and took four years of mathematics. Chemistry was his first love, and he planned to go on to college to train for chemico-medical research. Dr. Daniels encouraged Richard in many ways in his studies. They attended scientific conferences and conventions, and Dr. Daniels selected advanced texts for his pupil and suggested special projects. They usually discussed scientific matters for many long hours after school. Dr. Daniels was a man in his fifties who had reared two daughters to college age, but he had longed for a son with a propensity toward the sciences. Richard became that son.

The boy's typical teenage energy and enthusiasm led him to become active in many extracurricular school activities. Richard and his pals enjoyed long bull sessions lasting late into the night. There were hilarious conversations given to clever and rapid patter concerning politics, philosophy, and world nonsense of the day. Serious discussion aroused as much, if not more, interest as did fun and horse play. They derived much pleasure by dining at fine restaurants and by attending plays and opera, and they were no less interested in outings, sports, and traveling. Their schoolteachers regarded the young men highly because Richard and his friends had the happy facility of enjoying life without getting into mischief.

It is interesting to note, however, that when it came time for a school dance of importance, Richard and his group of friends managed to escort the young ladies of their choice. They all went on to college, and several earned doctorates in their field. They have since married, but they waited until they were established before pursuing a course of activity that leads to marriage.

Richard graduated from Steinmetz High School in June, 1944, which was when the Allied Armies invaded the European mainland. In order to get as much education as possible before being drafted into the armed service, Richard entered Northwestern University which offered a special, accelerated course. He could obtain a Bachelor of Science degree in two calendar years by attending summer classes and taking more credit hours of work than ordinarily permitted during each school term. Richard entered the college on partial scholarship at the age of sixteen. In his freshman year he completed three years of chemistry in addition to his regular studies in German, English, and physics.

The strain of this tremendous expenditure of energy was beginning to show on the boy. There was no housing available on campus, and his parents believed he was too young to live in a rooming house; therefore, he commuted from his home which was one-and-a-half hours from the campus. The work load and the transportation problem allowed a maximum of only two hours sleep per day including week-ends. Richard became quite haggard and thin, and a mental listlessness began to set in as he regarded the beginning of his sophomore year in college.

The war in Europe was still raging, and our offensive in the Pacific was making little headway; so it was natural that the feelings of uncertainty, if indeed not despair, that plagued most young men of that time should settle upon Richard too. At heart he was a conscientious objector to war, but his sense of patriotic duty was also strong.

He registered for the Spring Quarter which began his second year of college, and he began attending classes with little enthusiasm. Richard was sorely distressed by the war and especially because his entrance into it was imminent. The sights, sounds, and smells of war were vibrantly real to him, and he doubted that he would gain any advantage from being in the army. Some persons consoled him with the assertion that war experiences make a man of a boy, but he doubted that any emotional maturity was likely to be engendered by battle. That men must fight against invaders was a strong conviction of his, and he would willingly and without hesitation risk his life to repulse an attack on Chicago. But many of the issues of the war overseas were obscure, and he questioned the noble aims mouthed by the Allied nations. To die or be crippled for a politician's ultimate profit was to him a sin, and he wished fervently to know just what the purpose of American soldiers overseas was. Were they there to further commercial interests or to prevent eventual invasion of American shores by a madman bent on world conquest? The journalists of the period promulgated both views.

A long time had elapsed since he had thought about the Brotherhoods; and on an April night, as he rode home from the first day of classes, he found his mind turning to Dr. White and Berkeley. It seemed curious to him that he had let them slip from his consciousness so completely as of late. The concerns of studying and growing up had gradually displaced the Brotherhoods from his philosophical considerations. Richard felt remiss in this very important matter.

His studies had influenced his outlook to the extent that lately he was overly conscious of the precise and orderly world of science and its logic. The scientific attitude, however, could not provide Richard with any comfort in his moments of turmoil. There was no solace in logic, even were the facts of the young man's problem discernible and concisely presented for examination. It was, therefore, only to be expected that in the crisis of confusion he would turn to the source of comfort and peace he had experienced in the presence of the Brothers. As he sat forlornly gazing out the window of the street car at the bright stars above, he felt a strong need of contact with the Great Beings beyond. His silent prayer for guidance was so emotionally intense that tears blurred his vision.

CHAPTER 9

A Bit of Prophecy

The day following Richard's prayer, he felt much more content than he had for the past week. He awakened with a deep sense of peace; and when he arose from bed, he felt unusually sunny and refreshed. A dream which he could not recall seemed to be responsible for his contentment, but this was really only a vague suspicion on his part.

Richard attended his morning classes; and he went to eat his lunch, which he usually brought in his briefcase, at a pier jutting into Lake Michigan behind the Technological Institute of the university. He had just finished eating when a delightful sense of general well-being enfolded him. The pleasant view of the lake from where he sat in solitude was enhanced by the bright sun sparkling on the wavelets stirred by the clear, crisp April breeze. On sudden impulse Richard quickly turned to look behind him, and he was not at all astonished to see Dr. White standing patiently behind him.

"That's odd," Richard commented as he rose to his feet and approached Dr. White, "I had the strongest suspicion you were nearby!"

Dr. White smiled broadly at Richard. It was quite evident from the younger man's demeanor that he was overjoyed to see the elderly doctor. "I'm pleased to see you've come a long way in the past five years, lad," he said gently and with obvious esteem. The two shook hands warmly, and the meeting was very much like a reunion of father and son.

"If I'd known you would show up so soon after, I'd have called upon you much earlier," Richard joked.

"Please don't count on it," Dr. White cautioned. "You won't be able to look upon me again until after the Kingdom of God is established."

Richard puzzled over this statement for a moment as the kindly man looked at him steadfastly. He never knew what to expect from Dr. White, for he could be pretty startling at times.

"How soon will that be?"

"In about sixty years, let's say," Dr. White replied casually.

Richard did not expect such a candid reply. The fact that Dr. White was being very open was a clue that this interview was likely to be especially revealing. If this latter thought had not been uppermost in Richard's mind, it is possible that he might have thought at that time to relate Dr. White's present age to what his projected age would be in sixty years.

"How can you say sixty years so positively?" Richard queried.

"Because that is the schedule that was established long ago."

Richard was about to pursue this line, but Dr. White linked his arm with the young man's and guided him back to where he had been sitting. "Come, let's sit down while we talk. How have you been since I saw you last?"

The two men sat down, and Richard replied, "I've been in excellent health, and I think I'm beginning to learn a few things of importance."

"Good! Good!" Dr. White said with enthusiasm. "Do you still plan to be a physician?"

"No. I've decided to go into medical research from the biochemical aspect."

"I see. What caused you to alter your original plan?"

"Following your suggestion, I took a job as a laboratory helper during summer vacation the year before college to see if I really liked the job. I discovered that hospitals depress me. Perhaps it was because of the diseased tissues and morbid fluids that I was required to analyze or prepare for the pathologist, but I was also repelled by the atmosphere of the place. I'm not in the slightest afraid of disease, but patients and hospital personnel alike seem so negative and unwholesome that I knew that I was not likely to be happy in such surroundings for the rest of my life."

"But someone needs to care for the sick," Dr. White commented.

"True enough. I'm thankful that there are men and women who are drawn to alleviate the bodily ills of others, but I don't believe I would be very successful at it. The risk of diagnostic error as a practicing physician would probably haunt me to the point of ineffectualness. I believe I can better serve to relieve men's suffering by researching medicine. The actions of chemotherapeutic materials on the body fascinate me."

"You seem to have forgotten my admonitions concerning your life's work, Richard," Dr. White said cooly.

"It doesn't seem to me that I'm much inclined toward the tasks you have set for me; whereas I seem quite proficient at chemistry and the natural sciences."

"My friend, you are avoiding life," Dr. White said in earnestness.

Richard was taken aback by his assertion. "How do you mean?" he stammered.

Dr. White smiled compassionately. "You are not unlike most seventeen-year-olds. The world seems so complex and incomprehensible at your age that you cling to the concrete sciences where two plus two equals four and always will equal four. But life isn't like that. Psychology demonstrates that a man is likely to be just opposite of what he seems. Similarly, social science is beginning to document the complex interplay between human beings and their economic and social institutions. The investigations undertaken by psychologists and sociologists are invaluable to understanding politics which is the total expression of man's relation to man. These things are, and always shall be, far more important to all men than the sciences. If men are not practical philosophers, moralists, and politicians, a society conducive to the pursuit of scientific knowledge cannot even arise."

"I don't understand," Richard said.

"In short, scientists are subsidized by the practical stability afforded by sound political advancement. Science is unquestionably the key to our comforts and increased longevity, but the academic pursuit of science which flourishes today depends upon a previously established politico-economic organization. Civilizations have existed happily without the sciences. Our own culture is very advanced scientifically, but social stability and personal happiness still elude the great majority of us. Therefore, which is most important, science or social stability?"

"Social stability," Richard conceded.

"However, I wouldn't advocate the separation of science from society. Science is basically important to a modern culture. Man must eventually come to master a burgeoning technology so vast and complex as to be beyond your present comprehension. However, men must not be subservient to science or become trapped in the machinations of technology. On Earth, man is the measure of all things. Because mastery over one's self and one's environment is essential to one's spiritual advancement, each of us must perceive and command all science concerning our physical environment. But unless man also devises a stable political and economic society in accordance with God's natural laws, all will be transitory.

"The understanding of science is child's play compared with understanding human motivations, politics, and the effects of morals and psychological drives upon the fabric of a given culture. These knotty concepts are infinitely varied and difficult to reduce to formulae. Skill of observation and practice in the art of living are demanded of him who would lead men and gather them into a great nation. He must be a man who can courageously meet the fearful tasks involved in creating a national spirit and welding a people into ethnic unity. But such a man will never be able to rely on two plus two being four because in dealing with human beings there are no unalterable modes of conduct. He must continually measure the condition of his people and perceive the tenor of their moods so that he may ever adjust, balance, and forge ahead with his people. Only in this way will they have an effective, informed guide toward the perfection the Brotherhoods have planned for them.

"Science is often a recluse's retreat. However, scientists will soon come into greater acceptance by the general populace than they experience now. You, however, must become vigorously adept in the guidance of men. This requires a slow process of learning, but it will not be learned from guinea pigs and test tubes. You must deal with men in order to learn of men. Only the laboratory of life can provide the experiments and experiences which lead to proficient living.

"Tell me," Dr. White demanded, "what do you think of college now that you've had a year of it?"

"I'm quite disappointed with it," Richard confessed.

"In what respect?"

"I thought it would be much more advanced than it is. When I was in high school, the level of work seemed so shallow that I was eager to get into college where I presumed the nature of the study-material would be adult and advanced. But it seems that college is just a continuation of the very same teaching methods. The amount of homework expected is greater, but the same lack of emphasis on understanding is still operative. Perhaps I was childish in expecting my professors and instructors to be intellectual giants. They have the same tired attitude as my high school teachers. They're pouring a prescribed potion of information into yet another in the endless chain of classes which present themselves for talking to year after year. We do the assigned lessons and get a grade; and when we pass the exams, we're considered educated in a subject to the extent of so many credit hours. A certain accumulation of credit hours entitles us to a bachelor's degree. At the end we can't really be considered to have advanced in understanding or practical knowledge or ability. The degree, as I see it, is merely a measure of exposure to certain information.

"I don't feel that I've done anything so far that I couldn't have learned without the daily discipline of class assignments. All the laboratory work is mostly a matter of following recipes. I've done more original experimentation in my laboratory at home."

"Well, Richard, I give you credit for having seen the situation so clearly," Dr. White said smilingly. "It is unfortunate that college is no longer a repository of advanced thinking. A college degree is really a sort of 'union card' which is needed for an introduction to a better-salaried position. But most people who attend college are there for precisely that purpose and nothing more. Because employers often use the degree as a device for the elimination of job applicants, having a degree has become important to many who otherwise should have stayed out of college. A degree is presumed to be a measure of intelligence and an index of culture and knowledge. But I have seen educated dolts lose out to capable men of practical experience when put to test in the office or in the shop.

"A college degree is no indication of eventual success. The man of ability will get to the top with or without a college degree. A specific trade or phase of engineering unquestionably requires the understanding of the technical aspects of that trade, and a college degree in a technological field is really a sort of manual-training certificate. Extensive on-the-job experience is still needed before such a graduate is of value to his employer.

"What the world still needs is an institution of learning where men of real ability can be trained toward becoming humanly perfect, and this involves the whole panoply of intellectual endeavor. The colleges of today don't even tease the students' capacity for greatness. How wonderful it would be if a college were to become a magnificent spiritual and intellectual proving ground and thereby act as a prodding incentive calling upon the full depths of one's inherent abilities."

"That is what I dreamed college would be," Richard interjected.

"And that is the kind of institution that you are personally charged with establishing in the Kingdom of God."

Richard was nonplussed. "But I know absolutely nothing of such things!"

"You know more than you think you do! Furthermore, you have very little to gain by staying here in college—they don't teach what you must learn."

"But I'll have to earn a living," Richard protested.

"You'll do better outside the field of chemistry. You couldn't stand the routine little jobs you'd have to be content with if you take only a bachelor's degree. And you have neither the time nor the money to acquire the advanced degree which would entitle you to a more challenging and better-paying position."

"What shall I do?" Richard asked somewhat irritably.

"Quit school and get out into the world! You have so very much to learn about people, that you cannot delay your training. The Brotherhoods will see to it that you are exposed to the situations you need to balance your personality and to enable you to handle future problems. If you quit now during the first week of the school quarter, you will get a refund on your tuition here."

"I suppose it really doesn't make much difference," Richard shrugged. "I'll probably be drafted in six months anyway."

"I doubt that very much," Dr. White said.

"Huh? Why do you say that?"

"Because you've had enough of war in your past lives. You have little to learn from such experience, and you haven't the kind of negative karma that needs to be balanced out from that specific direction. In one of your incarnations you united the Jews into a nation symbolic of the foregathering Kingdom of God in which all the twelve races of Mu shall be represented. At that time you fully demonstrated your generalship and kingship. Having incarnated among the Jews at that time in order to help uplift their race, you earned their everlasting respect as one of their most endeared kings. Yet, truly greater things are in the offing."

"You amaze me," Richard chuckled.

Dr. White looked quite surprised.

"I mean," the young man continued, "that you flatter me so outrageously. I doubt you only when you tell me such things."

"Don't be impressed, lad. I reveal these vignettes of your past in order that you may better understand yourself and the Brotherhoods' faith in you.

"I wish to instruct you further on the training you are about to begin; so let's not digress until I have finished my thoughts.

"When you have been in a job long enough to learn the routine and you are offered a promotion, that will be your signal to quit and find another position."

"But that's foolish," Richard exclaimed. "I'll always be starting at the bottom. I hope one day to be able to afford some of the things other people enjoy. If I'm forever earning a beginner's wage, I'll never amount to anything."

"Never?" Dr. White chided.

"Well, that depends on how long this training period of yours will last."

"About fifteen years," was the bland reply.

"Holy Cow! I'll be an old man by then."

"If you adhere to the Brotherhoods' program for you, you will always enjoy a comfortable living. You will suffer only from your impatience. You have many things to make a part of your being which cannot be learned from reading or attending lectures. The varied industries and widely different jobs in which you will work are designed not only to teach you how to deal with men but also to show you how things are done in offices and factories. You will one day be instrumental in establishing the industries of a city and later a nation. The experiences you will have during the next years will be invaluable to you and your people.

"When you establish the Kingdom of God, it will be upon the great Isle of the West which will rise out of the Pacific Ocean at the end of this century. This island will for the most part have the same general boundaries as the long-submerged continent of Mu."

Richard was about to speak, but Dr. White held up his hand to delay the interruption.

"Obviously you won't be able to move people onto a barren, former sea-floor and hope to survive there. Much preliminary preparation must be made. You will first have to establish a community near the Chicago area in order to train the prospective candidates for the Kingdom of God. I will later explain the nature and purpose of this training. Until the time comes for the establishment of the community near here, the Brotherhoods will continue to bring about the development of Chicago as a balanced, diversified industrial area which can better nurture your special community into a strong city.

"Your city must always be totally self-sufficient and industrially strong because when the continent rises, most of the world will be destroyed. Raw material sources will then be non-existent; therefore, your scientists need to devise synthetic materials and have them perfected before that day. Since most of the United States will be several thousand feet below an ocean after the turn of the century, you will have to move your community to a place that will be safe during the cataclysm." Dr. White produced a small map from his pocket and pointed out the location of the place to Richard.

Continuing his discussion, Dr. White said, "The economic and political strife that will plague the United States and the rest of the world for the two decades prior to the coming inundation will make it imperative that you move your community between twenty and fifteen years before the end of the century. Before that time, however, the growth of the community near Chicago will be phenomenal. By various means, the Brotherhoods will influence the right persons to seek you out and to desire entrance into your budding city. It will be almost exclusively from among these citizens that the Brothers Themselves will select the persons qualified to colonize the Kingdom of God.

"Now that we have a general picture, let's go back and pick up the details."

"First, I'd like to know about this business of the ancient continent rising out of the ocean," the young man said.

"As you might imagine, lad, such an upheaval will produce far-reaching and disastrous consequences throughout the world. The event is of such importance that the Bible is full of prophetic references to it. The event is generally referred to as Doom's Day by scholars and laymen alike, and it is aptly named.

"The mechanics by which it shall occur follow the same pattern as has been the case over the long geologic history of our world. The Earth's crust continually is in the process of rising and falling—becoming alternately ocean and continent—and producing the stratified layers of rock so readily observed in mountainous areas. Our planet's surface rocks, which are about thirty miles thick at most, 'float' upon the denser underlayment. The underlayment is subjected to such extreme heat and pressure that it cannot crystalize, and although it is essentially solid material, it does not have the interlocking crystalline structure to give it dimensional stability. It is very much like a rubbery plastic and comprises the intermediate layer buffering our hard rock surface from the liquid core of the planet.

"You probably already know that Greenland was recently a tropical land even though it is now mostly covered by glacial ice. A *major* shift of the earth's land masses occurred with the sinking of Mu 26,000 years ago.[1] The Earth doesn't change its axis because the great inertia of the dense core gives our whirling sphere gyroscopic stability; however, our planet's crust slid several thousand miles to reach a tenable equilibrium which it had lacked before it shifted. The shift was started by vast, ever-widening glaciers of thick polar ice accumulating in a lopsided deposit on the spinning surface of the planet. Because of the inconceivable tonnage of these glaciers, the resultant imbalance

---

[1]A major shift of all the continents occurred about 7,500 years ago—3,000 years after Atlantis sank.

was sufficient to cause severe centrifugal aberrations in the Earth's rotation which literally shook the foundations of the continents. Although the ice was the trigger for the big slide of the Earth's surface, other factors contributed to setting up the condition of surface instability.

"The Earth is constantly undergoing a slight shifting of overall size; and since the rigid crust cannot conform to this change in dimensions as readily as the liquid core, the crust must adjust itself through a settling process that makes itself known by earthquakes. The faults produced by the settling process often permit rock at a depth of about ten to fifteen miles to liquefy as pressure above is relieved. The molten rock wells up through the fault and can sheet out over large areas to considerable depth. For about a thousand years prior to the sinking of Mu this type of terranean activity was quite prevalent in parts of the world and was particularly extensive along the southeast coastal lands of Mu near where Easter Island is presently located. Continental arches were also established by earthquake action which allowed the crust to rest more commodiously on the plastic intermediate layer. As time wore on, the whole surface structure became shot through with a maze of faults and pockets.

"When the polar ice cap began to slide, the whole surface began to break up and move over the plastic underlayment. The principal movement was completed within about seventy-two hours, but relatively minor adjustments continued to wreak havoc for some centuries afterward. New mountain ranges were thrust up, and continents were depressed or elevated. Oceans were displaced, and almost everything was changed seemingly overnight.

"The same situation is evolving in the world today. The crust is again out of a state of equilibrium; the continental arches are ripe for buckling; and the ice caps, though much smaller, are unbalanced. The trigger this time, however, will be from an outside source. On May 5th of the year 2000 A.D. the planets of the Solar System will be arrayed in practically a straight line across space, and our planet will be subjected to enough gravitational distortion to tip the delicate balance. Although one cannot normally expect mere planetary configurations to have such a spectacular effect upon us, many factors within our Earth are conjoining to produce great surface instability around the turn of the century.

"The developing state of the Earth's surface structure and the effect that the planets will have upon it was long ago carefully measured and analyzed by the Masters who, with the aid of Melchizedek, arranged Their program for the establishment of the Kingdom of God to coincide with this horrendous cataclysm. The Book of Revelation is mostly concerned with this period.

"Chapter sixteen of Revelation foretells the nature of the final years of this century. During the period which will begin after 1953, changes in the climate will be noted all over the world. Meteorologic upheavals will give rise to destructive winds, droughts, floods, and a generally high incidence of disruptive atmospheric conditions (*Rev. 16:1–12*); the final battle of Armageddon is then recounted (*Rev. 16:13–17*);and the chapter finishes with a description of the cataclysmic earthquakes which shortly follow Armageddon (*Rev. 16:18–21*). That the great earthquakes are an integral part of Judgment Day is stated in Revelation (*6:12–17*) and in the General Epistle of Jude."

"Would you please explain what Armageddon is?" Richard requested.

"Armageddon refers to the final great battle which will be so violent and destructive that nothing previous will be comparable to it. The viciousness and hatefulness of the combatants will reach new lows. The weapon of Armageddon is being forged at this very moment here in Chicago. The period of Armageddon began in the year 1914 and will rise intermittently to a crescendo of more frequent and progressively destructive wars. The battle of Armageddon will be the culmination of this series of violent outbursts. The last war will begin in 1998 and will end in wholesale obliteration in November, 1999.

"A few months later the seismic reapportionment of the world's land masses will come upon most of the survivors of Armageddon as a blessing. After Armageddon and Doom's Day, less than a tenth of the world's population will be alive to see the year 2001 A.D. The intensity of the earthquakes will be greater than has ever been measured by scientists. All the volcanoes of the world will burst forth, and a host of new ones will join them. Vast quantities of heavy gasses like carbon dioxide and sulfur dioxide will be hurtled into the stratosphere by the erupting volcanoes. The gasses will become super-cooled in the outer reaches of the atmosphere and then descend upon the surface of the Earth in convection currents of such magnitude that hurricane winds will howl over the face of the world. The skies will be filled with dust and choking fumes so that even the sun will not be seen directly for months. Walls of water a thousand feet high will roar across the submerging land and sweep away everything before them. Sea and land animals, vegetation, silt, and sand will be shredded into jumbled muck. Where soil is not washed away, it will be covered by boulders and stone; and the newly exposed sea bottom will be worthless for growing crops. The stench of decay and the bleak destruction everywhere will drive many human survivors hopelessly insane. Those who have the strength of their convictions will retain their civilization and rebuild the world. Those people, of course, will comprise the Kingdom of God, and they will be brought through the awful destruction soon to be visited upon the world. Doom's Day will not be without advantages, for it ushers in the Golden Age. After October, 2001 A.D. the Kingdom of God will be formed."

Richard was visibly shaken by Dr. White's account. "But why such a terrible way? Need so many lives be lost?"

"The karmic indebtedness of mankind as a whole will be taken care of to a great extent by these occurrences, Richard. It is really for the best in the long view. In Revelation it is promised that evil shall be 'bound'—which is to say that the influence of the Black Mentalists upon the righteous who shall still be alive will be restrained. Armageddon and Doom's Day are the Judgment. Those who are pure in heart will be spared; the careless and thoughtless will be removed. The selection will be based on Egoic advancement and personal karmic balance. The Kingdom of God must have no karma at its inception; therefore, each individual in that wondrous nation-to-be must have dissipated his own indebtedness so that he carries none into the new nation. The hardships which those who shall comprise the Kingdom must undergo during Doom's Day will be sufficient to off-set any residual debts. Of all the world's population they will suffer least, for they shall have had the advantage of the training of the Brotherhoods in the community near Chicago and shall

133

have put Their wisdom into practice in preparation against the great trial.

"The last half of the twentieth century will see much seismic and volcanic activity which, like the wars and atmospheric disturbances, will increase in frequency and destructiveness as the century draws to a close. Let these warnings be heeded by those who can comprehend.

"As a digression of interest, let me mention the apparent oversight of one Dionysius Exiguus who, in 533 A.D. proposed that the calendar years be counted from the birth of Christ instead of from the founding of Rome. His researches indicated that Christ had been born during the twenty-eighth year of the reign of Augustus Caesar. But here is where the Brotherhoods interfered with Dionysius' reckoning. He failed to uncover the fact that Augustus reigned for four years under his own name of Octavian before he was proclaimed Augustus by the Roman Senate. The Brotherhoods know that Jesus was born on October 4, 4 B.C., but it would have been awkward for Doom's Day to fall on the year 2004 A.D. since certain prophesies make 2000 A.D. the preferred year. The time of the great earthquakes is not being brought about by Higher Intelligence but is merely the natural consequence of geophysical forces. However, it suits the purposes of the Brotherhoods to make Their plans for mankind coincide with this scientifically predictable cataclysm.

"When the world has become quiescent again after this century, the Kingdom of God will flourish and know peace and prosperity such as no nation has ever enjoyed. After the Kingdom of God has been in existence for about ten centuries, Christ will come again as Melchizedek and use a physical body precipitated from 'basic substance' just as He did when He became the first Emperor of Lemuria. This will be as Timothy, in his epistle to Hebrews, described Melchizedek as 'King of Salem, which is, King of Peace. Without father, without mother, without descent, having neither beginning of days nor end of life; but made like unto a Son of God.' (*Hebrews 7:2–3*).

"Melchizedek will reign as the first Emperor of the Kingdom of God for a period of one thousand years during which time the Black Mentalists will be totally prevented from having any influence whatever over the human life-wave. This is the period known as the Millennium. Without any negative influences to hinder civilization, men will rapidly advance toward Mastership. Judgment Day will have removed evil men, and Melchizedek will have removed evil Mentalists. After Melchizedek's departure, men will be easily strong enough to resist and overcome any evil."

"Dr. White," Richard began thoughtfully, "I've read the Bible, and the term Kingdom of God seems to mean practically anything one wants it to. Does the Bible definitely refer to the Kingdom of God as a physical nation here on Earth?"

"The phrase *Kingdom of God,* as you say, can mean everything. It is used to refer to men, Heaven, and nations symbolic and actual. But the usage concerning the nation to be established on the Island of the West is referred to by Christ in *The Lord's Prayer* which He gave to us to repeat daily or oftener. He said, 'Our Father which art in Heaven, Hallowed be Thy name, Thy kingdom come, Thy will be done in Earth as it is in Heaven.' Inasmuch as Christ directs His prayer to the Father God, the kingdom to which He refers is the Kingdom of God. When it becomes manifest on Earth, God will be served by men as He is served by Angels in Heaven. So remember, whenever you repeat His prayer, you will be reminded of the Kingdom of God on Earth which Christ considered next in importance after praise of God."

CHAPTER 10

Lemurian Economics

Dr. White's visit was coming to be regarded by Richard with mixed feelings. He was happy indeed to see the man again, and there was little doubt but that he would be told much on this occasion; however, he was learning distressing things about the world, and the instructions concerning his personal future were disruptive of his own plans. Apparently sensing the young man's disappointment over the instructions to discontinue college and go to work, Dr. White began to enlarge upon the values of so doing.

"Working in industry will offer you the chance to see in action the many types of men with whom you will one day have to deal," Dr. White said. "You will also see for yourself the incredible inefficiency and muddling-through that characterizes all shops and offices large and small. The ineptitude of bosses to lead effectively and the disinterest of their employees will be clearly brought home to you. The prices of merchandise and services are high today because waste and inefficiency must be absorbed through excessive markups.

"Labor and management are constantly at one another's throats because the men of both factions seek to gain in excess of the services they perform. Given an opportunity, employers would cut wages and exercise despotic control over those who work for them. As in all too recent times, laborers would be employed at starvation wages as a result of collusion between employers to hold down the wages offered. Injured and aged workmen would be cast aside without concern, much like outworn machines. On the other hand, organized labor unions seek to work less and to demand ridiculous benefits by using extortion methods which have proven so effective to date. Both sides will war forever unless the economic principles laid down by Christ come to be observed fastidiously by all concerned.

"Unfortunately, the economic dead weight in the karmically unsound trade practices of our day cancels out the rightful profit margin to which manufacturers and farmers are entitled. If the middlemen, distributors, brokers, lenders, and taxers were eliminated, there would be enough money to pay every laborer an amount worthy of his effort. With such dead weight removed, retail prices would be lowered, thereby increasing the purchasing power of everyone's earnings. The manufacturer must now pass along to the ultimate consumer the costs of multitudinous taxes, interest payments on loans, and dividends to investors.

"The investor whose money earns a good rate of interest is a person who is deeply in karmic trouble if he contributes no personal service but collects rewards for which he has not personally worked. You may say that such profits are due reward for the risks of investment and the service of providing working capital for worthy projects; however, the investor reaps where he has not sown. In the Kingdom of God the people collectively will provide manufacturing capital from a commerce reserve fund. The commerce reserve will not be directly reimbursed nor will it be paid interest or dividends."

"That sounds kind of impractical," Richard commented. "Where does the money come from for the commerce reserve?"

"From a commerce tithe paid by every manufacturing company. There will be no taxes upon any individual, corporation, or commodity, ever. However, one tenth of all profits of every corporation will be willingly donated for co-operative upkeep of the retail marts and for coverage of the expenses of shipping and distribution. The excess from this commerce tithe will be placed in a manufacturing expansion fund which will be for the benefit of the commonwealth as a whole."

"But that system could produce new competition against the very industries that provided the expansion fund," Richard challenged.

"Not at all! Under the guidance of the Brothers, a board of engineers and manufacturers will decide on the firm most capable of efficiently producing any given item. The price will be fairly established by precise cost-accounting, and no firm will be required to compete with another. Cutthroat competition results in shoddy products manufactured down to a price and also results in eventual starvation wages for the workers. Just as the laborer is worthy of his hire, the company is worthy of its profits—but not to excess profits because excess profits are accompanied by karmic debits. Every laborer and every team of workers comprising a corporation must ever strive for efficiency, for in productive efficiency lies economic security and universal wealth. Any improvements in production devised and achieved by a given company will gain for its respective members a bonus from the extra profits. This is as it must always be."

"The whole deal sounds like price control to me," Richard said, "and the Office of Price Administration[1] has pretty well demonstrated that it doesn't work without somebody being unfairly squeezed."

"That's because no equitable philosophy guides that bureau's thinking. Furthermore, some influence groups have managed to have prices governmentally manipulated to their own benefit and to the detriment of their competitors and suppliers."

"It's disgusting that some businessmen will stoop to such things," Richard snapped.

"But those are the very things pursued for the joy of shrewd business," Dr. White explained. "All too many businessmen pride themselves on pulling a shady deal. If they can influence legislation and government policies ruinous to their competitors, that is the kind of manipulation clever operators gloat over.

"Fraudulent business practices that are barely within the law have become so widespread that they are inexorably undermining the commercial structure. Misleading advertising, salesmen who misrepresent contracts, manufacture of sleazy merchandise, and planned obsolescence are but a few examples of the extremely wasteful and exorbitant methods which have gained popularity among businesses. Each is out to exploit a captive market of ignorant suckers. In the United States we have come to the point of selling hokum to one another.

---

[1] A federal bureau during World War II.

"Big business today is conducted more and more in an alcoholic haze. Purchase agreements and sales contracts are signed in night clubs or on the bar of a cocktail lounge. The purchasing agent selects the seller who offers the best entertainment or the biggest secret rebate for his pocket. The best interests of the buyer's firm are not served, and the ultimate consumer pays the tab. Good value and efficient service have been relegated to the background while expense-account partying has taken their place. Business conducted by questionable influence is bragged about by men who really should be ashamed. But theirs is an arrogant need to triumph in their jungle-world of double-dealing transactions. Such men view the ideals of democracy as granting the freedom to grab whatever they can. To them equality of opportunity means that every man has the right to gouge his way to the top regardless of the station of his birth. The sacredness of contracts is being weakened by these sharpsters who rarely intend to keep their end of a bargain.

"Business is the principal contact a man has with his fellows. He spends more time at work than at home with his family and friends. Nowhere else in all of man's activities are the responsibilities and duties toward his fellow men so frequently tested as in business. This continual opportunity to demonstrate one's moral integrity should be met with scrupulous adherence to the laws of karma. All money transactions involve the exchange of karmic credits and must be handled with great respect and care. Everyone must eventually realize that all business is divine activity; and because government is business, it too falls under the same classification and deserves conscientious attention to moral considerations and economic efficiency.

"Nations today behave toward one another as badly as businessmen toward one another. But then, the main reason for government today is to provide protection for commercial interests and to administer certain internal services of general welfare. Cartels and monopolies on the international level supersede all considerations of war and patriotism. During this current war, munitions are being sold between enemies. Graft-hungry officials will wink at questionable shipments to neutral countries where transfer to enemy hands is completed. Millions of German boys and American boys are following their respective flags even to the death, but at the very highest business levels there are no national considerations. Their profit comes first! It is not money but the lust for it that destroys men. All honest, productive men deserve ample amounts of the medium of exchange, but the plutocrat has an insatiable hunger for money and for the power to gain more money."

"But men like Hitler and Stalin have a much different motive for power," the young man observed.

"It only seems that way, Richard. Communist Russia is a socialistic state that has as its head a plutocratic dictator who, in the name of the people, does in fact personally possess for his own use the entire nation and its workers. The aristocracy of Stalin's lieutenants shares in the fantastic loot and the privilege which attends it.

"Hitler is the product of a grand experiment which backfired. Powerful industrialists of Britain, France, and the United States conspired to put the industrial might of Germany into the hands of a socialist dictator and then control that dictator. A more fascinating aspect of their plan was to have the workers of Germany joined into an all-inclusive labor union which would be controlled by the same dictator. Hitler, being the leader of the Nazi socialist labor party, would have dual control of government policies and the workers. The big industrialists reasoned that were they then to direct Hitler to dictate laws conducive to tremendous profits for them, they would have solved all of management's biggest problems—especially the demands for human dignity made by laborers. The police-state tactics of Hitler's mob make labor strikes and personal complaints a crime against the state and an affront to their glorious leader.

"Germany was to be an experiment which, if successful, was to be extended throughout the world. All of Germany was to be reduced to the status of an industrial slave camp. Of the several political parties and leaders fomenting in Germany about the time of the depression, Hitler looked like the most promising tool to implement their plan, but they did not reckon with Hitler's personality. He too could see how well their plan would work, and so he decided to go it alone for his own glory and Germany's profit. Hitler signed Germany's death warrant when he prohibited the withdrawal of funds from Germany except in very small annual amounts. This act was tantamount to confiscation of foreign capital, and the big industrialists moved to retaliate. Now tens of millions of soldiers are trying to eliminate a man who was supposed to be a puppet of millionaires. Who is to be blamed for giving power to a man of such monstrous and perverted ideas?

"Don't ever feel secure that the original idea of the big industrialists will be discarded by future power seekers. Hitler really made the idea work, and the world will be plagued by his imitators for a long time to come. His methods of coming into power, his reign of terror, his confiscation of private property, his denial of human rights and justice, and his ruthless consolidation of power and control over the minutiae of daily living will be the world's legacy from Hitler and his international backers."

"How can you know such things?" Richard asked in amazement.

"The Brotherhoods are acutely aware of all such matters. The Brotherhood with which I am associated has maintained written records of the factors leading to the rise and fall of every civilization since civilization first began on the Lemurian continent 78,000 years ago. Our specific assignment from Melchizedek is to correlate and analyze every pertinent fact relating to the causes and failures of man's every attempt to organize socially. The schemes and rationales of his many social orders are fantastically varied. Some ideas have been sound, but most are childishly impractical.

"The purpose of the Brothers' correlation of these civilizations is to devise a sound basis for the government of the Kingdom of God. This final, great civilization must be flawless. No factors which can possibly lead to later dissension or karmic imbalance may be allowed to enter into the framework of the forming nation. The Brothers have done Their work well; and when the time comes for the physical formation of the civilization, it will proceed smoothly and efficiently because all contingencies and possibilities have been foreseen and prepared for. The community you will found shall be a city where men are to be educated and given an opportunity to put into daily practice the information that will be released to them by the Brotherhoods. They will be separated from the world around them in

141

order to free them from the negative influences of present-day civilization. After a generation—say forty years—they will have grown worthy of the Kingdom of God; for much like the Israelites having to wander in the wilderness for forty years before deliverance to the Promised Land, a long period of purification is essential.

"The economic principles of ancient Lemuria have brought wealth and economic security to every nation that has employed them; therefore they will also be meticulously observed and practiced in the new city near Chicago. Every consumer is entitled to the very best of everything. And so shall your credo be! Every product must be the finest possible. The best materials, the most efficient processes, and the soundest engineering principles must be employed. Farm produce must be the finest available, and prices must be kept at an absolute minimum.

"The success of the economy of the community will rest upon the mart system of distribution. One mart will be operated by a producers' co-operative which will sell *all* items at a mark-up of twelve percent. This figure has been established by the Brotherhoods after long research. The distribution of goods will be an operation jointly undertaken by the producers of all the goods sold, and distribution will be financed by the commerce tithe I mentioned earlier. Because the community will also be doing business with the world-at-large, its fame will be assured and its goods will be readily marketable if you adhere strictly to producing only the finest for a fair price. The world will soon come to respect the community for its dealings and efficient service.

"In spite of the unfair criticism and ridicule likely to be heaped upon the city by outsiders unable to understand the great work being undertaken there, those same scoffers will be among the first to seek the superior goods manufactured by you. Good value is appreciated and sought by everyone. Incidentally, you will have to be prepared for opposition that will come from the outside. The world cannot stand excellence and will seek to tear down whatever shows them up as lessers. The bad vigorously hate the good; the stupid jeer the brilliant; and the unjust despise the honest. This very prevalent tendency of mediocre humankind has been the destroyer of civilizations for ages past, and the city will not be immune from it. If your economic success is great, you may well find the community to be the butt of punitive and restrictive legislation designed to give relief to those who would presume to be your competitors in business. But were such laws to succeed in restricting you, the would-be competitors would still be unable to satisfy your markets or equal your low prices and excellent quality. Even knowing this, they would legislate against the community for personal satisfaction over its citizens who are striving for the Egoic perfection most of mankind rejects. This dog-in-the-manger attitude is universal among men.

"This is a strange world, Richard. However much the so-called 'good' people of the world hope for mankind's eventual perfection, they will tear down any individual whose personal perfection would seem to exceed their own; and so the 'good' maintain their mediocrity *ad infinitum*. It will require courageous men and women to take the grand step of allying themselves with the community, for their families and friends will bring social pressure to bear in order to dissuade them. But Christ Himself declared, 'I am come to set man at variance against his father, and the daughter against her mother, and the daughter-in-law against her mother-in-law. And a man's foes shall be they of his own household. He that loveth father and mother more than me is not worthy of me: and he that loveth son or daughter more than me is not worthy of me. And he that taketh not his cross, and followeth after me is not worthy of me.' (*Matt. 10:35–38*)

"So also shall be your own experience, Richard. Don't let your attachments to loved ones be so great as to supersede Christ's work. Those who cannot or will not follow must be abandoned. Those who are ready to advance *must not* be held back by their lessers. The lessers must be cut off without a backward glance, for they are as dead, and they shall lose life. We cannot save them all. Less than one person in five hundred will even be ready to come to the community; but the children incarnating to the families which have become established there will be very likely candidates for the Kingdom of God. Even many of the children who shall be born to your friends will have done so for personal contact with you. The last half of this century will see the very finest Egos incarnating as well as the foulest Egos—each

143

to fulfill his part in the grand scheme of things. Because of this condition, you can see why you must learn how to cope with all kinds of personalities.

"The many types of people you will encounter during the training period we have set for you will give you plenty of opportunities to learn how to influence them and get along with them with a minimum of friction. Moreover, these experiences will teach you about yourself, and we hope this will lead to self-analysis and personality growth. The expansion of your abilities and attitudes is a major task for you. To an important degree the success of the community rests upon your learning these lessons well. However, no man will be able to defeat the purpose of the Brotherhoods and Their establishment of the Kingdom of God. If you should fail in your tasks, others will take up where you leave off. This inexorable reality will obtain for every cog in the city. No one shall be indispensable!

"But it is equally true that every man is needed. The talents that each will bring into the commonwealth will be used to beneficial advantage. Because the work of each man is useful to the ultimate success of the community and the Kingdom, an equitable system of remuneration for each man's services shall be observed. In the present system of things, the executives usually draw large salaries as compared to the shop supervisory personnel and laborers. You will have to realize that there is no valid justification for this wide spread in wages for various kinds of work. The expert millwright puts in as many hours as the office man, and his skilled proficiency is just as valuable as the directive and planning skills of front-office personnel. Executives perpetuate overly high salaries for their own kind in order to establish and sustain prestige and social status for themselves. All too often the executives in a community are the only persons other than professional men who receive an income which affords a reasonably comfortable living.

"If a society is so ordered that every contributor to service and production earns an income compatible with decent living standards which afford comfort, luxury, and ample savings, then what practical purpose would be served by executives receiving extra income beyond their needs?"

Richard interrupted, "But isn't the person who takes the initiative to start a business entitled to extra compensation for the risks and extra effort he has undertaken?"

"Under the present system I must agree with you. But in the Kingdom of God new industry will be originated by the Citizens as a whole, and executives as well as all production personnel will be working for one another. I don't mean, either, that all men should be paid the same wage, because the skilled executive deserves more than the file clerk, the superintendent deserves more than the foreman, the tool maker more than the drill press operator, and the journeyman more than the apprentice; but the top men in all fields are really equals to one another in their respective skills—executive or productive.

"There is nothing intrinsically superior in paper work over manual work. Many highly educated men find more satisfaction in physical work than in sedentary occupations. But because of the higher salaries now paid for executive work, these men are constrained to work in an office when they would otherwise achieve greater contentment working with their hands."

"I doubt that I would be very content working with my hands like a common laborer," Richard declared. "I think there is greater opportunity for advancement in the executive field."

Dr. White fairly glared at Richard. "I detect not a little snobbishness in that remark. I'm sorry to see that you have the same erroneous notion so prevalent among young people. Where did you get such an idea?"

"It's just logical." Richard shrugged.

"I beg to differ with you," Dr. White countered firmly. "The laborer and the executive are two equal and essential halves of the same inseparable team. It is not possible that one is more valuable than the other. Much of the strife between labor and management stems from a very personal antagonism which revolves about relative social status. When one half makes it known by attitudes and actions that it is of infinitely finer clay than the other half, there is going to be resentment if not smoldering, smarting hurts nursed beyond reason. Every man *must* be rewarded according to his demonstrated ability without a partiality founded upon false status-standards. Each man must certainly come to respect the special skills acquired by both the machine-hand and the executive. Those skills are different, but no gradient prestige scale applies. True, a man charged with greater responsibilities deserves extra compensation, but it must be within reasonable bounds.

"In the Kingdom of God, laborers and executives will be next-door-neighbors in large, tastefully designed homes equivalent to today's luxury homes. They will both drive the best automobiles devised by industry and shall share their interests and tastes in common. Every resident of the Kingdom of God will have achieved at least the First Degree of Brotherhood in order to even have become a Citizen, and all will be striving for the same human perfection. The means of earning a living are immaterial to soul growth. The attitude of devout striving shall be a predominant characteristic of *all* the Citizenry. Streets must be cleaned, restaurant meals served, homes built, sewers laid, communities planned, machines designed, crops raised, children taught, men healed, windows washed, electronic calculators operated, machine tools fabricated—all are essential functions of a thriving community. Everyone provides a service, and all these jobs must be filled. Since there shall be nobody but college-educated Citizens permitted in the commonwealth, only Citizens will be available for filling the jobs. Would you care to judge which Citizen would have the greater spiritual advancement according to his occupation?"

Richard shook his head ashamedly.

"I'll tell you where you got that attitude of snobbishness, Richard. It was from your mother whose great ambition it is that you shall be educated and become a financial success. She has painstakingly implanted in your mind her prejudice against blue collar work as a source of income lest you should come to find a trade more to your liking. The attitude you have learned from her must be exorcised if you shall become a leader of men. Forgive her ambition, for it is peculiar to motherhood; nevertheless, you must grow away from her ideas."

"I can't help wondering what my parents will say when I tell them I'm quitting college," Richard mused. "I'm afraid they will think much the worse of me."

"I suppose they will, lad, but that is something you will have to get used to in your life. You cannot always enjoy the luxury of the understanding of men. The frustrations to which you will be subjected will be hard indeed, but they will teach you to bear ever greater frustrations concerning time, people, and economics. Patience is a virtue you must cultivate, assiduously, for it is the balm that ameliorates trying times. It is because of the conflicts and frustrations unavoidably inherent in the path we have devised for your education that certain personal powers have been temporarily removed from your use lest you employ them against your antagonists."

"What powers? What are you talking about?" Richard asked irritably.

Dr. White eyed him speculatively and said, "Do you recall that bad spill you took on your bicycle shortly after you graduated from elementary school?"

"Yes."

"Although you didn't experience much pain, you suffered damage to a certain part of your spinal cord as you landed on your neck and back. In years to come this damage will repair itself, and then the Egoic powers you have developed over many incarnations will return at a time when they can be more safely entrusted to you."

"You mean you were responsible for that?" Richard exclaimed angrily.

"The Brotherhoods were instrumental by your own prearrangement."

"It still makes me mad. My neck has been giving me trouble ever since."

"Yes, I can see that it would," Dr. White observed. "A spinal manipulation by a good chiropractor or osteopath should help to correct the distortion in your upper spine. I doubt that the spine can be completely straightened at this late date inasmuch as so much bodily growth has occurred since the accident, but relief from discomfort can still be afforded. Let me assure you, however, that the portions of your body through which those arrested abilities function shall be fully restored at the appropriate time."

"Why should you find it necessary to do such a thing to me?" Richard demanded.

Dr. White spoke compassionately as he explained, "The daily situations to which every person is exposed in this society are far too trying for an immature person to endure without striking back were the power to do so resident within him. You are in much the same predicament as a person would be if he were somehow projected into a primitive culture. That is why few Citizens care to incarnate into civilizations of inferior degree. It is much like expecting a polite gentleman to spend his life in a Neanderthal caveman's society. Too much Egoic advancement must go to naught during such reflexive incarnations, and the risk of losing hard-earned abilities is rather great. In an advanced civilization where almost everyone possesses occult powers, there is no need to surrender them temporarily. However, you seem to have learned how to overcome this drawback several incarnations in a row; so I am reasonably confident that you can do it again."

"I wish I had your confidence," Richard wisecracked.

Dr. White smiled, and then more seriously he said, "I've noticed that you seem to lack confidence in yourself in a number of ways. This is something which you must overcome, and only experience will bring about the social skills which lead to confidence."

Richard blushed in embarrassment. "I know. I seem quite shy in some situations."

"The day will come when you'll overcome shyness. Right now, it's more becoming that as a young man you be reserved and respectfully reticent; but as you enter manhood, you will most naturally be required to move among men smoothly and effectively."

"I just don't seem to be very outgoing," Richard apologized.

"That's typical of white occults, lad. Don't ever expect to be a hail-fellow-well-met. White occults are rather self-sufficient and are inclined to be aloof. But as is their way, you too are friendly, warm, and courteous when anyone approaches you or starts a conversation with you. I don't particularly expect that you will change much so far as being outgoing is concerned. You are easy to get along with, but you shall probably always be disinclined to presume upon another by initiating conversation or overtures of friendship. Your friendships are likely to be slow in forming but long enduring. This tendency of yours may put you at a disadvantage wherever you work, for you will find that promotions in the office usually go to the familiarly congenial men who may even seem to you to be brash, pushy, moderately unscrupulous, good party-goers, smoothly flattering to women, and convivial drinkers. Raises go to demanding smart alecks while the conscientious ones who seek to *earn* recognition are taken advantage of by the boss."

"That doesn't get anyone anywhere," Richard asserted, "not the smart alecks, the conscientious ones, or the bosses. I've been forewarned that promotions are based all too often on one's being a good golfer and going to the right cocktail parties; so I doubt that I'll ever be an executive or a salesman." A thought suddenly occurred to Richard, and he asked, "How can I become a leader of men when I don't like to drink anything alcoholic?"

"Well, lad, that has nothing to do with it, but I see the point you're driving at. No one in the community will have an inclination for strong drink; so the necessity will never arise."

"That seems strange," Richard observed. "Are we to be prohibitionists there?"

"Certainly not! The type of personality that makes a prohibitionist or censor is too fanatic to even be attracted to the Kingdom of God. The ancient and honored liquid foods like beer and fine table wines shall be appreciated until the very end of the world. But drinking as such shall not exist in the community because the type of physiologic need present in the drinker is incompatible with mental advancement."

"I don't understand."

"Persons who smoke tobacco, drink alcohol, or take narcotics suffer a hormone imbalance which causes an appetite for these drugs. The hormone imbalance is generated by mental distress and neurosis. The very real physiological need for these stimulants cannot be overcome on the physical level. One's endocrine glands are influenced by his Vital Body which is of the second plane of existence. The Vital Body, if you remember, readily responds to the Ego's mental activity. Emotional tensions and upsets produce a corresponding imbalance in the Vital Body and soon thereafter in the endocrines. Only spiritual peace plus mental and emotional well-being can reverse this hunger for detrimental chemicals."

"Are smoking and drinking immoral?" Richard inquired hoping to have this question answered authoritatively.

"What do you think about it, Richard?"

"Well, I suspect there's no sin actually involved in breathing warm smoke from a cigarette. People used to regard smoking as a mark of the libertine; so moral considerations are probably a hangover from those days. I can't see that it does anybody any good, but neither do I believe it hurts anyone too much physically. If people want to smoke, it's all right with me just so long as they don't blow the smoke in my direction. The only trouble I see with smokers is that they seem to feel that they are somehow entitled to smell up everybody else's air with their tobacco smoke. Did you ever sit down in a restaurant to enjoy a good supper only to have inconsiderate people at the next table envelop you in a cloud of cigar smoke? Everything you eat tastes like cigars."

Dr. White laughed out loud at the sad truth of the situation. "Maybe you're just prejudiced because you don't smoke," he said jokingly.

"I suppose some people do take up smoking in self defense," Richard said, "although most people I know started the habit because of social pressure from their group. A person is liable to become an outcast if he doesn't comply with his group's idea of what is fashionable and smart. Most kids who smoke consider the act as one which mystically confers adulthood. Then there are some who seem to have taken up smoking as an act of defiance."

"There is still a very significant percentage of men and women who do *not* smoke, Richard. These independent ones are more likely of the stable character needed in the community. You have pretty well pegged the causes of smoking and have answered your own question. Drinking is much the same kind of situation. No one was ever denied spiritual advancement for having enjoyed a cool stein of beer or a glass of wine at dinner. Those persons who drink for the purpose of intoxication impair their brain and spinal centers which are important to Egoic perfecting. The drunkard is small loss to Christ's great work, for the emotional perversions which led the person to drink were in themselves contrary to the mental attunement demanded for advancement.

"It is important that you learn to discern what causes the good and bad conditions operating in your life, and this requires alert observation and rational analysis. Life is a great teacher, and we have many examples provided for us. Fortunately, we need not suffer personally those things which can be successfully learned from careful observation of the misfortunes of others. Every occurrence in the world is the result of a thought or a deed. You must learn the proper actions to put into operation so that your environment may be more to your liking."

"What's this you're saying?" Richard queried with sudden keen interest.

"I'm pointing out to you that your environment is the result of your own thoughts and actions. You, and you alone, are responsible for everything you enjoy and suffer in this life."

"How is that possible?" Richard asked, no little amazed by Dr. White's startling assertion.

"Because everyone has the power of mental precipitation and uses it daily whether he knows it or not. The things we think about most become those which tend to enter our environment. To concentrate upon fear of disease and disaster will eventually bring them to pass. To desire a greater income will give rise to ideas, to a plan of action, and to attraction of sources of income. To have a mental attitude of confidence gives rise to undaunted living. To fear calamity brings one to see only the gloomy aspects of everything, and lo and behold, calamity dogs at one's heels. Bargain with life for a penny, and no more than a penny will be acquired. If you unwaveringly *believe* and *expect* life to bring you love, health, and prosperity, then these blessings become manifest in your life; for such is the power of mental energy over the physical plane of existence. Precipitation is a fact which, when one consciously uses it regularly, becomes a firm belief and practical tool. When you become a student of the Brotherhood, you will be taught further details concerning conscious precipitation.

"One's so-called 'luck' is determined by the status of his karmic account carried over from past incarnations and also by his conduct during the earlier years of the current incarnation. The actions put into operation by an individual come back to him in kind and intensity. Kindness shown to others returns as a kindly environment. A smiling demeanor elicits smiles from others; a gloomy disposition nets growls from others. Consideration to others brings consideration from others; selfish grasping results in loss of what one grabs. If one sows the seeds of hate, lust, or brutality, he shall reap a life full of these same things directed against him.

"Past and current thoughts, actions, and decisions account in every detail for the nature of each Ego's environment. No one else has determined it! Even the body one inhabits was chosen solely by the Ego before the egg was impregnated. And the civilization into which one has incarnated was earned by past effort.

"If you wish your environment to improve, merely uplift the quality of the thoughts upon which you concentrate. Initiate the actions toward others which you would have them show toward you. Perform excess service in order that your karma may improve. Make the virtues a part of your life, and ingrain them deeply into your soul.

"If your personality is not what you would like it to be, then change your attitudes. Your personality today is the result of your reactions to all the experiences you have ever had. Inasmuch as you today are the result of yesterday's thinking, the person you will be tomorrow is being determined by what you think today. Aim your thoughts toward the person you seek to become, and the years will see your desire come to pass. It is you alone who controls the nature of the thoughts flowing through your Mind. If negative thoughts crop up, do not pursue them; replace them with positive thoughts instantly. Do not dwell upon ugly, fearful, hateful, or lustful contemplations. Consciously switch to thoughts of a creative project, pleasant memories, love of Christ, vacation plans, or some other positive idea. After all, it's *your* Mind, and *you* control what passes through it. Carefully select the quality of the thoughts upon which you concentrate, for your thoughts have direct action upon your personality and your environment.

"Hoping that the good things of life will enter one's environment but fearing all the while that they might not will surely result in failure to secure the desired good, for fear and lack of confidence preclude effectual precipitation. Faith is the antithesis of fear, and to acquire a firm faith one needs only to test the principles of Universal Law to see that they always work. Faith is the unshakable knowledge that God's Laws never fail.

"One should learn to have confidence in the essentially benign nature of human existence. It is a truism of all mankind that there is no such thing as chance. We are always in the right place at the right time. One may be killed as an innocent bystander wholly blameless of the immediate circumstance; yet no one has ever experienced an untimely death or died in an unwarranted manner. We may unwittingly find ourselves in the locale of the 'accidental means' of our death, but our work is fulfilled before transition can occur. We are never the victims of chance. Happenings of life are determined by our *own* previously instituted causes, and never is anything like predestination imposed upon us by Higher Beings."

"Don't the past lives and past personalities of an Ego affect his present personality?" Richard asked.

"Less than you would like to believe, lad. It's better that you forget the past and not seek to rest upon laurels earned in previous incarnations. This lifetime is your present point of contact with reality. Meditation upon what used to be is a poor substitute for the challenges of life and the opportunities for advancement here and now. If at times you enjoy envisioning other times and places, then contemplate the future you wish for yourself—not only for this life but also for the next incarnation. You are planting the seeds now for the environment you will enjoy or suffer the next time."

Richard was thoughtful for a moment, and then he said, "You told me I was at one time an Egyptian Pharaoh who, because of his work, was murdered by the priesthood. How was it that I became subject to murder? Wouldn't I have had to murder someone in order to become karmically liable to the same fate?"

"Not always, Richard. Indiscriminate and foolish acts can bring sudden death upon anyone, but your case had a yet different twist. Your reign as Pharaoh was unusually benign for the times, and no executions or tortures were conducted under your reign. However, you knew the risks involved in clashing with the powerful priests of Egypt and of the virtual inevitability of your elimination by them. Even though you had no karmic debt of murder to be balanced, you were assassinated after your work had been brought as far as you could personally promote it. The mode of your transition was the logical result of your kind of battle against sly and murderous Black Mentalists."

"It would seem logical that now I can commit one murder without suffering karmic indebtedness," Richard said speculatively.

Dr. White raised his eyebrows in shocked surprise. "What kind of talk is that?"

"I mean that it would seem that I'm one up on the tally sheet and that I'm entitled to one murder to even my score. I don't think I could ever hurt anyone, but I'm curious from a hypothetical point of view."

"It just doesn't work that way!" Dr. White said, much relieved. "Every murder has its karmic repercussions regardless of the past. Any person who interferes in the life of another to this ultimate degree will suffer dire consequences regardless how many more times he may have been murdered than he has murdered."

"Well, don't I have some sort of karmic credit due me for having been done in so unfairly?" Richard's eyes twinkled as he posed this question to the elderly doctor.

Dr. White smiled, and he said, "I don't know if you deserve an answer to that question, but I know it's based on a genuine question you have about karma. Let me remind you that regardless of how valuable your work for mankind and the Brotherhoods was at that time, your demise was not unfair or unwarranted in the eyes of the priests and their followers. Your murder was their just due in their opinion. You were their blasphemous enemy, and so they dealt with you as they felt fitting. Such excuses are a moot point, but they felt your reforms were detrimental to the long-established order of things. In the democratic states men use votes and political pressure to subdue political rivals; whereas elsewhere the custom has been to liquidate rivals before they liquidate you.

"Furthermore, you have already evened your score with your Egyptian assassin during a subsequent incarnation."

"I killed him?"

"Not exactly. It's not unusual that karmic accounts are settled through situations which arise naturally. It was during your next incarnation among the Jews that this erstwhile assassin also came into incarnation. The fellow became an exceptionally loyal soldier in your army; but because you were enamored of his wife, you arranged to have him killed in battle. Your feelings were understandably strong toward this woman, for, unknown to either of you, she had been your Egyptian queen in her former incarnation. But because of your selfish act against your loyal soldier, you and she both suffered certain losses even though the man had karmically earned his death at your hand. She too had to suffer because she had been the instigator in the matter. Afterward, however, she became the only *real* wife you had in that lifetime.

"I hope this little example impresses upon you the seriousness of operating in the environment of another to *any* extent. If ever you do, you will suffer the consequences. Karmic justice will always be brought down upon evildoers; but even though retribution must come, woe unto him through whom it comes. Therefore, be content to know that no person may commit a wrongdoing but that he must one day suffer for it. "Vengeance is the Lord's; so don't usurp the execution of karmic justice from its rightful, all-knowing Executor. Stay clear of the karmic situations of other people. Rather, have pity on those who are heaping eventual misery upon their own heads by their present foolish abuses of others.

"In the Kingdom of God, men will have been taught how to avoid the kind of situations which demand karmic retribution. By living their lives in such a way as to not initiate deeds, words, and thoughts that might cause trouble, the vicious circle of human antagonisms can be eliminated. The Lemurian way of life will be recaptured only through careful observance of every detail and nuance of karmic interplay between human beings. The laws of karma will be taught to the community by the Brotherhoods so that they will understand the proper course to follow in many varied circumstances. Thereafter, the actions they put into operation will be governed by knowledge of the results to be expected. The discourtesies, personality frictions, and irritations

155

of life can be overcome when men observe the rules which have been discerned and tested for ages by the Brothers. The Laws of Karma will show men the way to tranquility, security, happiness, and prosperity."

"When you mention prosperity, it reminds me of a question that's been bothering me," Richard said. "Where is the money coming from to build the city you speak of?"

"One day you will see whence it shall come, but let it suffice for me to say that it shall flow to you in amazing amounts when the time has come to build the city. The money will come from your own pockets and from the thousands of people coming into the city and also from philanthropies, legacies, and spontaneous donations. None of it, however, will come from the Brotherhoods. The people must build the city themselves and govern it themselves—that is the way they will learn best. The Brothers will give advice to help you over the rough spots if you have exhausted all your own knowledge and effort upon a problem without arriving at a solution."

"Will we go back to the gold standard again?"

"No. As long as you are in the United States you shall be bound to use its currency. But the Kingdom of God won't use such an arbitrary base for money as precious metals. Gold, for instance, has no intrinsic value, but the fact that it doesn't tarnish or corrode makes it an ideal material for coins. Yet, sea shells or tobacco do just as well as mediums of exchange.

"The only true measure of value is human labor. Wealth is not created by finding a large deposit of gold in the ground. Gold cannot harvest a crop or build a house or make a plow. True wealth resides in the usefulness of the item to man, and the cost of the item is determined by the amount of human labor required to make it or process it. No power in the world has usefulness until man harnesses it, and no material resource has any value until man gathers it and refines it. Wild berries feed no one until a man picks them.

"The cost of every item shall be determined by the amount of labor required to prepare it for market and deliver it to the buyer. A tree which has grown wild has only potential value which becomes real value after it has been cut down, moved to a mill, sawed and dressed, and delivered to market. The cost of each board foot of lumber is a pro-rated portion of the total labor expended upon the tree which yielded it.

"No one in the community or in the Kingdom of God shall be able to own or control natural resources. God created the Earth and all its bounty for the benefit of all men equally. If a man is allowed to gain control over a commodity needed by all other men, he soon demands exorbitant prices for the privilege of purchasing it. Because other men must have it, they are obliged to pay whatever the monopolist decrees. Petroleum, water, iron, and lumber are the property of all and are intrinsically free of cost. The Angels who created them for us have done so for love of us and seek only thanks in return for Their wondrous gifts. The only cost that can be charged to a buyer of a natural resources is in the amount of human labor expended to supply it to the buyer in the form he desires it. The government shall supervise the companies assigned the task of gathering and preparing basic resources for the commonwealth in order to assure the lowest cost possible.

"Transportation facilities will be publicly owned and operated because privately owned airline, rail, and trucking firms tend to charge as much as the traffic will bear, and often they show partiality to certain industries in their rates and rebates. The best service for the least price is a right to be enjoyed equally by every citizen and corporation. The philosophy of economics established long ago by Melchizedek on the continent of Mu must be rigidly adhered to lest karmic discrepancies weaken the overall stability of the economy.

"A salutary feature of the economy will be the impossibility of inflation or depression. In the Kingdom of God, prices will not fluctuate for thousands of years at a time. Therefore money saved by Citizens will have the same purchasing power when withdrawn as when deposited even though a lifetime has passed. Panic-makers and speculators have no place in the Lemurian scheme.

"A man will still be able to earn as much money as his skill and brains will gain for him, but it is not likely that becoming a millionaire will be the ambition of many Citizens. The purpose of the highly developed civilization to be fostered in the Kingdom of God is to promote spiritual advancement toward the goal of Mastership. Were it not for this purpose, Melchizedek and the Brotherhoods would not be so concerned with its evolvement.

"No person will be allowed to own land or manufacturing facilities. Long experience has proven that as real estate and factories are passed along from generation to generation, family dynasties are developed which consolidate the wealth of the nation into the hands of relatively few persons. The power over others that is inherent in comparatively great wealth is invariably used to the disadvantage of the poorer citizens. Therefore, whatever wealth a man may amass in his life will revert to the commonwealth upon his transition. Minor children will be supported to age twenty-one, and a widow will receive the same income that had been earned by her husband. In all cases, the retired man or his widow will be maintained in the same manner to which they have been accustomed until the end of their days.

"All homes shall be rented from the commonwealth, and retired couples shall be entitled to remain in their life-long home as long as they choose. If they wish, they will have the option to pass the lease to an adult offspring of theirs. The government shall build all homes, factories, and other buildings, and it shall maintain them. It will thereby be able to unobstructedly replace them as they age and can keep the appearance of the neighborhoods co-ordinated and free from dilapidation. Each renter will care for the home as if it were his own property, and he shall be free to decorate and remodel it to fit his purse and tastes.

"Children will be required to attend school until age twenty-one. To maintain the schools and to provide for such city services as garbage removal, street building and maintenance, fire protection, and the general miscellany incident to operating a municipality, the citizens will be requested to contribute ten percent of their wages. This will be wholly voluntary, and there will be no taxes whatever in the Kingdom of God. Based on past experience during the Lemurian civilization on Mu, there will be ample surpluses in the nation's treasury by using this system."

Richard pursed his lips in concentration and said, "It seems rather unfair that a young man should be denied the financial assistance that a legacy from his father could afford him. It's pretty hard for a fellow to get started in the business world if he has to save from scratch."

"Your thinking is undoubtedly influenced by the fact that your father is a manufacturer of some means. It is much fairer that every young man start from the same starting point. If a man uses his brains and energy, there is no limit to how far he can rise. Your sentiments are based on life in the present system. The big trouble with inheriting money is that the heir must compensate for it karmically. The acquisition of an unearned windfall brings with it a corresponding karmic indebtedness. Until mankind learns that no one can long retain anything for which he has not personally compensated, men will strive to grasp for sorrow-engendering advantages."

"Well, is it safer to be poor?" Richard asked seriously.

"Of course not! Poverty, or living on the margin of one's wages, is too harrowing and is consequently a barrier to the emotional well-being that is important to spiritual uplift. Don't ever let a rich man kid you that money brings unhappiness. That's merely a smoke screen to discourage you from competing with him. Certainly, money cannot bring happiness, but neither is there anything about a medium of exchange which can bring unhappiness. Living on the verge of continual want is depressing to anyone. The sense of self-respect and security inherent in having a surplus of cash after each week's expenses is much to be desired by everyone.

"Money in sufficiency is necessary for the gracious gestures of everyday living. One must be able to entertain friends, respond in gift giving, and have the wherewithal for attending social and cultural activities without impairing one's budget. Money in sufficiency permits one to be perfectly honest in all things great and petty. One need not be wealthy in order to live well; one needs only to have a surplus over regular expenses.

"It will be the community's responsibility to provide all the vocational training and philosophical instruction necessary for every wage earner to provide his family with a comfortable living. If he cannot, or will not, adapt his way of thinking so that he becomes a self-reliant, productive individual, he must be returned to the world outside. The relentlessness of karmic accountancy demands that every Citizen contribute beneficially to the overall balance needed for the success of the community and the Kingdom of God."

CHAPTER 11

Today Versus Tomorrow

An expression of concern clouded Richard's face as he complained, "What you have told me of the economic system to be employed in the Kingdom sounds distressingly like socialism or even communism."

"Well, then I had better point out some of the major differences between the ancient Lemurian philosophy and socialism and communism:

"The socialists arose as a voice against social and economic subordination of poor laboring classes by aristocratic landowners and domineering industrialists. However, the socialists' proposed system of having everyone share equally in the wealth of the state is an impractical answer to the abuses of class consciousness. To take wealth from the rich and distribute it among the poor will not benefit the poor to any appreciable degree because there are so many among whom to divide the loot. The mere act of reapportioning the property of big landlords into small farms for the landless farmers does not create prosperity any more than does giving anyone equal title to the factories or railroads or mines. Prosperity results from efficient productivity and distribution.

"The great fault of socialistic schemes lies in taking the fruits of the labor of capable and self-reliant citizens in order to raise the standard of living for the apathetic and indolent citizens. Socialism penalizes the energetic creators of wealth by awarding unearned benefits to dole-eager louts. The system results in a continual leveling down of the standard of living and retardation of progress. Only a fool would continually labor to his own disadvantage; and it doesn't take long before the able citizens realize that the greater their own productivity and efficiency, the greater proportional sacrifice they are making to the populace as a whole. Even state propaganda encouraging noble self-sacrifice for the general welfare fails to keep skilled persons from becoming disenchanted. The less a person does toward earning his own way in a welfare state, the more he profits from the system. Not that we should do away with all social benefits for the aged and the helpless, but public relief rolls are loaded with sharpsters, malingerers, and schemers.

"A social conscience is the mark of an empathetic, humane person. One should certainly be sensitive to the misfortunes and hardships of others. One *must* respond to a genuine need for help. It is important to the whole community that a stricken member be helped to his feet again as quickly as possible. The welfare state, however, puts an economic crutch under the fallen one but somehow discourages complete recovery. The added karmic indebtedness from unearned benefits heaped upon the already karmically insecure sufferer is to his further disadvantage.

"The Lemurian system helped a fallen Citizen to change occupations if necessary or to become self-sufficient again in some other way. The educational system saw to it that every man was trained to be skilled in needed work so that he could earn a good living. Today the inept are fed and clothed with public funds and left to waste away in the backwash of human productivity.

"No such wastefulness of life will be tolerable in the Kingdom of God. The Lemurian aims are soul enlargement and spiritual advancement. Living off the efforts of others is karmically incompatible with these aims.

"The advantages of economic co-operation among members of a community have been well proven. Sharing burdens common to all lightens the load upon each individual. There are obvious benefits when a town's residents pool their resources to create, let's say, a municipal water well and distribution system rather than each person drilling his own well and buying his own pump. This co-operative principle has long been employed by towns, farmers, and businesses. Business corporations are essentially co-operatives designed to increase efficiency and profits of human enterprise. The principal concern of local and national governments is to provide those services which are more efficiently and inexpensively performed on a co-operative rather than private basis. This is the Lemurian way—the way whereby government serves its citizens.

"Now let us briefly discuss communism. Karl Marx deplored capitalist management of industry as the prime evil of our society. He asserted that if the down-trodden laborers of his day were to rise up and wrest control of industry from the upper classes entrenched in control of capital, then the workers could administer the fruits of their production to the overall benefit of everyone. His proposals were militant and rang of glorious results to be gained by what he pictured as an inevitable war between the classes of society. Marx declared for the abolishment of profits in order to reduce prices, and he envisioned a government of the proletariat with their representatives chosen by a sort of electoral process.

"The Communists enlarged upon Marx' socialistic ideas by proposing to collectivize human effort and to do away with all private property. Nihilist and anarchist theorists among them fomented for complete governmental reform in order to eliminate corrupt rule and the privileges it confers to administrators in power. Lenin and his Bolshevist Party seized power in Russia under the guise of revolutionary reform and proceeded to ruthlessly liquidate political opponents and to eliminate the voices of the theorists and idealists. To bring order out of the chaos of revolution required practical measures far different than communist theory, and the means used by Lenin to achieve effective controls over the nation led to dictatorial central authority more despotic and enslaving than Russia has ever known. As a result, Red Russia practices state capitalism under totalitarian tyranny. The government dominates the nation's inhabitants, and the people are subservient to the state which is considered supreme. The individuals existing under the Red regime are expendable pawns.

"In contrast, the Lemurian philosophy abhors collectivized labor, and it encourages profit incentives to reward the individual. Anyone has the opportunity to accumulate a fortune, but he will be legally unable and ethically unwilling to use his wealth as a club over the heads of others. Neither will he be able to pass his money to a succeeding generation or be able to amass real estate or productive capital. This, of course, is designed to prevent the growth of family dynasties that would eventually be able to challenge the rightful government in the making of public policies. During a man's life he can rent the use of fine homes and luxuries without having to buy them; so he will still be able to enjoy any surroundings he is wont to desire with less expense than actual ownership entails.

"Russia's leaders lay claim to a workers' paradise on earth when the Communists have conquered the entire world. The hardships endured by persons presently living under communism are justified as the price of waging war against nations who do not choose to live as wretchedly as Russians. Remember, Richard, that Russia has become an armed camp dedicated to the premise that it shall bring the entire world under its domination. Unfortunately, the Red leaders have demonstrated their full intention of subjugating the world's laborers to their rule. They seek absolute power over every activity of every person— the kind of limitless power to make another suffer privation or die at their whim. They exult in their terrifying grip on the throats of men, and their viciousness is typical of those under the sway of the Black Mentalists. Slavery, torture, horrifying savagery, and extermination are the devices of sheer evil.

"Since communal co-operation has become identified in most people's minds with the Communist revolutionary movement under the guidance of criminals and calloused killers, the advantages of co-operative endeavor are tainted by association with Bolshevist politics and their reign of terror and slaughter. The Fascists, I hasten to add, are equally vicious, for they maintain totalitarian political control in essentially the same way as do the Communists. Economic reform will be regarded with suspicion for a long time by Americans because of the bullies who have used the good points of such reform as sheep's clothing to disguise their bid for wolfish power.

"The greatest disadvantage to socialistic governments is that they tend to become dominated by bureaucrats and dictators. Looters who publicly mouth their devotion to the general welfare manage to gain control over the vast public resources of the state for their own gain. The laborers are all too receptive to the power-seeking politician's promise of legalized seizure of envied wealth, but the politician's promised and much-vaunted classless society somehow soon gains a new aristocracy embodied in the bureaucrats. Clandestine pilfering by government officials later gives way to thinly veiled grabbing of vast sums. The economy becomes ever weaker from these blood-sucking officials; and when financial chaos looms on the nation's horizon, a battle for power is inevitable among the officials over the dwindling revenue available for pilfering. The strong man who arises victor in such a contest is usually the most unscrupulous of the lot, and he takes over as dictator.

"The blame for this situation falls squarely on the citizens of the ravaged land. Because they are stupid enough to believe they can get something for nothing, they hasten to put a man into power who promises them a pot of gold at the end of an economically improbable rainbow.

"The Citizens of the Kingdom of God will be of sufficient perception to forestall any such antics from a would-be dictator. To usurp power in the Kingdom of God is an absolute impossibility. Furthermore, if a public official were to yield to graft or pilfering from public wealth, it would soon be detected by the foolproof Lemurian accounting method. After full restitution is made by a convicted thief, exile from the Kingdom is mandatory; and this penalty is too great for any Citizen to risk. No person or group of persons shall ever be permitted even the slightest inroad to gain power or privilege at the expense of the Kingdom of God or any one of its Citizens. The nation will be forever opposed to socialists, communists, capitalist tycoons, or a priesthood's domination."

"Maybe it's because I'm prejudiced," Richard began, "but the free enterprise idea still sounds like the most rewarding system to me."

"In many respects I agree with you, Richard," Dr. White said. "The concepts of free enterprise, supply and demand, and laissez-faire have made America the strong and prosperous nation she is. America has demonstrated the benefits of unfettering the creative soul of man from feudal paternalism and the artificial status quo enforced by those who fear that new products might upset their positions of power and profit. American patent protection on new ideas and inventions has stimulated the astonishing growth of technological developments. However, there are certain dangers inherent in the free enterprise system which have already become apparent.

"The idea of competition in industry breeds beneficial productive efficiency and less expensive manufacturing processes; but when competition gets too fierce, industrialists will protect their capital investments by any means. The better manufacturer may find himself displaced by a competitor who is panicky enough to engage in unscrupulous, illegal, and even forceful measures to monopolize the market. Wealth is power in America, and the men who control it are all too willing to expand their wealth in ways ultimately detrimental to the public welfare. Even a country's empire-building is the inevitable result of market expansion and competition. A nation may rationalize colonization of another nation as being for the protection and advantage of that weaker nation; but expanding nationalism, capitalism, communism, or fascism is ulteriorly motivated by the seeking of private profit.

"In Lemurian economics, the present free-enterprise idea is closely duplicated in order to encourage every man to do his best and thereby enjoy the rewards of extra effort and skill. Inventors and innovators must be especially rewarded because they contribute far more to the commonwealth than the producer. An idea is a commodity which can serve to profit all posterity; whereas, the manufacturer of a product can only serve his customers to the extent of his lifetime's energy and the durability of his products.

"The Lemurian limitations placed upon the private garnering of resources, real estate, productive capital, and personal power are a reluctant necessity; for even if enlightened men motivated by the highest social ideals were to acquire great wealth, they couldn't be assured of altruistic personalities in those who would succeed to their power. Therefore, freedom to expand one's private enterprise to the limit of one's resourcefulness must be subordinated to provisions which will forestall abuses of power and assure social, economic, and political stability over the centuries to come.

"As industrial societies developed on the planets Venus and Mercury about one hundred millennia ago, it was again demonstrated that men cannot long be entrusted with private control of productive capital. The regulations developed on those planets to insure economic plenty for all their citizens and to maintain equal opportunity for every man were brought to us through Melchizedek and were incorporated into the laws of the first civilization formed on Earth 78,000 years ago. The government of the Kingdom of God will recapitulate those very same laws."

"What kind of government will the Kingdom have?" Richard asked. "I'm sure it won't be a monarchy as the name implies. Will it be a republic or a democracy or what?"

"The Kingdom of God will not be ruled by anyone or by any group. There will be no king, regent, or strong man at its head. All executive functions will reside in a council of twelve men which will later become a board of governors. A thirteenth member will be elected as president of the council. The government will be a republic only insofar as the election of the members for the council is concerned. Election will be for life, but this rule will not apply to the community in Illinois. The laws of the Kingdom of God will reside in a constitution, and all laws will have to be voted upon by the democratic procedure of referendum. The voters obviously will be required to be much more alert politically than people are today.

"The judicial arm of the government will be under the jurisdiction of the Brotherhoods, and They shall also decide the eligibility of candidates for public office. The Brotherhoods will give special training for a period of seven years to Citizens especially inclined toward governmental administration. The greatest value of having the Brothers decide the worthiness of prospective candidates resides in Their ability to perceive the inner heart and Mind of a man."

"What kind of laws will be in the constitution?"

"The Constitution of the Kingdom of God will be closely patterned after the Constitution of the United States of America which was itself directed by the Brotherhoods. The Bill of Rights will also be included and so will the basic laws of the Lemurian Empire."

"I'm acquainted with the first two documents, but what are the Lemurian Laws?"

"There are ten of them. I shall repeat them for you now, but you will have to wait until you are actually a student of the Brotherhood before you will be given full understanding and examples. They are as follows:

One: No one may profit at the expense of another.

Two: No one, nor the government, may take anything from a person or another nation by force.

Three: All natural resources shall belong to the commonwealth of all citizens and shall not be owned by any person or corporation of persons.

Four: Every Citizen is due equal education and the freedom to choose his vocation, and he has equal rights before the law.

Five: All promotions shall be based only upon personal merit and proficiency.

Six: Everyone must compensate fully for every personal possession he receives and hopes to retain.

Seven: No person nor the government may operate in the environment of another unless specifically requested to do so by that person. The government, however, may enforce the law in treasonable, criminal, and civil suits.

Eight: No one may kill or injure another except in the defense of his life or his state.

Nine: The sanctity of the home is inviolate.

Ten: If no violation of Natural Law is involved, the majority rule will apply and will be subject to approval of the Brotherhoods' direct representatives whose decisions will be final.

"As you will later learn, all the Lemurian Laws are based on Universal Law or, if you prefer, Cosmic Law or Natural Law. These are guides to help men avoid karmic repercussions in the living of their lives.

"While we are on the subject, we may as well discuss briefly the organization of the community to be inaugurated here in Illinois."

"Already I have a question," Richard said quickly.

"What is it?"

"Where exactly is this community to be located?"

"That is entirely up to you. But keep it within a sixty mile radius of Chicago."

"May I name it as I choose?"

"It will have a name which means *the place* in a European

language. I'm certain that when you discern that name, you would have it no other way."

"I see," Richard laughed gaily. "I have Hobson's choice!"

Dr. White smiled and quickly added, "Let me forewarn you to figure enough expansion room for accommodating a city of at least a quarter million persons. The community is likely to become the second largest city in Illinois. When it starts growing, its increase will be phenomenal because the Brothers will pour thousands of persons into it as quickly as the new members can be assimilated. The problems of expansion must be solved by you and your council, and in so doing you will prepare yourselves for the subsequent building of the Kingdom of God's initial city in the Pacific Ocean. This second city shall be named after the City of Brotherly Love."

"Phew!" Richard exclaimed. "Let's not get too far into the future just yet! First tell me how I'm supposed to get the first city started."

"That too is something you must solve for yourself. The training you shall receive during the next decade will aid greatly in helping you approach this great work with ability and confidence. Do you recall that about five months ago you had a very vivid dream about building a great city?"

"Yes!" Richard said in surprise. "I remember that dream more than any other I've ever had. It was so unusual that I even mentioned it to my mother that morning after I awoke."

"What was unusual about it?" Dr. White urged.

"In it I was in the midst of construction works which extended as far as the eye could see. I spoke with many persons about many things, but what struck me upon later review was that the course of the dream maintained a logical sequence of events quite like a real experience instead of the nonsense of usual dreams. Another wonderful thing about it is that it was the first dream I've had in color."

Dr. White smiled. "That dream was actually an induced vision of scenes of activity which you will some day view again in actual reality. It was granted you so that you might have some concept of the magnitude of the work awaiting you."

"All in all, it was a pleasant experience," Richard said with evident delight.

Dr. White gripped the young man's upper arm affectionately and gazed at him with fatherly pride. The elderly doctor cleared his throat and said, "We must examine the governmental set-up for the community; and as we proceed, you will note that the Lemurian philosophy must necessarily be modifed for use in the community. Since the members of the community shall be living in the United States of America, they, as citizens of that nation, shall be obliged to abide by its laws fastidiously in both letter and spirit. In fact, they will adhere to the spirit of the Constitution to a greater degree than any other citizens of the United States.

"The community will be organized as an incorporated, non-stock, non-profit religious organization, and a board of trustees will be charged with the proper administration of the assets of the corporation. The inhabitants will be encouraged to incorporate their community into a city and to administrate it according to the laws of the land. They will have to pay federal income tax which, unfortunately, will detract from the full realization of the Lemurian economic system during this transitional period; however, there will be many benefits to be enjoyed from those facets of Lemurian economics which in no way conflict with present laws. Co-operative purchasing, low-profit mart-distribution, low-cost housing, and a competitive wage advantage in manufacturing goods for outside consumption will all contribute to the comforts and well-being of the members of the community to a degree exceeding that which they had formerly known while in the world-at-large.

"Until such time as you are established in the Kingdom of God, you may have to employ women in industry and offices; but in the Kingdom of God this practice will be forbidden forever. It is significant that the ancient empire quickly crumbled when, near the end, women sought to compete in industry and politics with men. Women shall be permitted to work only if they choose not to marry, and the employment in which they shall be permitted will be limited to nursing, teaching elementary school, and serving as clerks in the women's and children's departments of the marts. Try to keep the employment of women at a minimum in the community as a preparatory step toward the Kingdom. (Please see Appendix.)

"The purpose of this rule is not to suggest male superiority but to halt the current deterioration of home life. Nothing is so important to civilization as the proper rearing of the succeeding generation. The intensive college education of women will be particularly slanted toward this all-consuming task. Women must know a great deal about everything in order to fulfill their challenging responsibilities as perpetuators of civilization. Marriage, too, will come to be recognized as a far more demanding and rewarding institution than men and women recognize today. Most of our conventional attitudes toward motherhood, marriage, love, and sex will have to be adjusted upward in the community.

"The strength of the Kingdom of God will rest upon the sanctity of women and the home. The home is the basic unit of society where children are educated to appreciate the finer things of life and where happiness, security, and patriotism are learned by first-hand experience. Morality in a people is established primarily by parents and is merely augmented by schools or churches. All adults will be required to assist lovingly in the proper guidance of all children as the opportunities arise. Discipline, of course, will be administered only by a child's parents if they deem it necessary. Good manners, respect of elders, and self-discipline will be instilled in every child for the successful perpetuation of the high ideals for which all Citizens aspire. Children learn best by observing good examples of the behavior they are expected to emulate. Respect for elders comes naturally through the parents' earned respect rather than from fear of punishment. All disciplinary measures must be aimed at inducing self-discipline in the child.

"Courtesy is the keynote of serene living. Children must at an early age learn to observe the courtesies which smooth the paths of life. In order to be courteous, one needs only to consider *first* the effects that the satisfaction of his desires will have upon others. The common annoyances of life are eliminated through this simple observance. Why should anyone discard trash on the public scene, deface property, shoplift merchandise, selfishly demand undue privileges, or disturb the peace?

"Silence is important to the human soul. It is during quietude that Egoic advancement is gained. Peace and tranquility within the city will be an observance jointly required of everyone.

Soundproofing of factories, offices, and homes will be required. The playing of radios or music so loudly that it can be heard beyond the confines of one's house or auto must be guarded against at all hours of the day. Persons should no longer be subjected to the loud talking of others or to the sounds of the automobile's horn, roaring motor, or squealing tires. Industrial and transportation sounds must be reduced to a whisper.

"Noninterference from external noise is a basic right of every person. Noise is an invasion of personal privacy. Without noise, productive efficiency surges upward, tempers are in repose, and tensions ease. The tyranny of noise in present-day cities is costing men dearly in inefficiency and fatigue. Your city shall be able to demonstrate that urban life can become tranquil merely by practicing courtesy. How can one help but be courteous and thoughtful of others when everyone he encounters considers his feelings before their own wishes? These attitudes are best instilled from birth so they become second nature.

"Children learn discourtesy and destructiveness from others; and parents can easily guide their children away from detrimental influences when, as in the community, there are few examples to mislead them. Children in primitive tribes, whose safety and very lives depend upon their being undetected by enemies, are trained to silence even while in active and joyful play. These children do not suffer a disturbance of personality because they aren't permitted to scream and shout while having fun any more than city children are disturbed because they must play on narrow sidewalks instead of in the broad boulevards. In both cases the preservation of the children's lives depends upon their respective restrictions. Children are exceedingly adaptive in this respect. Raucous behaviour in children and adolescents stems from lack of easily practiced rules of noiselessness.

"The easy adaptability of children will be used to condition the first generation arising in the community for the way of life as it is to be lived in the Kingdom of God. Hitler, for instance, embarked on a predetermined plan to condition tiny tots over a period of years into young men who are now savage killers and vile rapists devoid of kindly consideration for the peoples Hitler characterized as being less than swine. The hardened and depraved creatures he created are so unique among mankind as to

171

be hardly recognizable as human. Conditioning techniques can be lovingly extended by parents to make their offspring the very opposites of Hitler's corrupt prodigies. Just as he molded men in the image of Evil, the community's high ideals will mold men in the image of Christ. To be sure, training children to observe certain desirable behavior cannot confer Egoic advancement to even a slight degree, but it will produce a generation of men among whom advancement can proceed as readily as in the ancient Lemurian culture.

"You will learn as you grow a little older that many influences are developing in the United States which will tend to brutalize and coarsen the sensitivities of children toward the fragility of life. This will be a sad trend indeed, for an adult's mores are an extension of his general attitudes as a child. To combat this, the community must do its best to re-establish in children a sense of empathy with and respect for all life forms.

"Because of ever-worsening world tensions, the toughening of children in the hope that they will be more courageous and effective in war will seem desirable to the nations. This concept will certainly backfire. A man who is a 'tough guy' has no consideration for the feelings of others; so when war suddenly brings him up to date in his considerations of human pain and frailty, he sees only his own susceptibility. The result is a forlorn, craven, useless soldier on the battlefield. Courage in battle comes from a willingness to protect those at home from the horrors of defeat. Courage arises from morality and an appreciation of life's sweetness for the persons one loves. The clod can think only of himself, and he is the first to flee battle. One's self-control and resolution in war are products of the knowledge that there are ideologic principles transcending the individual which are worth defending to the death."

"Why do you talk so much about war and battles?" Richard asked somewhat alarmed. "Will the city or the Kingdom have to fight a lot?"

"No, lad. I merely wished to point out the falsity of the justifications to be given for the coarsening of children's sensitivities and the blunting of their moral consciences.

"Can't you see that an ever increasing number of tough-acting and inconsiderate children includes girls as well as boys? The kind of women into which tough-acting girls grow are not fit to raise the succeeding generation into capable, industrious, and reliable citizens. Only two generations are needed for a culture to collapse from its citizens' compounded selfishness and crudeness.

"Lemurian home life must be much more stable than families are today. Mother shall be queen and treated accordingly. Women will earn respect and honor for being the foundation of the stability of civilization and its continued advancement. Furthermore, the father shall be king in his household. I don't mean as an absolute ruler but as director, protector, provider, devoted father, and masculine lover. It is a truism that a man is respected and obeyed by his wife in direct proportion to the degree he cherishes her and is lovingly devoted to her."

"It won't really be necessary for *me* to get married, will it?" Richard asked hopefully.

"Why in the world do you say that?" Dr. White exclaimed.

"I doubt that I would know how to court a girl," was the frank reply.

"Who does?" Dr. White laughed. "You're only seventeen years old. The art of courtship isn't inborn; so you're in the same boat as every other man in the world. You'll just have to blunder along like everyone else until you become accustomed to the company of young women. Girls are really quite easy to get along with."

"Frankly, they seem so much more poised than I," Richard admitted shyly. "They treat me like a kid."

"I think you should consider the fact that you've been about two years younger than the girls in your classrooms. They're ready for boys older than themselves, not younger. Don't buck nature. Girls mature socially earlier than boys."

"What would you have me do, go out with fifteen-year-old high school girls?"

"That's a good start! You're not going to marry all the girls you go out with, and the best way to find out what girls like to do and like to talk about is to become more closely acquainted with them."

"It sounds like you're trying to encourage me to date girls," Richard smiled.

"I certainly am!" Dr. White answered. "It's about time you started."

"But I don't want to," Richard protested genially.

"That's because nobody likes to do things in which he feels inadequate. You'll make embarrassing mistakes just like anybody else who's learning something new, but you needn't go out with the same girl more than once. Anyway, it's better that you find out what different kinds of girls are like so you can better judge the qualities you'll want in a wife. I suggest, however, that you not discourage yourself by seeking the most glamorous and poised young women for your first dates; they'll only try to impress you with their superiority. Start out with a girl who is even less experienced than you in dating."

Richard chuckled out loud. "It seems strange that a man like you who is so philosophically and spiritually inclined should encourage me to go out with girls."

"Don't let anyone tell you that marital love and sex are laughable, impure, or in any way unworthy of a man. God divided the human life-wave into two equal sexual polarities in order that men and women should be inexorably drawn to one another. There were three major purposes to be accomplished by the device of bisexual attraction. The first is the most obvious to everyone: procreation in order to continue the race.

"The second purpose was to provide a spiritually regenerating fount for both men and women. Sexual orgasm releases an occult energy which balances certain elements within the creative make-up of human bodies. Intellectual power and procreative power are the two factors of human creative energy. The greater one's Egoic advancement, the greater are his powers of creativity. Therefore, the greater one's Egoic advancement the greater are his intellect and capacity for sex. Intellect and sex counterbalance one another in every Ego. If either factor is used to a much greater extent than the other, mental and spiritual imbalance results.

"The third purpose of God's creation of sexual polarity is the most important by far. The compelling desire an Ego feels for extensive companionship with a mate is a means for teaching human beings how to get along with at least one other person on an intimate day-by-day basis. After thousands of incarnations of practice at co-operation, the emotions of mutual concern slowly developed between mates. While man was still in prehistoric times, he began to extend these emotions to family members and his neighbors, and he gradually evolved tribal co-operation and humane considerations. The social growth that arose from sexual attraction was according to God's intention.

"Sexual attraction is much more powerful than people realize. The magnetism which draws men and women together is a force beyond the Physical Plane of existence. Perhaps this accounts for sex being so mysterious and baffling to the scientists who seek to explain it. It is a matter of great importance that the joining together of two Egos of opposite polarity creates a neutral, balanced entity in the Universe which is a true marriage. Until an Ego is united in such a polar coupling, he feels a vague, restless, yearning dissatisfaction with life which defies description or analysis. Each Ego is but half of a unit which seeks completion.

"Unfortunately, all marriages do not result in a balanced polar coupling. When the respective Egoic advancements of the man and his wife are not equal, the marriage becomes forced and does not result in polar neutrality. It is sad, indeed, when a man and a woman join in wedlock primarily for the satisfaction of sexual passions or for convenience or for money reasons and the like; the union likely will be strained for its duration. Seeing that marriage is for a lifetime, it is very important to examine one's prospective marriage partner from every viewpoint in order that a balanced coupling will be most likely. There are many Egos assigned to this planet and many degrees and sub-degrees of Egoic advancement; yet there are literally scores of Egos of opposite polarity who will satisfactorily meet any given Ego's requirements for achieving a spiritually sound marriage. Generally speaking, Egos of equal advancement incarnate in such a way as to become available to one another for courtship and marriage. However, astute perception is needed to determine the suitability of any prospective couple. In the Kingdom of God every facility will be available for assisting men and women to secure a balanced marriage conducive to the continued Egoic advancement of each partner.

"So far as you're concerned, Richard, you will have to determine the suitability of a prospective wife just like any other person these days. For that reason, I have been encouraging you to get out and learn about girls so you can later learn about women."

"I don't know," the young man said hesitantly. "I think I prefer to stay single."

"Don't tell me you don't like girls," Dr. White scoffed.

"Oh, no! It's not that!" Richard exclaimed. "I find girls very attractive and delightful."

"Well, you know what they say about faint hearts and fair ladies."

Richard smiled wanly and said, "I still doubt that there will be any ladies in my life. I'm too bashful."

"Nonsense! There will be many lovely women in your life, and there will be four in particular who shall be major turning points in your life."

Richard stared wide-eyed at Dr. White. "Is that for sure?" he stammered.

"Certainly! That's the trouble with adolescents; they can't imagine themselves being any different from what they are to-day. You're all so certain that your attitudes have reached a permanent plateau. What a surprise you're in for! Your tastes, desires, philosophy, mentality, and morality are still just in a formative stage. The maturing process continues until death."

"I've suspected as much, but the future is pretty much an unknown to me. You're looking back with surety at where you've come from, but I can't look forward with any surety." He paused, then said, "Be that as it may, let's get back to this business of the four women. That interests me. Who will they be?"

"To disclose your personal future in detail would deprive you of your courage in some cases and from self-effort in others. However, I can characterize the four so you will be able to recognize them in retrospect. They are: Emotional Passion; Sly Calculation; Virtuous Chastity; and Devoted Love."

"That doesn't mean much," Richard complained. "Will I meet them in that order?"

"Not necessarily."

"What value do you intend for me to gain from this information?" Richard asked in puzzlement.

"Perhaps you will find it useful sometimes in the future. Perhaps also you will then be convinced that your future is known to us." Dr. White then recited a verse to further identify the four women in regard to the times of their relative appearances. Richard rehearsed the verse until the elderly doctor was satisfied that the boy had it memorized.

"Which one shall I marry?" Richard asked.

Dr. White smiled, and with a wink he admonished, "That is something only the future will reveal."

"But at least I shall have a son," Richard countered. "Berkeley already told me that much."

"He did?" Dr. White said in mock surprise. "What were his words? Do you remember?"

"Let's see," Richard said haltingly. "He said I shouldn't reveal the name written upon me until the first boy is born in my household."

"Good! Remember that exactly," Dr. White commented mysteriously.

Richard paused to gauge the possible reasons for Dr. White's evasiveness. Whenever the elderly man conducted the discussion of a subject in an abtruse manner, there simply was no way to extract detailed information from him. Richard wisely let the subject drop.

"Getting back to the community," Richard began, "I'm interested to know what kind of people will come to live there."

The elderly doctor seemed pleased with the young man's obvious shift of subject, and he embarked on a discussion of the new topic with enthusiasm. "I suspect that you are afraid the city will be a hodgepodge of eccentrics, fanatics, and bearded cultists. Such persons have no place in a balanced society. You will be able to identify them and exclude their detrimental influence from the city. Sincerely interested persons will inquire about the city in a much different manner than the merely curious and argumentative seekers of information. Avoid like the plague any applicants who harbor a tendency toward fanatic, self-righteous, puritan, or churchy demeanor. These characteristics indicate emotional imbalance and immaturity.

"For the most part, only the proper persons will be attracted to the city. They will be practical minded with a leaning toward the physical sciences. They will be a faithful, conscientious people, romanticists in the adventure of life, essentially philosophers. They shall have a high sense of social justice, be especially free from racial and religious prejudice, and have a fine regard for the rights of others. Each will exemplify his belief that the home is the basic unit of society where children are properly prepared for the good things of life and its responsibilities. As a people they will be joyous, enthusiastic, and energetic."

"I see," Richard said. "They will be mostly scientific, intellectual, and liberal."

"Maybe you *don't see*, lad," Dr. White said rather harshly. "That all depends upon what you mean by an 'intellectual' or a 'liberal.' I personally do not care to use those two terms because they mean widely different things to different people.

"Most persons who arrogate to themselves the status of 'intellectual' are seeking a distinction among men to compensate for their social ineptitude. A deep sense of inferiority compels them to proclaim their superiority over intelligent men of good sense. Intellectuals like to believe that they are so far above the rest of society that common men can't understand them or appreciate them. To prove this contention, they have an esoteric jargon of their own. When intellectuals gather, they spend the time impressing one another with their culture and education. Such intellectuals form a sort of lunatic group of writers, artists, poets, and bizarre nonconformists who parrot clever things they've learned from published intellectuals. Because they really try to believe they are above men, they will go to any extreme to demonstrate their contempt for society's hard-gained concepts of proper behavior and morality.

"Intellectuals behave in a bohemian manner not so much for the sake of enjoyment but because it is the very opposite of prudent convention. They flout religion because they feel their intellect is beyond such opiates. They contrarily profess radical, revolutionary movements and would secretly love to gain control over their country in order to mold it to their own liking. Inasmuch as they cannot fit into society, their antagonism toward it makes them want to command all who comprise it. They would force everyone to acclaim their kind as exalted beings. Intellectuals are notorious for having promoted revolutionary ideologies which have resulted in the overthrow of established governments, and in effect, they have carelessly and unconscionably delivered whole nations into the hands of dictators. This they may do in hope of reward from a new government, but almost without exception they are removed as dangerous inciters of revolution by the very scoundrels to whom they afforded power.

"Most intellectuals are prone to harmless self-pity, retreat, and erratic behavior; but the liberal is a real villain. He will take no firm stand on anything even if his very survival depends upon a soundly reasoned plan of action. He will tell you that one must be open to both sides of every question at all times. He will bend over backwards to demonstrate, for instance, that Nazism and Buddhism are similar or that the concepts of good and evil are wholly relative so that no absolute moral laws can exist or insist that the notion that the sun revolves about the Earth can never be entirely disproven. Under the guise of open-mindedness and intellectual fairness, we have a person who will not think constructively or conclusively. Ironically, he usually is college educated, smoothly persuasive, and well polished socially, and these attributes aid in his appointment to positions of trust and respectability. But his devious, unanchored morality and his adeptness at evasive double-talk make the liberal an easy turncoat and traitor—after all, his loyalty is only relative to his non-absolute code of morality. He can rationalize any immoral behavior by his shifting standards which allow him, above all other men, the ability to live any way he pleases and never sin in his own eyes. This he can do without inner conflict because the liberal can argue that his intellect may in some respects exceed God's wisdom—if indeed he even recognizes a God. The liberal, as you can see, is without common sense, logic or morality. He is creation's most dangerous fool."

"I withdraw my summary," Richard said laughingly, and he covered his face in mock chagrin. Then in seriousness he asked, "How do people come to be like the liberal you describe? I myself have met the type, and I've often wondered what could make someone act that way."

"I believe it's a case of lack of proper moral guidance when they were children," Dr. White replied. "The public school system seems to be largely at fault. The public school teacher is

179

firmly enjoined from discussing anything remotely religious in his classrooms lest he express his personal moral tenets and come into conflict with the various religious heritages of his pupils. Many parents leave the moral training of their children to the very schools which *may not* engage in moral training because morality is considered a part of religious philosophy. These same parents are the ones who don't go to church and who don't send their children to Sunday School. Where in the world do people expect proper morality to come from? Do they suppose right attitudes and acceptable behavior spring naturally from within the children's brains or that they breathe it in with the air? Between irresponsible parents and hobbled schools they are producing far too many brilliant but unprincipled scoundrels.

"The exciting ideals of our Christian heritage and our American heritage are being neglected. The heroes held up to children today are baseball stars, movie stars, and romanticized gangsters. I doubt that adults intend to displace Washington and Jefferson with Dizzy Dean, Wallace Beery, and Jesse James, but children don't know any better. They will strive to emulate the way of life of the heroes glamorized by modern ballyhoo. What's even worse is the glamorization of battle in current war propaganda and movies. If ever an uncensored film of an actual battle were shown in our movie houses, voluntary enlistments in the armed services would fall to zero. Furthermore, I deplore the idolization of warriors merely because they have killed an unusual number of the enemy. By so doing, we glorify the taking of human life and evade humane concern for our opponents' widows, orphaned children, and forlorn mothers. Extraordinary gallantry and courage in the face of the enemy are admirable qualities in a man and deserve recognition, but skill in killing men and thereby gaining notoriety is rather a negative admiration. The character of such an 'ace' is all too likely to be vicious and blood-thirsty.

"Here I am on the subject of war again," Dr. White reminded himself disgustedly. "The stupidity of the whole affair distresses me beyond words. You shall see, lad, that it will settle nothing. The hatred, fear, pain, misery, and destruction that it causes will be to no avail. We seek to destroy Hitler and Tojo, but others like them will always sprout up wherever a nation's gullible populace permits. Why are men so willing to die for a self-seeking dictator who surrounds himself with an aura of nationalistic splendor? Man is entirely too willing to believe that he and his nation are superior to all others and that his alleged superiority reduces other nationalities to contemptible subordinates unworthy of just consideration.

"The man who loves his country's honors, ideals, and traditions is likely to be a patriot rather than a nationalist. The patriot is *for* his country instead of *against* other countries. One who loves his own country can respect the love that another nation's citizens have for their homeland and its lore. The patriot can be trusted to avoid war. The nationalist, on the other hand, easily succumbs to the base tendency to become organized *against* someone or something. It seems that only nobler souls can be organized *for* something.

"The schools in the community and in the Kingdom of God shall not be lax in the moral training of their students. Since all Citizens will adhere to the philosophy of Melchizedek, teachers will not be in conflict with variant religious concepts. The continuance of the Kingdom of God will depend heavily upon its school system.

"To encourage the maximum acquisition of knowledge in the community and in the Kingdom, education at every level will be free of charge to the student. Adult education will be available on the same terms. The whole community benefits in manifold ways from every dollar expended for the education of its members. There will be much leisure time for the Citizens of the Kingdom, and they shall be inclined to use it to further their spiritual advancement which, after all, is the main purpose of civilization.

"Americans are surfeit with luxuries, comforts, conveniences, food, and possessions; yet they suffer a gnawing spiritual discontent. This makes Americans forever seek some new experience or diversion in hope of pacifying their undefined craving. They unknowingly seek a worthy goal to strive toward but cannot even find it in conventional religions. In the teachings of the Brotherhoods, men at last will have found the source of joy and inner peace from which they have been cut off for so many long millenia. When you yourself have undertaken the Brotherhood's studies, you will begin to fathom my meaning."

"But you've told me so much!" Richard corrected. "How can there be more?"

"I have told you virtually nothing, lad—just general outlines upon which to focus your attention as you proceed through life. The outline Berkeley and I have provided you will serve as a framework upon which to organize your thoughts concerning the experiences which you shall have. The millions of words that you will have to read and comprehend before you'll have completed the Brotherhood's detailed training will greatly enlarge the meager information so far revealed to you. Advanced personal instruction from the Brotherhood will serve as a springboard for many flights of profound contemplation."

"I've already found and read a couple of books which will help," Richard commented.

"Oh?" said Dr. White reservedly.

"Yes. I've discovered some of James Churchward's books on the lost continent of Mu and some books on yoga."

"Undeniably, Churchward did some good archeological detective work," Dr. White observed, "but, unfortunately, he had to deal with evidence gathered solely from Mu's colonies. Some of his deductions and datings are consequently a little wild, but his collection of data is impressive."

"I haven't been able to get hold of any writings about Atlantis yet," Richard offered further, "but I will have a little more time if I'm quitting college."

"Stay away from anything about Atlantis, Richard," Dr. White admonished firmly. "There is little other than nonsense and misinformation in any available publications concerning it. I'm sorry to say that the subject of Atlantis has been adopted by the Black Mentalists to confuse and ensnare persons who seek to investigate the legend.

"I also suggest that for the time being you stay clear of any publications having to do with yoga. At a later date you will be further enlightened in the subject. Until then, the very dangerous practices in yoga are to be completely avoided."

The young man was astonished by Dr. White's evident insistence, but Richard quickly nodded his acquiescence. "Incidentally," the young man said, "I was reminded of a question when you mentioned Mu's colonies a moment ago. You told me long ago that representatives from all of the original twelve tribes must be reassembled into the Kingdom of God, and this obviously would also include the community. Does this mean that all twelve races will intermarry?"

"Yes, lad. Does that bother you?"

"No. Not at all. If anything, it very much pleases me. It seems the perfect answer to racial discrimination. If there shall some day be only one race, that old source of conflict will be eliminated."

"Very true. But there would be no racial antagonisms in the Kingdom of God in any event. Such fears and hatreds are incompatible with the spiritual and social advancement required of its Citizens. Intermarriage is important to bring the Universal Race into being for other reasons."

"I have to admit to some prejudices taught me by my parents, but I have not been able to substantiate them. I have Jewish friends and a Japanese friend, and I cannot see any justification for claiming them to be inferior to other nationalities. A Negro boy in my English class here in college is so far superior to me in our studies that I'm ashamed to hear people defame a man on the grounds of his color or religion. The people of other nationalities and races with whom I've become acquainted are so personable and congenial that I delight in their friendship."

"In this respect all aspirants to the community will be in agreement," Dr. White said. "The Brotherhoods are constantly working to bring about mutual acceptance and understanding between races. Inasmuch as all advancement in position in the city will be based solely upon personal merit and ability, members of the various races will have authority over persons of other races. If the infantile prejudices prevalent in the world-at-large were to prevail in the city, strife would be incessant.

"Incidentally, if you would like to read books helpful in your attainment of proper attitudes preliminary to your formal instruction by the Brotherhood, I suggest that you study psychology and make practical application of what you learn. I also recommend that you learn the philosophy of government expounded by Lao Tzu because his wisdom can be usefully adapt-

183

ed to the community's best interests. Except for following these two specific suggestions, leave the rest of your education in the hands of the Brothers. They will see to it that the information relative to your proper education will be provided at the most advantageous moments.

"We would also like to see you get out on your own and away from your parents. You are too protected at home, and you will learn the lessons of life required of you only if you have to shift for yourself. You must come to understand personally the frustrations and hardships of the men and women who must earn a living under present economic conditions. In this way you will be able to serve the needs of men more effectively when the community forms. This lesson will be a difficult one, and you shall not be done with it until your appreciation of their plight is genuinely learned."

"I doubt that my father will stand for my leaving home, Dr. White," Richard warned.

"It will do you both good to get away from one another for a while. At this stage of your developing manhood the conflict between father and son is likely to be greatest. Both of you have such strong personalities that antagonism between you is inevitable. One day, however, you will arrive at a state of mutual respect. This means that you will have to appreciate his viewpoints as much as you would like him to be tolerant of your ideas and wishes."

"Boy, that'll be the day! He's just plain bull-headed and strict. He won't even listen to reason."

"Well, that surely sounds typical of an adolescent," Dr. White laughed. "But perhaps you will one day be grateful for the comfortable life he has provided you. The restrictiveness you complain about is a good sign of parental concern. It takes effort to consistently discipline a child. It's far easier for a parent not to sustain continual concern over the proper control and guidance of his troublesome offspring. If your father has effected unusually restrictive disciplines which are not placed upon most other children your age, it is very possible that he has a greater interest in your welfare than the average parent. Although you are unaware of it, your father loves you. Because he does not believe in a show of affection between males, he may appear stern, forbidding, and distant. He would never let you hear him praise you; yet he boasts to others of your achievements. In his own way he seeks to cause you to strive harder by withholding praise. And if you think about it, you will realize that he instinctively gives you freedom to make your own decisions as you demonstrate your ability to govern yourself in an adult manner. Even though the standards by which he judges your maturity are overly hard, the advantages you enjoy by his grace are quite advanced for a seventeen-year-old boy. You rankle under his restrictions because most of your young friends whom you use as standards of comparison are older than you. When you become a parent, your understanding of your father will become more lucid."

"We shall see," Richard said grudgingly.

"I'm sure you will," the elderly doctor said with a gentle smile. "Incidentally, when you leave your parents' home, seek the city of the 'Violet Domes by the Sea' and make your home there. In the Valley of Saint Mary near that city, you will find peace and wisdom. There you will be readied for your tasks."

In a tone that revealed his long, troubled concern with the question, Richard asked, "When the proper time comes, how will people know that I'm all those things you said—like the 'Judge of Israel' and the 'Builder of Lemuria' and that I'm the founder of the city to be in Illinois?"

"You will tell them, of course."

"But any crackpot could make such claims!"

"Yes," Dr. White conceded, "but what you will claim shall ring of evident truth, and those who are able to comprehend the validity of your assertions will quickly uphold you."

"But wouldn't it be better if some well-known, respected person stated such claims in my behalf?"

"No! If this were done, which of you would be the greater authority: you or the person who proclaims you leader? Christ and Isaiah spoke for Themselves to inform the people of Their positions of authority."

"That may be, but look what happened to Christ on account of blasphemy."

"It was intended that Christ should be crucified," Dr. White countered.

"That's small comfort! To do what you've suggested, I'll be sticking my neck out awfully far. One person is too puny to have much influence over the world or to protect himself if the world is out for his scalp."

"To the contrary, lad. One man armed with truth and a practical plan can change the whole world. You will know this by the time you are ready to begin your work; until then, remain obscure and continue to play the fool. Even though you will face opposition all through your life, never fear. You will not be without protection and help. The Comforter will be with you in times of need."

"The Comforter?" Richard exclaimed. "Do you mean the Holy Ghost?"

"More exactly, the term is Holy Spirit."

"Is there really such a thing? That's a concept I've never been quite able to accept."

"What do you think is meant by Holy Spirit?"

"I suppose it was intended to explain the miracles attributed to the Apostles. I also remember our pastor in confirmation class telling us a person is supposed to come to faith through the Holy Spirit. However, my own opinion is that there was no need for theologians to personalize this aspect of God's power as a third individual comprising a Triune Godhead."

"Well, I will admit that the idea of three entities being one God does strain a man's credulity a bit. There's no real mystery about it though. Christians worship Christ for good reason. His performance of miracles and the whole conduct of His ministry on Earth are proof enough of His divinity. The Holy Spirit also worked 'miracles' but through the media of ordinary mortal men. Actually, there is no such thing as a miracle. If even one exception to the laws of the universe were to be permitted, it would open the door to total disorganization on a cosmic scale. The strange and wondrous powers exhibited by Christ and the Holy Spirit were entirely within the bounds of mental precipitation and according to the laws of the higher planes of existence.

"Those disciples who enjoyed affiliation with the power of the Holy Spirit had the ability to understand and speak any language, to raise the dead, and to heal the sick. The Holy Spirit gave insight to greater understanding of hidden truths and thereby inspired the Prophets and their writings. The awe inspired by the works of the Holy Spirit was too great for Christians not to venerate it.

"The warranted worship of Christ and the Holy Spirit put the early Jewish Christians on the horns of a dilemma, for the first Commandment of Mosaic Law demanded that God *alone* shall be worshipped. They solved their problem by 'perceiving' a mystery wherein God is composed of three entities: Abbará, who is the Father God; Christ, who is the Archangel Melchizedek; and the Holy Spirit who represents God on Earth working directly among men for their soul advancement."

"But who *is* the Holy Spirit?" Richard asked directly.

"Holy Spirit is a translation from the Ancients' term *Essence of Divineness,* which refers to the Masters and High Adepts of the Brotherhoods. By means of Their near-Angelic power these Elder Brothers are the preservers and comforters of the human life-wave. It is They who further man's understanding of his destiny.

"So if I say that the Comforter shall be with you, Richard, it is the same as my saying the Holy Spirit shall be with you. The Holy Spirit, or Brotherhoods if you prefer, shall prepare your way and shall influence those who will come into the community. The world will soon see wondrous signs, and it will know the Kingdom of God is at hand. The first steps are being undertaken, and the great plan for mankind is being put into motion. Nothing and no one can stop the timetable now."

Dr. White smiled in a way that revealed all the loving wisdom inherent in the elderly man's personality. Some inner contemplation made his face radiantly serene. Then to Richard's dismay Dr. White was gone in a twinkling. The young man trembled from shock, and his senses were numbed by the unnatural and unaccountable disappearance.

After a moment he cried out involuntarily, "No! No! Don't go away! Not so soon!" Richard's chin and lips trembled uncontrollably with emotion as he got to his feet. Not knowing what to do, he stood looking about in a distracted manner. Then, without thought of his lament being heard, he blurted out the feeling that welled up within him. "Oh, I wish you had stayed a little longer! I speak to you so casually; yet I really wish to almost worship you. I thought for years how naturally I would bow down to you if I should ever see you again, but I have shown you no real respect at all! You put me so at ease that I act like I was talking to an old friend whom I can see again tomorrow. I love you, Dr. White! Strange as that may seem, love is the only word strong enough and even that falls short."

"Don't be so forlorn, my son," Dr. White said.

Richard quickly turned toward the source of the voice, but Dr. White was not there.

"Be comforted, for I shall be with you always," the elderly man's kindly voice continued.

Richard stared at the place where his ears told him Dr. White's voice was originating, but there was no one to be seen. "Where are you?" the young man called. "What's happening?"

"I'm still here, but I've imposed a mental barrier upon your sight so that I may depart without your seeing where I go. From now on I shall maintain constant contact with you. If ever you are confronted with a problem that is beyond your ability to solve, I shall be available to you telepathically.

"I must go now. Peace be with you!"

CHAPTER 12

Wisdom of an Essene

Richard went forward from the day of Dr. White's visit happily expecting frequent communication from his advisor. However, this was not to be—the young man had to make all his own decisions. There were many of life's lessons to be learned by the method of trial and error, and Richard had to discern the causes of the conditions in his life for himself. Despite his desire for guidance, it was not forthcoming lest it interfere with his Egoic growth and acquisition of knowledge through first-hand experience. Many times he failed, and his confidence wavered; but his hard-won solutions to personal problems made him all the stronger.

His withdrawal from college was a trying experience for Richard. After much argument and discussion with his parents, he terminated his formal education within two days of Dr. White's instruction to do so. His father was sorely disappointed by his failure to go on with college; and his mother was so disgusted that she never forgave him for bursting her dream of his becoming a brilliant professional man. The tension which developed between Richard and his parents over this situation caused them to behave quite curtly and sternly toward him. They could not understand why their son should quit school without warning—especially since his grades were excellent and his skills as a scholar were well developed.

At his father's insistence, Richard looked for work immediately. His parents decided somewhat punitively that since he was embarking on a lifetime of wage earning, he should begin to contribute to the family's income. Richard took a job as an assembly-line worker in a defense plant which manufactured aircraft radios. He remained only until the end of the war in Europe and then went to work at his father's woodworking factory. That summer Richard decided to enlist in the Regular Army instead of waiting to be drafted, and he was accepted into the United States Army Combat Engineers. While he awaited notice to report to a training camp, Japan surrendered on Richard's eighteenth birthday. The young man was subsequently notified by the army that although he had passed his physical examination, he must now be rejected because his eyesight didn't meet peacetime enlistment requirements.

About this time, his parents sold their home in Elmwood Park and purchased another in the city of Chicago. Shortly after moving into the new house, Richard contracted a serious case of double pneumonia. He was still flat on his back when he received a notice from his draft board to report for his pre-induction physical examination, but he was so emaciated that he was adjudged ineligible to serve in the armed forces pending a future examination. In conformity with Dr. White's prediction that Richard was not likely to serve in the army, there never was another examination.

Richard returned to his father's factory in December as a machine operator; and when he had grown strong and healthy again, he took a job as a mimeograph operator in an office. Here he learned the methods and functions of a large merchandising organization. In accordance with Dr. White's admonition about promotions, Richard left the firm when after eight months he was promoted to the firm's sales department. Concurrently he persuaded his parents to let him visit California. The science teacher who had encouraged his studies in high school, Dr. Daniels, offered to let him live with him and his wife in Los Angeles where they had recently relocated. Richard had saved quite a sum of money during the past year of work, and so his trip would impose no financial drain on his parents.

In January of 1947, he left for California. Dr. Daniels was genuinely happy to see his protégé, and Richard was thrilled to have the honor of staying at his favorite teacher's home. Their modest house was situated in the shadow of the University of Southern California where Dr. Daniels was employed. His wife, who had been a teacher of high school English in Chicago, attended classes at the university in order to earn a degree in music. Inasmuch as her two daughters had married, she was able to indulge this long cherished ambition. Mrs. Daniels was a sweet and outgoing soul who gladly welcomed Richard into her home as if he were long lost kin. Like Dr. Daniels, she was a gentle and amiable person with a heart big enough to love the whole world. This elderly couple's very apparent mutual love and respect for one another made a warm household indeed. Their lifelong devotion to the education of children and their understanding of adolescent needs and problems made them the ideal persons for Richard's further education.

Their home was a scholar's delight. They had a rather extensive reference library and subscriptions to several scientific periodicals which fascinated Richard. The central table of their study was heaped high with literature, and the room was usually a clutter of books. There was a never-ending symphonic concert being played on their phonograph, and since Richard loved that kind of music, the whole atmosphere seemed close to heaven to the young man.

Dr. Daniels had arranged for Richard to work at the university, and the young man was on the payroll just a few days after he arrived in Los Angeles. When their workday was done, Dr. Daniels and Richard would walk home together and talk of all manner of scientific and philosophical topics. The pleasant evenings at home before the study fireplace were enriching hours for both the teacher and his student. Richard learned much of the rationale of the scientific method and gained understanding of the world of scientists far beyond the scope of his college training.

Both Dr. Daniels and his wife were earnest Fabian Socialists, but their efforts to convert Richard to the socialist camp were in vain. The elderly couple was active in the American Socialist movement and were friends of Norman Thomas, the Socialist Party's perennial candidate for President of the United States. The demagoguery Richard associated with promoters of social reform was refreshingly absent in Mr. Thomas, and Richard was favorably impressed by the man's sincerity and evident good sense when he talked with him. This favorable opinion relaxed much of Richard's resistance to Dr. White's ideas on government for the Kingdom of God. Richard now knew that other people had independently arrived at an understanding of the short-comings of mankind's attempts to achieve an equitable government. But he also saw that the socialists had no well-developed safeguards against political bullies and corruption in their scheme. Their proposals were but another patch upon the patchwork economy which has haphazardly evolved over the ages. The socialists still borrow heavily from present concepts of money, property, and production; but without cognizance of karma, their ideas are largely without stability.

The Daniels took Richard on their frequent picnics and outings, and the young man soon learned that in many respects there was very little difference between young adults and elderly adults. The activities they enjoyed in common and their witty conversations and congenial good fun were all shared on equal footing without condescension on either side. This was a far cry from the young man's experience with his parents and relatives. The balanced relationship possible between the enthusiasm of youth and the experience of maturity was practically demonstrated to Richard. He began to see the mutual advantages of their working together. For a young man, he exhibited an unusual understanding toward mature caution; and his appreciation of the value of men beyond the vigor of middle age grew increasingly greater from that time forward.

Late in the spring of 1947 Richard returned to a cool reception at his parents' home in Chicago. Richard was glad to be back, but he was accosted with the accusation that he had, by his deference to Dr. Daniels, rejected his own parents. This deeply puzzled him, for the thought had never occurred to him. The nagging that he endured for the next few days on this theme irritated him to the point of exasperation.

A high school friend of Richard's named Raymond had recently been discharged from the army and was enthusiastic about going on a trip to Miami, Florida, before he settled down to working for a living. Raymond persuaded Richard to share expenses with him and spend a month or two on the ocean shore together. The adventure was appealing, and Richard was ready and willing to escape the nagging he had been suffering during the week he had been home from California. Neither did he intend to be intimidated by either of his parents; so he informed them he was going to Miami with Raymond and simply went.

The two adventurers took the train to Florida where they rented a room in a Miami Beach hotel overlooking the Atlantic Ocean. After about a week of loafing in the sun, Richard began looking for employment in town. He soon found a job with a company that did small printing jobs and mimeographing. He worked a few days in the shop, and then Richard's boss felt that he was the man with the right personality to be the firm's salesman. Richard was provided with a convertible automobile and a list of clients to call upon. Raymond knew a good thing when he saw it; so he too came to work for the same company. However, Raymond was assigned to work at another location, and the two friends usually saw one another only after working hours. Both young men did everything together and had a relaxed vacation for about a month in Florida. Only for one night did they separate, and that was because Raymond had been invited by a fellow worker to attend a party. That evening Richard wrote some letters and went down to mail them about nine o'clock. The night was warm and humid; so he decided to take a stroll down the shorewalk. The shorewalk stretched for a few blocks south of Richard's hotel and ended at the harbor channel to Biscayne Bay and the port of Miami. Palm trees lined the walk, and lights from the nearby buildings were subdued enough not to interfere with the starlight overhead. There were very few people walking at this remote end of the walk, and in the peaceful quiet only an occasional rustle of palm leaves in the breeze was to be heard.

Richard was somewhat alarmed when he detected the sound of footsteps of two men overtaking him from behind. He stopped as the men came near, and he turned alertly to face them. They came to a halt about five feet distant. Both men were smiling as if in anticipation of greeting an old friend. Suddenly, Richard was flooded with a feeling of sweet tranquility, and at once he sensed the benign intentions of these two men.

The younger of the men advanced and extended his hand in friendship as he addressed Richard using the name given him by Dr. White.

"We had rather hoped to see you tonight," he said. "My friend and I drove in from the west coast of the state so he could visit some old acquaintances here in Miami. However, it's been in the back of his mind to meet you ever since he learned you were in Florida."

With this brief introduction, the other man hesitantly came forward. He was an aged man whose hair, including his eyebrows and neatly trimmed goatee, was pure white. This older man, perhaps eighty-five years old, was corpulent and moved heavily; but his face was agile, and it revealed the presence of a keen mind and a cheery humor.

The younger of the two men was of nondescript middle age and built like an athletic instructor. He was tall, blond, and handsome, and he carried himself like he was an extremely capable and successful business executive. He appeared to be a type that would brook no nonsense, but his smile was calculated to put others at ease in his presence.

The elderly man falteringly shook Richard's hand and pressed it fondly between his hands as if he were patting his infant grandchild's cherished little hand. Richard became confused, and he felt awkward and embarrassed. "I don't understand," Richard stammered. "What's this all about?"

"Forgive me," the old man began apologetically, "but I don't expect I'll still be around until the day when you will have fulfilled what's been promised of you. My kind friend and teacher there has told me much of the future and . . . and . . . well . . ." he shook his head dejectedly. "I guess I'm just an old fool to embarrass you this way." He released Richard's hand and stepped back.

"Please don't feel that way," Richard said spontaneously. "It's just that you have the advantage of me. You obviously know my name, but I don't understand what you want."

The old man looked to his companion for an indication of what to do next, and Richard automatically shifted his glance to the tall man in expectation of explanation. For a moment the tall man smiled warmly at his elderly friend, and then he turned to Richard and said, "This fine old fellow has been my most apt and devoted student. You must please forgive me for having confided to him things that he has long hungered to know. His respect for what I have told him precludes his revealing it to anyone else. He is a rare Ego, and it is my sorrow that he did not come to us much sooner, for he could have risen high."

Richard began to have some inkling of the nature of the relationship between these two men. "Who is *us?*" Richard inquired pointedly.

"I am associated with the Essenes," the younger man replied. He extended his arm toward the old man in a gesture that could have become a pat on the back had the two been standing just a little closer together. "And my friend here is a retired physician who moved to Florida to pass his declining years but found inspiration instead."

"It's true!" the old man said enthusiastically. "I found out that life has a purpose only after I existed in wondering despair for a whole lifetime. How I wish that I had known at your age what you know already!"

"But what do you want of me?" Richard persisted.

"Perhaps it is hard to comprehend," the old man said, "but all the greatness and excitement for which the world has long waited will soon occur. I shall not see it; yet to see *you* is to touch those future events which I wish I could witness for myself."

"I think I begin to understand," Richard assured him. "What I await has not yet happened to me; but if you find some satisfaction in seeing me, then I should be pleased. But let me explain that there is no reason for me to be accorded honors. Your expectations for me are very likely greater than my own."

The old man nodded happily and turned to his companion. "It is as you said," he smiled. Then his expression became serious as he observed, "I've examined his hands as best I can in this light, but I don't see the sign."

"There is still time," the younger man replied obliquely.

"Yes, I suppose so," the old man mused. "Well, I'll be going now," he said briskly, and then to the tall man he added, "I'll see you in a few hours over at the house." He then turned to Richard and bowed slightly in the gracious manner of gentlemen of the last century, and he hurried away. His departure was as precipitous as had been his appearance.

Richard peered after the bulky figure receding down the dim walk, and he felt irritatedly mystified by this abrupt encounter. He looked at the tall man at his side.

The man anticipated Richard's question by saying, "I have

come in answer to many questions you have pondered since you last saw Dr. White. If you have time, perhaps you would like to discuss some of them tonight."

Richard's heart leaped with excitement. "I have all the time in the world," he replied cheerfully. Two long years had passed since he last enjoyed contact with Dr. White, and the prospect of information concerning things of real importance was always exciting.

The man became distracted for a moment as he watched his elderly companion turn down a side street a block away. Richard followed his glance in time to see the old man pass from view behind a building on the distant corner.

"I can see that you are wondering why I should have permitted the awkward meeting between you and my old friend. When once he learned that I was to see you, he pleaded with me that I allow him to see you too. He promised me that he would be as unobtrusive as possible and depart quickly. He would have much preferred to linger with us, but he is a man of staunch word of honor. That old man means much to me. He has brought much joy into my heart. He will savor this meeting over and over again in future discussions with me, for you have provided him with more than you shall ever realize. His embarrassment was far greater than yours, and the fact that he went through with his intention to shake your hand and talk with you proves to me that it meant a great deal to him. I wasn't able to deny him his desire because . . . well, Richard, you see . . . he'll go through transition within a week."

Richard caught his breath. His voice choked as he said, "He acts so cheerful! If I had known it meant so much to him, I could have been more understanding with him." Richard was ashamed to have failed to take full advantage of an opportunity which was now gone forever. He thought silently for a moment and then asked, "Does he have cancer or something like that?"

"No. He's not ill. Neither is he aware that his body will so soon fail him. Heart failure during sleep will effect his transfer to a greater existence and release him to higher teachers."

A sense of sadness swept over Richard. He had never before felt the pain of foreknowledge so personally.

"Don't mourn for his sake," the man admonished. "He

doesn't expect to live forever, and he looks forward to the day when he may again function freely on the Astral Plane."

Richard took up the thought and added, "Yes, I'm sure it must be wonderful to see old friends and loved ones who have gone on before. The prospect that I myself find worthwhile about death is being rid of the limitations of the brain and body. To be able to know instead of surmising is an exciting prospect."

"Transition is not a passport to omniscience, Richard. To be relieved of the physical vehicle does not confer mental attitudes or knowledge not already learned. We, as Egos, are the same after the body dies as we were in physical life. Our Heaven or Hell is within us, and we mold the nature of our afterlife during our life on earth. Fearful, hateful, and spiteful people carry these personality traits into their astral existence and thereby fix limitations upon the happiness they will experience on the Astral Plane. Their negative emotions attune these Egos with the lower vibratory rate of the lower Astral Plane."

"Isn't the lower Astral Plane what is commonly called *Hell?*" Richard asked.

"That's right. There are various levels of Hell ranging from the lowest, where murderers and the vile Egos who associate themselves with the Black Mentalists have bound themselves, to the other end of Hell's spectrum where dwell the unhappy Egos who dubiously refuse to learn that the mere elevation of the quality of their thoughts can promote them to upper astral existence. The lower Astral Plane is confused, dark, and dejecting. By comparison, the upper astral is bright, musical, joyous, and expansive.

"Egos who are happy, loving, wise, and helpful naturally gravitate to the upper Astral Plane upon transition. There they may receive instruction from the Higher Beings of our life-wave in order to be better prepared for subsequent incarnations. But if you remember, it is only upon the Physical Plane that we gain the knowledge which becomes a *permanent* part of our soul equipment, and this restriction applies until the Ego attains Adeptship. The type of personality and character a person evolves during physical life determines the status he will suffer or enjoy on the Astral Plane. However, after he arrives upon the Astral Plane at the station corresponding to his character, he can

197

modify his situation there by changing his emotions, thoughts, and desires."

"Doesn't one's good deeds or evil deeds have considerable bearing on rewards of happiness in Heaven?" Richard inquired.

"Not acts but character determines one's status in Heaven. The criminal murderer kills because of his depravity, but so may a gentle nurse kill by careless or indiscriminatory administering of medication to a patient. Karmically, both the criminal and the nurse during a later incarnation must suffer deaths similar to the ones they inflicted. One of them killed by intent; the other killed through lack of due attention. Karma will settle their accounts on the Physical Plane if they haven't in the meanwhile compensated for their hurtful deeds by the rendering of appropriate excess service to others.

"If you recall, karma means *carry-over*. That is because karmic accounts are ignored on the Astral Plane. The Astral Plane is not concerned with reward and punishment but rather with the uplift of an Ego's character if he so desires. The ignorance which binds a man on earth will also bind him in Heaven. But as rapidly as a man uplifts his attitudes in Heaven, his level of spiritual attunement correspondingly rises toward the higher vibrations of the upper Astral Plane.

"It's a sad commentary on human beings that many sink lower on the Astral Plane while they are there. For example, soldiers who are slain in battle often continue their hateful and vengeful contention after they arrive on the Astral Plane. The dark emotions they persist in sustaining tear down whatever spiritual advancement they may have gained in former lives. Unless these Egos come to a state of forgiveness, peace, and serenity, they cannot hope to see upper astral life."

"What exactly did you mean when you used the term *vibrations* a moment ago?" Richard asked.

"Let me explain it this way: the nutational rate of the Astral Plane is constant; therefore, it is not nutational frequency to which I refer but rather to certain astral radiations analogous to electromagnetic radiations of the Physical Plane. It is these astral radiations which afford sympathetic attunement between similar Egos.

"Just as there are many classes of society coexisting in a large city, so it is on the Astral Plane. The different classes of culture that exist in society may impinge on one another in stores, factories, and places of amusement, but the members of any one class seem unable to find much in common with the members of a different class. Socialites, poor Negro slum dwellers, intellectuals, skid row bums, middle class Christians, underworld hoodlums, unskilled laborers, college-educated executives all live together in the same city and are known to one another, but the mores and customs distinctive of each class seem intolerable as a mode of life for any of the other classes. Analogous to these coexisting worlds within a society, the Astral Plane is likewise compartmentalized.

"On the Astral Plane, mental precipitation is practically instantaneous. The surroundings in which one finds himself are the direct result of the kind of thoughts he sustains. Egos who share the same level of happiness, serenity, helpfulness, and love would naturally be attuned to one another and would be surrounded by the same kind of environment because similar thinking determines similar corresponding environment. They would find themselves together yet distinct from those Egos above and below their respective level of advancement.

"Each type of emotion has its own characteristic vibrational frequency. When an Ego experiences an emotion, his Mind generates a radiated energy upon the fourth plane of existence. This vibratory energy is radiated whether the Ego resides on the Astral Plane or is incarnated in a physical body. The clairvoyant person actually sees these vibrations as colored auras enveloping the Ego's Astral Body. Each character trait and emotion is definitely related to a radiation of specific color. Love is at the highest end of the vibrational spectrum and exhibits a clear violet color in an Ego's aura. Hate is at the lowest end of the spectrum and is indicated in an Ego's character by the presence of murky red in his aura. Because almost everyone at any given moment possesses the full range of all the traits possible to human character each in a varying degree of refinement, he simultaneously exhibits the whole color spectrum of emotional vibrations. The amplitude, or intensity, of each vibrational frequency—that is, the relative brightness of each color in his aura—is determined by the extent to which the Ego has developed the corresponding characteristic or emotion.

"Love and hatred, for instance, may easily coexist in an Ego's emotional makeup. He may profoundly love Christ and all mankind; and because of this supreme refinement, the amplitude of his love frequency will be intense and dominant in his emotional spectrum. But he may also suffer great hatred and fear of the Black Mentalists. This negative emotion will also appear in his Egoic aura in proportion to the intensity of his hatred and fear.

"You may say that hatred of the Black Mentalists is fitting and proper, but it isn't! The Ego's hatred doesn't hurt the Black Mentalists; it only holds down the overall level of refinement of the Ego doing the hating. That is why Christ commanded us to love our enemies—because such love enhances one's own Egoic advancement. Indeed, Christ loves even the evil Black Mentalists. They are human beings struggling in darkness along the path toward unity with God. Their perverse and negative attitudes are truly pitiful.

"Angels and Archangels are without hatred. Were They to hate, think how disastrous such emotions charged by Their highly advanced powers of precipitation would be to our universe. Angels are, and must be, the embodiment of loving patience and compassion.

"A human Ego's overall spiritual advancement can be measured by averaging the amplitudes for each of his emotional vibratory frequencies. An Ego is highly advanced when his positive emotions are of intense amplitude and his negative emotions are of correspondingly feeble amplitude. His overall spiritual advancement automatically determines the quality of his astral companions and the level he will occupy in 'Heaven' or 'Hell.'

"An Ego resting upon the Astral Plane who plans to reincarnate must be of spiritual advancement equal to or exceeding the average spiritual advancement of the two parents of his proposed new physical vehicle. In this way no parents suffer a child of lesser spiritual advancement than themselves. This is guaranteed by Cosmic Law."

"By the way," Richard asked, "what was this business about my hands?"

"My companion was looking for a sign promised to the Sons of Tubalcain to indicate that the Judge of Israel shall be a man of practical nature and a laborer in the trades who shall be sympathetic of their needs. The sign grew out of rumors among the builders of the Temple of Solomon. Their fancy grew into tradition, and it was finally formalized into prophesy. In order to satisfy this prophesy concerning the founder of the Kingdom of God, you will have to be marked with their sign. It need only be a token."

"But *I'm* not the founder of the Kingdom of God!" Richard exclaimed. "The Brothers in charge of the project are the founders, and They in turn are following the suggestions of Melchizedek."

"True. But you are the instrument, and your physical body is the vehicle."

"It seems to me that you fellows feel free to do almost anything to my body. You specifically set out to ruin my eyesight, nearly break my neck, and send a plague of pneumonia upon me so that I'm bound to follow the course you've set for me. Not only do you write on my body, but now I hear there's yet to be a sign on my hand."

"Your body is also the Lord's," the man firmly reminded Richard. "He shall bring about His magnificent plan for mankind through it—but only with your willing approval. You are enjoying a privilege which you've earned. Other men would gladly endure torture for lifetimes to have your present opportunity."

"I didn't intend to sound ungrateful," Richard said. "I know that each apparent physical hardship I've suffered has been part of a well-devised plan. It's just that you seem to do as you please with my body, but it's *my* nerves that do the hurting."

"I'm not a callous person, Richard, but perhaps you are being overly resentful about your pain and your rights. You have never in your whole life had to endure suffering. You aren't deformed or crippled or sickly, and your mental and physical health are exceptionally sound. Look around you to see what handicaps and hardships others suffer, and then be thankful.

"Furthermore, I really don't believe you are as unhappy or as indignant as your little speech seemed to convey. You are sometimes facetious at the wrong time, and you give the wrong impression of yourself. I'm aware that you are supposed to play the fool, but let's be a little more precise at the moment. The time that is being devoted to you by the Brotherhoods is precious indeed. Be worthy of it!"

Richard stood corrected, and he became very much aware that

this tall man had a personality that commanded respect. They sat down on the large blocks of stone which bordered the harbor channel at the end of the shorewalk and continued their conversation.

"You must take good care of your body, Richard, because it must serve you well for a very long time. Keep it vigorous, strong, and youthful, for your life's work will demand a great deal of energy. Strengthen your body with physical labor, and eat pure food. Use your knowledge of chemistry and medicine to avoid harmful foodstuffs. Maintain a balanced diet of natural foods, for the body can be no better than the building materials provided it. The responsibility for its proper nourishment is yours alone. If your body fails you, the Lord cannot use you. Moreover, a sound Mind cannot exist in a poor body, nor is a sound body compatible with a distraught Mind. Spiritual harmony and advancement demand a vigorous, stable Mind and body. Be watchful over your vehicle. But I don't mean for you to become a hypochondriac, for a hypochondriac is a worrier who frets his body into illness by being overly solicitous toward every imagined pain.

"The human body was designed to sustain tremendous strains; however, you must use good sense to enable it to do so. Respect it for what it is. You are not superhuman; so until you are further advanced, you won't be able to keep it alive and useful beyond a hundred years or so."

"You mean it's possible to stay alive appreciably longer than that?" Richard asked incredulously.

"Certainly! There's no reason why not. If an Ego is sufficiently learned in the science of human physiology and has the ability to precipitate effectively, he can sustain his physical vehicle indefinitely. The normal body has a built-in aging mechanism so that a lifetime lasts only long enough for the average Ego to derive the optimum benefit from an incarnation. This aging mechanism can be overcome by an advanced mentality so that balance between the catabolic and anabolic forces of the body's cells can be maintained for prolonged periods without the disadvantages of decrepitude. So long as the Vital Body on the Etheric Plane is integral, the physical body can go on and on."

"Do you have to take special hormones or something?"

"No. Everything needed for the body can be produced within itself provided that ample, wholesome food is ingested. The key to longevity is mental precipitation and contemplation upon certain centers within one's body. Adepts, should They need to incarnate, can maintain vigorous life for several hundred years; and Those Masters who have chosen to work directly on the Physical Plane to help mankind can sustain Their bodies indefinitely."

"That sounds fantastic!" Richard exclaimed wonderingly.

"Nevertheless, it is a fact. Jesus still uses the physical vehicle He loaned to Christ nineteen hundred years ago, and it's in far better condition now than when Christ was using it."

"But His body was hung on a cross, speared, and buried deader than a doornail," Richard protested.

"What about the Resurrection?"

"As far as I'm concerned, whatever it was that *really* happened on that matter is beyond human comprehension," Richard declared.

"Then let me explain." The tall man sat thinking for a moment, and then he said, "Perhaps it would be better if I reviewed Jesus' life from the time He was born. I think it will make more sense to you that way.

"To begin with, you are already aware that Jesus was born to two Adepts who were united in a Virgin Marriage. Mary, His mother, was the daughter of a wealthy lawyer. She was brought up as a devout Jewess and was taken to the Temple in her early adolescence for consecration to God. There she was personally instructed by an Adept named Hillel who was at that time Chief of the Sanhedrin—the Jews' supreme council and tribunal. Joseph, Jesus' father, traced his lineage directly from King David (*Matt. 1:1–16*) thereby fulfilling the many prophesies of Jesus' genealogy. Joseph was a devoted Essene who received his instruction at the Essene headquarters on the shore of the Dead Sea."

"I thought Jesus was conceived by the Holy Spirit," Richard interrupted.

"In a sense Jesus was. Joseph was an Adept who consequently was part of the Holy Spirit!

"After Jesus was born in the manger of the inn at Bethlehem, the little family stayed at the home of a sheperdess in that town until Jesus was forty days old. His parents then consecrated Him to the Lord at the Temple in Jerusalem and stopped again at the shepherdess' house on their way home to Nazareth. The three Magian priests from Persia met them there and presented gifts to the infant Jesus. Kaspar, the great Master who lived in Persia, had sent these three wise priests of the Zoroastrian religion on their mission. He did so to acknowledge that Jesus' birth had occurred under the properly 'starred' auspices of the then well-known astrologic prophecy. The birth of Jesus had been arranged to immediately follow a series of three rare sets of multiple planetary conjunctions in the heavenly sign of Pisces—the astrologic House of Hebrews. The honors that Kaspar extended to Jesus verified to the sages of the world the identity of the human instrument for Melchizedek's approaching advent as the Christ.

"The three Magi warned Joseph to flee the country because of the jealousy of Herod the Great. Joseph heeded their advice and took his wife and child to the Essene temple at Zoan, Egypt. Shortly thereafter, Herod the Great had all the boys in and near Bethlehem who were under the age of two years old slain so as to kill the Messiah. The High Priest, Zacharias, father of John the Baptist, refused to reveal the whereabouts of his infant son, and so he too was slain. Members of the Essene Brotherhood rescued John and His mother, Elizabeth, and brought them to Zoan. For three years Mary and her cousin Elizabeth were instructed in the proper ways to rear their advanced Sons for the work that They would perform. When Their instruction was finished, Mary, Joseph, and Jesus returned to Nazareth. Elizabeth and John resided with a relative in the Engedi Hills. John's education was undertaken when He was nine years old by Matheno, an Egyptian Jew who was a Master from the temple at Sakkara. Elizabeth died when John was twelve, and so Matheno took John to Zoan where He remained until He was thirty years old.

"Jesus began His formal training under a wise Rabbi by the name of Barach. Jesus, as you might imagine, was a brilliant scholar who could read with profound comprehension at the age of five years. Because He had earned the eleventh degree of

Brotherhood before His incarnation as Jesus, His Egoic powers were able to overcome the physical limitations of His infant vehicle. By the time He was seven years old, Jesus had memorized verbatim all the Jewish books of prophesy. Rabbi Barach brought his amazing student to the council of the Sanhedrin when Jesus was eleven years old, and Hillel was so entranced with the youngster that he personally educated Jesus for the next year. Their mutual admiration for one another grew quickly, and they were almost inseparable companions. Many of the knottiest points of the law which would perplex the Sanhedrin, Jesus could clearly explain to Hillel through the logic of loving justice.

"Joseph and Mary came to take Jesus home after their Passover pilgrimage to Jerusalem, but Hillel delayed His return for another day in order to show Him off to the elders who had come from the outlying reaches of the Holy Land for the celebration in Jerusalem. This is why Joseph and Mary were required to return for Him when they discovered Jesus was not with their entourage returning to Nazareth.

"Prince Ravanna of the royal house of Orissa in India was present at the Passover feast in Jerusalem, and he heard Jesus dispute with the doctors of law. He later inquired of Hillel about the child and thereupon went to Nazareth to pay homage to Jesus. Ravanna took up residence nearby, and eventually, with Hillel's intercession, persuaded Joseph and Mary to allow Jesus to accompany him to India where he might be taught the wisdom of the Brahmins.

"For four years Jesus was a student at Jagannatha Temple where several Great Sages became His teachers. These wise men taught him much of value; however, He constantly came into conflict with the local Brahmic priests over their doctrines of caste and transmigration. The time came when He bid his friends and teachers farewell because He could no longer stomach the offensive lies by which the priests in Orissa maintained their power over the people. At the age of seventeen Jesus felt compelled to go among the people and preach to them about the evils of caste, and the oppressed lower castes took up His arguments to foment revolt against the excesses of the priesthood. Jesus' sermons on the brotherhood of man resulted in His being hunted as a seditionary by the officials of Orissa; but the common people saved Him, and He escaped from India to Nepal where Buddhist priests of the city of Kapilivastu welcomed Him eagerly.

"Jesus stayed in Nepal for several months to read sacred ancient literature stored there in a great library. The Master in charge at Kapilivastu readily perceived the status of the young man, and He arranged for Jesus to journey to Lhassa in Tibet so that He could study at the vast archives secreted there. It was in Lhassa that Jesus met Meng-tse, the famous sage of the Far East who was several hundred years old at the time.

"After studying earnestly under Tibetan Adepts and Masters for about five years, Jesus turned toward home when He was twenty-three years old. The Persian city of Persepolis was His first stop, and He stayed to teach for a few weeks as a guest of Kaspar before He resumed His journey by heading southward to Assyria and thence to Galilee. He finally arrived home to visit His mother after having been absent for twelve years, but He did not stay long. Jesus hurried on to Athens, where He delayed for a while to teach the Grecian sages and to preach to the people. From there He sailed to Zoan, Egypt, to visit His cousin John at the Essene temple, and a little later He formally entered the Brotherhood at the temple in Heliopolis, Egypt. Jesus was twenty-five years old at the time, and for the next five years He was a student under the guidance of Masters congregated there specifically for His education. During this period Jesus perfected His physical vehicle for Melchizedek's use.

"John, in the meantime, returned to Judah and made His home in the Cave of David at Engedi, thereby becoming known as the Hermit of Engedi. He ventured forth to the Jerusalem market-place to exhort the people to reform their ways and to denounce their wicked priests and rulers. After having established His presence in Judah, John began to baptize at Gilgal on the Jordan River and to preach at Bethany.

"When Jesus was thirty years old He left Egypt and journeyed to Cana to see His mother. After a short visit, He went to the Jordan to hear John. For several days Jesus remained obscure among the crowds who came to be baptized and to hear John's promises of a Savior soon to come. Each day at the end of His sermon, John would wade into the river and look skyward as if in intense contemplation. Simultaneously, Jesus would walk near the shore and also look into the heavens. No one seemed to notice this routine, but one day as Jesus and John were enacting the procedure, a brilliant light manifested just above Them that only an Adept or Master could perceive. The great Archangel Melchizedek was at hand to undertake His ministry as the Christ. The long awaited and meticulously prepared event for which the two men lived was at hand.

"Jesus stepped into the water, and John baptized Him. When His body was fully immersed, Jesus vacated His physical vehicle. He functioned thereafter upon the Mental Plane of existence using His Mental Body. John supported the momentarily lifeless body until Melchizedek's Ego entered and revitalized it. Behold! An Archangel becomes a man and lives on Earth! Yet only He and John and Jesus were aware of it at that time. There was a strange stirring in the witnessing crowd, for they sensed something extraordinary. While John and the 'stranger' He had just baptized were conversing privately in subdued speech, a dove suddenly flew to the shoulder of Christ. John's demeanor immediately changed, and He spread out His arms and proclaimed hallelujahs. What a thrill for John to realize that He was talking face to face with a God. Of all the persons Christ later encountered in His ministry, the only ones who knew His true identity were John the Baptist, Mary, Joseph of Arimathea, and the Masters of the Essene retreat at the Dead Sea.

"The crowd pressed upon John and Christ, but Christ confounded them by veiling Himself with invisibility. From that day forward, John evangelized joyfully and fearlessly. His mission was accomplished; so He spoke truth regardless of possible consequences from the authorities.

"Christ devoted His first forty days on Earth to placing limits and controls upon the Black Mentalists. These controls exist to this day so that man can achieve Egoic advancement. It was by this act that He saved the world. He also removed vast karmic indebtedness from the nations of the world which was the crushing legacy from the national sins committed by preceding generations. He and the Archangelic Host took away the sins of the world for the time being, but now the nations are up to their necks in karmic debts again. However, the events at the turn of this century will wipe the slate clean.

"Christ went on to a three-year demonstration of His divinity in order that men would be moved to hear, wonder, and remember. The impact of His advent was far more tremendous than the Bible or history conveys. Men literally set themselves upon new paths! He was God of Infinite Power; and although He did not walk proudly, neither did He cower. His demeanor was kindly, loving, compassionate, joyful, and serene. He remained unperturbed and confident in any situation because he was in total command of all He surveyed. No wonder that a person of those times would be intensely moved by contact with Christ!

"Imagine the wonder Christ must have excited daily in His Apostles. He spoke a great truth when He told them, 'He that believeth on me, the works that I do shall he do also; and greater works than these shall he do.' (*John 14:12*) Melchizedek saved our world from destruction by evil, removed evil barriers to advancement, provided His protection, relieved us of our debts, and showed us the beginning of the way to duplicate His advancement. Unfortunately, our finite human comprehension keeps us from a true appreciation of all He has done for us. Instead, we praise ourselves for our blessings and condemn God for our hardships. We are ungrateful and thankless, but still Christ's Love for us is unwavering and forbearing. He seeks only that a person attune himself with the ideals He preached during His ministry so that He may fill that person with His blessedness and love. Wherever we turn, we encounter God's wonders; yet we are as blind men. We seek strength within ourselves and consequently are fainthearted. Christ is always ready to help, but we turn to Him only as a last, desperate resort.

"Christ labored among us for three years to uplift us; and men crucified Him. But what a triumph the Resurrection was! This demonstration of the fallacy of death gave man hope against his most dreaded enemy. There is an important fact to bring out here: although *Christ* was crucified and gave up the ghost on the cross, it was *Jesus* who occupied the resurrected body. As soon as Melchizedek vacated the body when it died on the cross, Jesus and fellow Masters functioning from the Mental Plane of existence sustained certain chemical balances within

Jesus' lifeless physical vehicle until its burial. Joseph of Arimathea had the body entombed in a new sepulcher after having spoken for the corpse from the governmental authorities. Two unusual circumstances are to be noted about Jesus' body after Christ's transition: the leg bones did not have to be broken to hasten death, and the body was taken down quickly so as not to hang over the Sabbath. Once the body was interred, Jesus and the other Masters labored over it in the tomb until it was fully restored to perfect functioning. Jesus once again vitalized His physical vehicle, and the Masters who assisted Him passed outside and caused the soldiers guarding the seal upon the tomb to fall asleep. Remember that an Ego who functions upon the Mental Plane is not bound by the seeming solidity of material objects on the Physical Plane; so rock presented no barrier to Their coming and going. The Masters signaled Adepts who were waiting outside to roll away the stone closing the sepulcher, and Jesus stepped out into freedom.

"Jesus was the Ego occupying His body when He appeared thereafter to the Apostles. His wounds were sealed against bleeding and infection, but they were left open so that the Apostles would know certainly that this was the body that had died on the cross. Jesus then gave intensive instruction to the Apostles and other disciples over a forty-day period following His resurrection. The final appearance to the disciples was undertaken by Melchizedek using an astral shell He created in the image of Jesus. Christ caused this astral shell to be visible to the disciples, but He forbade them to touch Him for the same reason that Christ asked Mary Magdalene not to touch Him when He appeared to her the first Sunday at the empty tomb. As He gave them His blessing, He rose a short distance above the ground and dissolved the astral shell in a shower of glorious golden light. The disciples needed even this great sign to convince them of Christ's divinity. It's no wonder, Richard, that men are hard to convince of things beyond their perception when those who had personally witnessed so many miracles needed even this last sign.

"Sophistication, cynicism, and a fear of being thought gullible have caused many Egos to reject truth when it came their way. There are so many cults, 'isms,' and religions fostered by charlatans for their own profit that thinking persons tend to reject all unusual information of an 'occult' nature. However, the truly discriminating intellect will unprejudicially weigh and further investigate all ideas it encounters. Those Egos who have had prior knowledge of truth from previous incarnations will experience an affinity for facts concerning human existence whenever they happen upon them. Among these are the Elect who shall people the Kingdom of God."

Richard sat in thoughtful meditation after the man finished talking, and he impressed upon his mind the things he had been told. At last he asked, "Are you Jesus?"

The man smiled broadly and answered kindly, "No. I most definitely am not. Jesus resides in western Europe. He was the Elder Brother in charge of the entire Essene Brotherhood until not so very long ago. Like all Masters who have been the head of Their Brotherhood, He is now a member of the Order of Melchizedek. He uses His physical body whenever He goes among the ordinary populace of the world; but for the most part, He functions upon the Mental Plane in His Mental Body."

"How does He keep His physical body alive if He isn't present in it?" Richard asked.

"He sustains it at a distance by precipitation. The body rests in a somnolescent condition in a protected cell. It breathes, and its heart beats, but it remains asleep. It is nourished by Jesus who mentally precipitates nutrients directly within the bloodstream."

"That's fantastic!"

"Truth is indeed stranger than fiction," the man smiled.

"And you say that everyone can one day duplicate this feat?"

"It is knowledge inherent in Mastership. Even men without spiritual advancement can extend their lives in vigor well beyond normal life expectancy by certain principles of yoga."

"Ah yes!" Richard exclaimed. "That subject interests me. Tell me about yoga."

The man smiled and sighed. "Yoga is not for the occidental personality. I must warn you to avoid its disciplines. I'll tell you of its rationale and explain to you why it is so terribly hazardous.

"The term *yoga* means *union*. An adherent is called a yogi, and he seeks to achieve simultaneous awareness of the three of his four bodies which function respectively upon the Physical, Etheric, and Astral Planes of existence. When he has achieved this end, he is able to perceive happenings upon the Etheric and Astral Planes. Although he may have achieved conscious contact with the higher planes, he is still a long way from functioning upon them. His clairvoyant powers are enjoyable and enlightening but not really conducive to spiritual advancement. A yogi's contact with the higher planes is not the proper natural outcome of Egoic refinement but is a forced experience brought about by physical exercises and breathing exercises of a bizarre nature. These practices are the disciplines of Hatha Yoga which means *union through courage*. This is aptly named!

"The devotee of Hatha Yoga strengthens his body by following an austere ascetic regimen of strenuous exercises and careful diet. To the yogi, the physical vehicle in glorious good health is but the normal starting-point for his journey into astral experience. The violent strains to which his body is submitted during the course of his efforts to perceive the great-beyond would simply destroy a normal physical vehicle. The yogi subjects the plexi of his body, which are the control centers of his autonomic nervous system, to many years of a type of mental concentration that is designed to result in conscious control over normally uncontrollable body functions. A practiced yogi can change the rate of his heart beat or stop it; he can mentally induce his endocrine glands to excrete their hormones in any quantity; and he can regulate all his digestive processes. By coupling his developed bodily control with certain breathing methods, he causes the plexi of his physical body to enter a state of imbalanced excitation. In this state, he can perceive the life-forces emanating from another Ego and can contact persons residing on the Astral Plane. There are many wondrous experiences to be gained by such glimpses of 'Heaven,' but the terrifying and dangerous prelude to this 'paradise' hardly makes it worthwhile.

"The yogi who forces his way into the higher planes must first encounter the *Dweller at the Threshold* of the lower Astral Plane before he can proceed further. The Dweller at the Threshold is a human entity of hideous malevolence. Most yogis who struggle successfully to this point of contact with astral existence are riven by convulsions of sheer terror as they encounter the Dweller. The vile Egos and Black Mentalists at the lowest end of the

Astral Plane then have a perfect inroad to the defenseless yogi's body, and they drive him hopelessly insane. Those rare yogis who have successfully overcome the dreadful fright of their meeting with the dweller avow it was an experience they hope never to go through again.

"Only as a means of achieving physical health and vibrant well-being does Hatha Yoga have something worthwhile to offer. The preferred path to clairvoyance and conscious functioning upon the Astral Plane while still living in a physical vehicle is through *Rajah Yoga*—the Kingly Union. This is essentially the way of the Brotherhoods, and it is proper for the occidental mentality. No physical exercises or systems of breathing are involved. Moreover, it provides natural protection from the lower astral entities when the Ego's breakthrough to astral clairvoyance occurs. Its method requires only that one gradually increase the frequency of one's spiritual vibrations through character uplift, mental and emotional refinement, and proper development of virtuous living. This is a relatively slow course but the foolproof one which was followed by all those Great Ones who have achieved Adeptship and Mastership. Attempted short cuts to spiritual power almost invariably lead to sorcery and mentalism through enthrallment by the Black Mentalists.

"The road to spiritual greatness may seem surprisingly simple—but only because it is. Man was intended to rise naturally in smooth sequence from the clod he was at creation to the perfection of Mastership. Attunement with Christ principles, harmless living, karmic balance, and a fervent and burning desire to be a Brother comprise the path to advancement. And of these, the last is perhaps the most important.

"Living among people and solving the problems of life are essential to the development of virtue and soul enlargement. The quiet life of contemplation and meditation in an 'ivory tower' sort of existence is a blind alley. To avoid life and its vexing aspects is merely to delay the mastering of social situations and karmic pitfalls which must eventually be disposed of in another lifetime if not tackled now. If one runs away from a painful or difficult situation instead of facing it until it is solved, it will only reappear later as a similar situation of even greater difficulty. When a problem is successfully solved, it ceases to be a bothersome or distressing thing. Should the same circumstance ever arise again, it is easily disposed of because one has the knowledge and experience to overcome it. Fortunately, no one is ever exposed to a situation he is not able to handle successfully. Rest assured that you will never be tested beyond the range of your ability. If you fail, it will be because you have not fully applied yourself to the task presented."

"I see that yoga is not the panacea I envisioned," Richard admitted. "Isn't the body-building aspect of yoga good for persons of occidental mentality?"

"Yes, it is. Furthermore, there are many beautiful concepts in its religious meditations that are useful and should not be rejected because the goal of Hatha Yoga is spurious. However, if yogis devoted as much time to their Egoic advancement as they do to seeking a glimpse of the higher planes, they could soon *function* upon the Astral Plane as Adepts instead of risking the loss of their souls to the Black Mentalists."

"How about the yoga systems for increasing longevity?"

"Those also are effective when kept within reasonable bounds. There is no sure formula for retaining one's youthfulness, for it is mostly a matter of many sensible little practices. Moderation in all things and the maintenance of a sunny and youthful mental attitude are perhaps the best that can be advised for those not yet Adepts. The elimination of the harmful waste products of bacteria from within the body is a very efficacious course for forestalling aging processes. It's understandably impossible to completely eliminate bacteria from our bodies; but if a person maintains a habit of daily bowel evacuation, the principal source of bacterial toxins is removed. The colon's function is to remove moisture from feces; and the longer the waste products remain in the colon, the more the deleterious substances of bacterial decomposition are absorbed into one's blood. The stool should be light in color when eliminated; for the darker it is, the longer it has been stored in the bowel. Another big source of microbial toxins is the foliage on the tongue. This should be brushed off with a toothbrush every morning and rinsed out with water.

"Be wary of food fadism. To maintain a strictly vegetarian or meat diet is destructive to the body and eventually results in

213

mental aberrations which are not conducive to spiritual advancement. Man needs the nutriments of both vegetables and meat: his body is designed to digest both. There is absolutely no spiritual value inherent in one food over another food. To abstain from meat in one's diet because it has base animal vibrations which might lower the aggregate vibrations of the human vehicle is outright nonsense. No one ever ate his way to Heaven, or to Hell either, for that matter. Admittedly, the optimum proportion of meat to vegetable foods in any one individual's diet is different from everyone else's. This proportion is each person's responsibility to discover for himself through trial and error. Be wise in maintaining a balanced diet, and never try to impose *your* optimum diet on another person for his improvement. What is beneficial to your system may be literally deadly to his."

"What about the yogi's evident success in attaining clairvoyance?" Richard asked. "Isn't that something of benefit?"

"No, I'm sorry to say. To force onself into realms where one's spiritual advancement and intellectual understanding haven't as yet paved the way will inevitably result in contacting Black Mentalists. The deliberate misinformation the Black Mentalists foist upon conscientious but misguided persons seeking voices and visions from 'heaven' are worse than useless. Many persons, especially women, may be spontaneous mediums who hear spirit voices and see ectoplasmic processes. Without exception, these contacts are inspired by the evil forces. Egos of high advancement can contact the upper Astral Plane and can see and hear the persons with whom they are conversing there. But these advanced persons *never* disclose their ability to perform such feats of true clairvoyance except to authorized Brothers. The commercialized clairvoyant, however sincere, is an unwitting tool of Evil. The person who consciously seeks such occult powers by deliberate courting of the forces of evil is known as a witch. The end cost of such an alliance with the Black Mentalists is Egoic enslavement by them and destruction of soul.

"To try to push your sense perceptions beyond the level of your spiritual advancement is folly. The senses naturally become able to perceive the higher planes in direct proportion to achievement of balanced Egoic advancement. No special effort to intensify one's extrasensory powers is necessary as spiritual advancement is being attained. But I can see, Richard, that you are discontent to await the slow, proper outworking of these developments; so I'll tell you of a project on which you can work now.

"In accordance with their present knowledge, psychologists have divided the human mind into the two main classifications of conscious and subconscious. This is a fallacy, for no such division actually exists. The apparent barrier existing against full, conscious utilization of all the brain's potential can be dispelled with just one word, *awareness*. Egos who have achieved several degrees of Brotherhood have fully penetrated this so-called barrier. They are exceptionally balanced and serene persons because they do not suffer phobias, prejudices, fixations, and other personality disturbances brought about by obscure feelings lurking in the subliminal backreaches of the brain. All the functions of the brain are available to these Advanced Ones.

"So if you wish to embark upon a very worthwhile yet harmless exercise, work to increase your inner awareness. Self-analysis, astute soul searching, and meditation upon the attitude-forming events of your early life will tend to penetrate the veil between your buried past and your present consciousness. The vast storage facilities for information within the 'subconscious' mind can also be made available through awareness. Everything you've done, thought, and seen in this lifetime is recorded there in infinite detail. Picture the advantages of making such a fund of information readily available. The 'subconscious' possesses fantastic prowess in mathematical calculating, and it can also be assigned to conveniently govern routine tasks like driving an automobile and performing repetitive operations so that one is free to concentrate upon more important matters at the same time. Awareness is the key to full use of your brainpower."

After a moment of silent consideration of the ideas for achieving better mental awareness, Richard returned his thoughts to the previous subject. "I've read that Christ is called the *Great Yogi* by some philosophers in the Far East. Does this have some bearing on His ability to walk on water as some yogis are purported to be able to do?"

"A little thought, Richard, would disclose to you that comparing the Archangelic powers of Christ to men's yogic achieve-

215

ments on our human life-wave is rather ridiculous. It is more reasonable to refer to *Jesus* as a great yogi, but even so, an Ego of eleven degrees of Brotherhood far surpasses any yogi. It is very true that effective use of the principles of yoga can enable a man to overcome the vibratory phenomena of heat and gravity. Even natives of certain primitive tribes whose ancient ceremonies often require ordinary men to walk upon burning coals are able to come away without even a slight burn. This amazing feat has been authenticated by scientists innumerable times, and yet to science the source of the natives' immunity to burns remains a mystery. This seeming miracle is the result of the natives' absolute, unwavering faith that it can be done. The firewalker *knows* that it can be done because he's seen his father, brothers and acquaintances do it. Once he himself has done it, no scientist will ever convince him it's an impossibility to walk on fire unharmed. His faith literally works wonders. The medicine men of his tribe cure his diseases by the same device. The patient firmly believes the medicine man can cure him with hocus pocus, and behold, he's cured.

"What faith can cure, it can prevent. The germ theory of disease is incomplete because it does not take into account mental attitudes of the human being. Fear of disease is a principal factor in its contraction. To have confidence in the knowledge that one can overcome the adverse influences of microbial infection by mentally reinforcing the natural defenses of the body is a force of such magnitude that positive outlook alone will prevent illness from ever threatening. By the same token, worry over one's health can precipitate susceptibility to sickness. The common cold is a plague because almost everyone is conditioned to accept its inevitability. Scientific investigations have demonstrated that only one cold sufferer out of four actually has an infection to account for the symptoms. The other three are suffering identical symptoms which merely mimic the true cold. These people were so sure that a momentary stuffiness in the nose or a sneeze was the prelude to an inescapable head cold that they suffered for several days with a false cold.

"There are many organic diseases which the clairvoyant physician is easily able to perceive as being the result of anxiety, tension, fear, hate, and worry. Notable among these are cancer, stomach ulcers, heart trouble, endocrine abnormalities, and a vast array of emotional and mental disorders. No germs are involved in such illnesses, but rather they consist of a breakdown of normal, healthy, bodily functions through the action of continual negative thought upon the Vital Body."

"Did Christ cure people during His ministry through the sick person's own faith?"

"Undoubtedly He did; but when it came to raising the dead, it was strictly His *own* knowledge at work."

Richard commented, "I presume that when Elijah caused the dead to live again, He was essentially an instrument of the Holy Spirit."

"Elijah, who later incarnated as John the Baptist, was of eleven degrees of Brotherhood like Jesus was. Being just one step below full Mastership definitely made Him a *member* of the Holy Spirit. Elijah used His own mental powers of precipitation to perform His miracles. When He brought down 'fire' from Heaven and was fed in the wilderness and caused rain to fall and drought to occur, He was merely exercising personal powers inherent to High Adeptship. Moses, as a High Adept, was the one who precipitated manna for the host of Israelites to eat in the wilderness. In the same way, Christ precipitated fish and loaves of bread for the multitude who came to hear Him preach. The very great Prophets of Biblical times were in Themselves the force of God manifesting to the Jews.

"They were all devoted to the principal tasks of stamping out idolatry and to building belief and obedience among the Israelites until that people's collective intellect and faith should arrive at the point where understanding could replace blind obedience. All 'miracles' were staged as if they were the will and acts of the *Living God*. As man's concept of God has expanded, the methods of representing Him have been enlarged by the Brotherhoods. Childish deceptions were necessary only for childish minds. The time is at hand for the mystery of God to come to an end.

"Now, Richard, I see that it is getting late, and I think we had better call it a night. I have many things to attend to yet; otherwise we might talk longer. However, your questions have been answered; so I'm sure you'll understand that I must be on my way. I want you to walk back to your hotel alone. I'll wait here until you've gone a few blocks."

He put his hand on Richard's shoulder and said sincerely, "I'm very happy to have had the privilege of talking with you this evening. I hope I've been of some help."

"You certainly have."

"Good. My very best wishes go with you, Richard."

Richard turned and walked along the shorewalk to his hotel without turning around even once to see if the man was still standing there. He preferred it that way. When he entered his room, he stood leaning on the door knob after he had closed the door behind him; and suddenly he realized that he had not learned the name of his latest teacher.

CHAPTER 13

The Women

Richard settled down to learn the woodworking trade at his father's factory in Chicago. He found many satisfactions in creating with his hands, and he developed a flair for the work once he permitted himself a genuine interest in it. Within a year he was set-up man for the plant and was gradually taking on the work of foreman which entailed sample-making and the choosing of machining procedures. The less supervision he was given, the more responsibility he took upon himself until he found he was learning more and inquiring deeper into the techniques and intricacies of woodworking. He even became skilled at making tools, jigs, and fixtures by teaching himself.

During the summer of 1948, Richard began to keep company with Sylvia—a Jewish girl of high intelligence whose political and philosophic sophistication was attractive to Richard. She was in her final year of high school and was an excellent conversationalist and entertaining companion. Richard came to date her with increasing frequency until he saw her almost daily, and what had begun as intellectual companionship rapidly warmed into a love affair. She drew him out of his natural reticence to openly display his affections.

Richard and Sylvia seriously discussed marriage, but they both came to the conclusion that it would fall short of the best. Family opposition was mounting from both sides on religious grounds, and the situation augured a poor start. Their feelings gradually dwindled to a warm friendship, and finally each went his own way after seven months of happy companionship.

In the process of growing up together, they discovered they were not suitably matched emotionally. The episode came to a close when Sylvia went away to college in Michigan.

Three months after Sylvia left for college, Richard met Dorothy at a square dance sponsored by Northwestern University. Dorothy's demeanor was reticent, and this ingenuous behavior was attractive to Richard. It wasn't long until Richard was going out with Dorothy exclusively. Although she had been sure that only a career in journalism could be important in her life, Dorothy managed to go out with him very often.

Richard's courtship of Dorothy was not smooth by any means. There was frequently a clash of wills which usually had to be resolved through a patient defining of differences and then meshed into a satisfactory compromise. Their mutual willingness to work out their opposing views and to examine problems and new ideas was a most valuable point in their favor. Eight months after Richard and Dorothy met each other, he asked her to marry him. She accepted, and they made arrangements to marry two weeks later during her Christmas vacation from school. Their stormy separations and stressful reconciliations had indicated that they couldn't continue seeing one another without soon being legally wed in order to relieve the tensions of their desires. Dorothy insisted that their marriage be kept secret from her parents because her father had asserted that when she became a wife she had to look entirely to her husband for support. Although Richard had already promised to put Dorothy through her final two years of college, she didn't want to have to move from her dormitory until the following June.

Richard was disturbed by the realization that he couldn't very well invite his parents to his wedding when Dorothy was excluding hers; and as he drove home, it seemed doubtful to him that marrying secretly was the right way to start their life together. He again began to wonder if Dorothy was really the right woman to assist him in his life's work, for he had often tried to visualize what her reactions might be when one day he would tell her of the business he had to conduct for the Brotherhoods. However, Richard reasoned that her ambition and trenchant character were likely to be helpful qualities in undertaking such an arduous enterprise with him.

About halfway home, he brought his automobile to a halt for a stop sign, and just then Richard's musings were interrupted by a strange occurrence. Dr. White suddenly said, "Pull your car onto the shoulder of the road. I wish to talk with you for a while."

Richard was so startled that he jumped. He looked around in the car and felt the seat alongside him. "Where are you?" he asked excitedly. "How long have you been here?"

"I'm quite a long distance away, Richard. This contact with you is by audial induction."

It was a curious experience. Dr. White's voice was just as clear and distinct as if he were sitting nearby, but the sound had no direction. It seemed to come from within Richard's head.

"Pull your car over," Dr. White reminded him. "You'll be obstructing traffic if you stand where you are."

The little rural intersection was dark and sparsely traveled. Richard usually came by this route for the twelve-mile trip from Evanston to his home in Chicago to avoid congested traffic. After crossing the intersection, he parked on the shoulder and turned off the ignition.

"It's wonderful to hear your voice again," Richard said warmly.

"This will be a rather impromptu discussion," Dr. White replied. "We hadn't planned to contact you until quite a bit later, but your surprise move tonight impels me to speak with you now."

"Why? What's up?" Richard asked with concern.

"The woman you intend to marry is not for you!"

"What makes you say that?" Richard demanded. "What's wrong with her?"

"Nothing is wrong with her. But does she love you?"

Richard answered frankly, "No. But I think I can get her to."

"You mean to tell me that you are aware that she doesn't love you, and yet you are willing to live a lifetime with her in the most intimate of human ties?"

"She needs me!"

"The question is do you really love her?"

"Yes!"

"Perhaps you only feel tender and pitying emotions for the girl—and pity is no grounds for marriage. A person always feels warmly toward another whom he feels he can serve and uplift, but this borders on arrogance. Moreover, I wonder if you've ever asked yourself why she'll marry you when she doesn't love you."

Richard thought about that for a moment and answered, "I guess I really don't know."

"It's because she's clever enough to sense your abilities. Has she not said several times that she's sure you'll be a millionaire at an early age?"

"She's had a rather deprived childhood; so it's only natural that she'd dream of riches. Even though I'll probably never have much money to call my own, she'll at least enjoy comfortable circumstances as my wife. With the security of marriage and a sufficiency of love, Dorothy will come to love me too."

"Why impose such a task upon yourself when another woman might love you naturally and readily. Think of Sylvia's warmth and outgoing love. Why deprive yourself of the greatest blessing man can enjoy?"

"I can get along successfully with anyone," Richard asserted.

"I suppose you can; but at what cost to you? At what cost to your efficiency as leader of the city and the Kingdom? She is too much unlike yourself! Unfortunately, you are in a mood for marriage, and you are taking the first girl who has happened along and are hoping for the best. Just because most marriages are contracted because it seems to be the next logical step is no justification for *you* to reject my instructions concerning the choosing of a mate and the spiritual importance of marriage. You have taken her apathy toward love as a challenge to your masculinity, and so you pursue her elusive favor even to the point of offering marriage. Your sex drive is dictating the urgency for a wedding, and pity is your rationalization."

"My heart is given to Dorothy for the rest of my life. Your appeal, if that's what it is, to dissuade me from marrying her is too late. A man simply can't back out on a girl after talking her into marrying him."

"Now is the time to reconsider, Richard! Children and inescapable responsibilities come fast in marriage. Later you may repent of your proposal. Living a lifetime with a partner unsuited to you is a living hell. Measure your contemplated move from every angle. If you persist in this romantic chivalry at the continued expense of careful analysis, you will find the penalty severe indeed."

"Dorothy is a bright girl, and after I've taught her the wonderful things you've revealed to me, she can't help but be a good wife. She's willing to learn and will soon come to enrich my life far beyond what you can see in her at the moment."

"I can see her for her whole lifetime to come," Dr. White retorted. "Whether you marry this girl or don't, I must unconditionally demand that you refrain from disclosing to her your real identity or purposes in life or any of the information I and the others have imparted to you. You have the prerogative of free will, Richard. We will not interfere with your desire to marry Dorothy if that is what you decide to do, but consider well what I have said tonight. If it were not important, I would not have troubled to talk with you in this way."

Richard was about to reply when it became apparent that Dr. White was no longer in contact with him. He sat with his thoughts for a minute and then started the engine of his car and drove home.

During the next day, Richard resolved to cancel his plans to marry Dorothy; and that evening he returned to explain his change of mind. He felt pretty certain that Dorothy would have independently arrived at the same decision because of her rather reluctant acceptance of his proposal. To his surprise she had grown enthusiastic over the idea and had even asked one of her girl friends to be her bridesmaid. Richard hadn't the heart to suggest a cancellation in view of her happiness. As a matter of fact, her bright-eyed anticipation of the coming wedding was delightfully infectious, and Richard quickly subdued any doubts he might have had about marrying her.

They were married New Year's Day, 1950, in Chicago. Their two-day honeymoon came to a close when Richard brought his bride and her baggage to her college dormitory for the resumption of the school year; and then he went home to break the news to his parents. His mother's rage and revilement were far beyond Richard's expectations. Her furious denunciation brought about a breach in their relationship which would not mend, and thereafter his mother was determinedly cool and resentful toward him.

The next eight months were a troubled time for Richard. His marriage to Dorothy brought few delights but many detriments. His wife was too preoccupied with her studies to permit him visits during the week; so he had to be content with telephoning her when she'd return to her dormitory for the night. He still lived at his parents' home and worked at his father's factory; so he was continually exposed to their biting innuendos designed to keep him mindful of their vigorous disapproval of Dorothy. But worst of all, he began to fear his status with the Brotherhoods had been severely impaired. He grew more irritable and dejected, and he could only hope that the drawbacks he was experiencing would be resolved when he and Dorothy could set up housekeeping on their own. For the present, he had to resign himself to the position of being, in effect, neither married nor single.

One warm May evening when his parents had gone out on a supper date, Richard decided to go to a restaurant rather than prepare his own meal. Calvin, a Chinese friend he had known for several years, worked in a small Cantonese restaurant which Calvin's parents owned. Richard went there for supper; but as luck would have it, Calvin had gone out with some friends just a few minutes before Richard arrived. Calvin's sister, Grace, served Richard his meal; and although they had only a sort of nodding acquaintance, she sat down at Richard's table to keep him company while he ate. It was a quiet evening in the restaurant, and she was happy to pass the time with someone. Richard had always guessed Grace's age to be in the young teens because of her diminutive size; so he was surprised to learn that she was twenty-two years old and only two days younger than he. Grace stood not quite four feet eleven inches tall and weighed about ninety pounds. She was a girl of considerable beauty and immense personal charm. Richard was amazed at her vitality and sparkling personality, for he had previously regarded her as a timid wisp of a girl of whom he usually caught but a fleeting glimpse behind the kitchen doors of the restaurant.

They had a wonderfully entertaining conversation, and Richard discovered that her bright and witty company had raised his spirits to a semblance of his usual self. He was reluctant to bid goodnight to this happy little pixie. Just as he was finishing his dessert, Grace locked up shop for the night; and he asked her if she would like to go for a walk to enjoy the balmy spring night. She too had found their talk delightful, and she readily agreed that it would be a fine night for a stroll. Grace changed from her waitress' uniform into a strikingly feminine dress and fresh make-up. They walked for about two hours, and in that time Richard came to learn that Grace suffered from a chronic, systemic ailment of such severity that on occasions it nearly claimed her life. Yet she was cheerful, outgoing, and concerned over the problems of others even though she herself was often confined for long periods in a hospital. The cause or identification of her mysterious ailment eluded her doctors, and her future was uncertain. She confided many inner thoughts to Richard that she had never told anyone before: her dreams, her fears, her struggles in a predominantly white-race society. Richard's sympathy went out to this lovely girl; and as they walked down the sidewalk of a quiet side street, he had a sudden warm impulse. He stopped, gently turned her face to his, and bent down and tenderly kissed her. Grace kissed him back. She kissed him very hard and pulled his arms tight around her.

Their prolonged embrace was a dizzying experience for both of them. Silently, they slowly resumed their walk without saying much for the next ten minutes or so. Richard and Grace were each in deep thought about this spontaneous happening and its implications. Richard suspected that he filled a long deprived need in Grace's life, and he could feel her exultation in having charmed him to such a delicious extent. But unknown to him, this was more than a flirtation on her part, for she had entertained a daydream longing for him even before this evening. Fortunately, both of them were aware of the explosive potential of their newly discovered compatibility. Theirs was a relationship that could have blossomed into a richly satisfying love affair, but neither would permit it. Richard had Dorothy—his woman for life. Nonetheless, Grace confused his feelings to a great extent. He lavished his love upon Dorothy, but it was Grace who regarded him affectionately. Richard saw Grace very rarely. Only if he was feeling especially depressed would he seek out Grace's companionship, for her pert gaiety could quickly dispel the mood.

Dorothy came to live with Richard at the end of her summer school session, and he left his father's employ in order to take a job as foreman of a woodworking plant. Richard's new job required him to plan a factory, purchase machinery and tools, hire and train the personnel, and have a production line in operation within fourteen days after he was hired. Production was rolling in twelve days. He worked seven days a week at an excellent wage, but he stayed with the firm only three months. He learned that his new employer was a notoriously unscrupulous operator who rarely paid his suppliers. When Richard's bank notified him that three of his paychecks had bounced, he attached his employer's bank account in the amount of the paychecks and promptly quit.

This happened shortly before the turn of the year, and Richard took a brief trip to Southern California where he unexpectedly found the "Purple Domes by the Sea" on Point Loma in the city of San Diego. These domes of violet-colored glass capped an abandoned temple and several of its associated structures. Inasmuch as Dr. White had suggested four years earlier that Richard make his home in the city where he found the domes, the young man persuaded his bride to move to San Diego with him.

Richard's first job in San Diego was as a die maker in an aircraft plant, but he soon quit in order to make more money as a millman in the United States Navy Civil Service. Later he established a one-man cabinet shop on El Cajon Boulevard where he built custom furniture and cabinets of fancy woods. Dorothy, in the meanwhile, graduated from college and found a job as assistant editor of a local magazine. This position didn't last long, however, because she became pregnant just in time to exempt Richard from the Korean War. At this period they developed the closest feelings ever to be experienced in their marriage; and as her pregnancy neared term, she seemed especially dependent upon her husband's devotion and gentle concern.

The pace of Richard's business was far too strenuous; and in the light of his coming added responsibility, he had to modify his operations so that he could hire employees to relieve the load upon him. After much negotiations, he found a customer for large quantities of mass-produced woodwork items. At this time, on June 20, 1952, Dorothy gave birth to a baby girl. The child was a pure delight to Richard, but his long hours at the shop kept him from his family far too much.

Richard's contacts in the business world provided an engagingly varying environment for him; whereas Dorothy's loneliness and her basically dissimilar tastes led her in pursuit of entirely different interests. During the many months of limited contact with each other, the areas of disagreement in their philosophies grew apace, and their personal views actually became antagonistic. Richard's rather limited income and the frustration of Dorothy's career due to motherhood fostered attitudes of resentment and feelings of deprivation in his wife. Unfortunately, the activities in which each of them derived the most fulfillment were outside the realm of their marriage, and as a result, home became essentially a place for sleeping and eating.

Richard moved his place of business to a factory in the LaMesa Industrial District in order to have the necessary room for his new operation. He hired help in the new place, but like most budding entrepreneurs, he had to be his own salesman, shop foreman, office man, and bookkeeper. He plunged into the added expenses and problems inherent in the expansion of his business happily confident that the Brotherhoods would see him through to success and prosperity. The Brothers, however, move in ways strange to the comprehension of mortal men. Richard's business soon began to experience some serious difficulties. The main setback was the Canadian Government's removal of its socialist subsidy on lumber. Richard's profits were based on a low-cost source of lumber in Canada; so when the Canadian mills had to raise their prices, his livelihood threatened to vanish. In addition, a competitor in Los Angeles cut prices to recapture the sales he had lost to Richard's firm. Richard had neither the time nor the capital to buffer his losses until he could learn if there might be another economical source of lumber; so in November, 1952, when the indebtedness of the firm grew to equal the book value of its assets, he dissolved the business. Richard took the loss of his business rather hard. His world, which had seemed so secure only a few months earlier, was now a shambles, and he was depressed and perplexed by the turn of events that had brought him to such a state. One day when Dorothy left the house for about an hour to go to the grocery store, Richard stayed home to look after their sleeping baby; and as he slouched in his easy chair deep in thought, Dr. White's voice broke the silence.

CHAPTER 14

Years of Trial

"Why are you so depressed, lad?" Dr. White asked compassionately.

For the first time in many days, Richard became alert and enthusiastic. He sat up and almost wept with happiness. He had feared that he would never again hear from Dr. White, and now that fear was gone. Richard immediately sensed that the contact was again telepathic because the sound of the voice had no direction. Richard smiled and exclaimed, "Dr. White! Thank God, you've not abandoned me!"

"Did you forget my promise that I will be with you always, Richard?"

"No."

"You have given way to despair and have failed to call upon Christ in your trouble. That doesn't seem like very courageous faithfulness to me. Your dark and troubled thoughts will only afford an inroad to the Black Mentalists if you persist in them."

"I guess I've been pretty disappointed with things during the past month," Richard allowed. "We might as well face it; I'm a pretty miserable failure."

"A failure?" Dr. White laughed gently. "How can a young man of twenty-five years count himself out as a failure? By whose standards are you a failure?"

"My wife knows I'm a failure. And there's no doubt that the rest of the world will also consider me one."

"Time alone will tell, lad. Be patient! As it is, you certainly have no call to be disappointed over the loss of your business. Weren't you told that you must thoroughly learn the lot of the workingman? It's not likely that you would have achieved this goal as a businessman."

"But I have already learned what they endure," Richard protested.

"Not nearly so, Richard. Be more gracious in bending yourself to God's will. He tests thoroughly how well one has absorbed His well-taught lessons. Observe, analyze, and learn! Your lessons in this life are but just begun."

"Did you bring about the ruin of my business?" Richard asked.

"If so, it was by omission rather than commission."

"What do you mean by that?"

"Well, Richard, you expected *Us* to help your company to become a success instead of using your own intelligence to predetermine the likelihood of continuing profits. You had the ability to carefully analyze and weigh the risks of that venture before you committed yourself. But instead of determining the quantitative values of the contingencies that could possibly arise to threaten your business, you merely guessed at them qualitatively. Now you know the bitter consequences of guessing instead of knowing. Never gamble. Every move in life involves risk, but he who combines logic and knowledge enjoys luck."

"I guess I did tend to lean on you. I was too eager to earn a better income, and I admit I plunged. But I have a strong suspicion that the loss of the business is mostly punishment for having married Dorothy against your advice."

"Now that's an angling comment if ever I heard one," Dr. White said jovially. "No, Richard, your failure in business was due to the reasons I've just pointed out. You are not being punished for having married Dorothy. Whatever lack you feel in your marriage is due solely to mismatching of Egos. What is even worse, however, is the disruption of the plans of several other Egos because of your marrying her."

"Before you and Grace incarnated for this lifetime, you prearranged to provide a physical vehicle for he who would have been your son by her. She specifically incarnated in a body of Chinese descent because the important Ego who planned to come through you two sought that specific combination. Grace devised her body so that it would fail her after about ten years of marriage. Then, as a widower, you were to encounter another woman who would help raise the boy to manhood."

Richard was sorely troubled. "What am I to do now?" he groaned.

"There is nothing you can do now except release Grace from her bond with you."

"What do you mean?"

"I mean that the *Union of Minds* which you built with her just prior to this incarnation and then later augmented during the times you saw her in Chicago constitutes a third entity, or etheric corporation, which is as a marriage. Unless you specifically and unselfishly release her from this union, she shall remain bound to you by promises made while both of you were still on the Astral Plane. Although neither of you are consciously aware of the concreteness of your mutual pact, it attracts you to one another and holds you together."

"What about the son I would have had by her? Will he be born to Dorothy and me?"

"He cannot afford to come through Dorothy. He who would have been your son will have to make other arrangements. If you are considerate, you will release Grace so that she too may modify her circumstances if she be so inclined."

"I've messed up things worse than I feared," Richard said dejectedly. "How may I rectify my blunder, Dr. White?" he pleaded.

"Like in all things, you have to deal with this situation as it exists. You chose your fortune inadvisedly; yet you must make the best of it. What might have been or what should have been is useless to meditate upon. Don't indulge in fantasies about things which can no longer be recaptured. You have a wife and a child. These responsibilities are inescapably yours. You can either be happy with the lot you've chosen, or you can be miserably discontent—it's largely dependent upon your own attitudes. You told me once that you could get along with anybody. Since you and I both believe you can, there should be little problem in this respect. In spite of your basic incompatibility, you and your wife still enjoy one another's company on frequent occasions and maintain a good degree of communication.

"The tasks the Brotherhoods have assigned to you remain unchanged. Unless you should at some future time personally reject the great work for which you are being prepared, your

231

training shall continue and the original schedule be maintained. Any personal burdens are privately yours to work under, but your executive and organizational talents belong to the Kingdom of God. If you do your best, We shall assist in bringing about an overall beneficial balance into your life. But we can transmute your environment only to the extent you allow."

That was the end of the interview. The information Richard received brought no joy to him. If anything, the news concerning Grace and the son who would not be his disturbed him. The reassurance of the Brotherhoods' continued efforts in his life, however, wrested him from the grip of his despondency, and within the week he accepted an office position at a utilities company. Although the salary was not very good, it was somewhat above the average wage being earned in San Diego; and in order to augment his income, Richard worked nights in addition to his office job. His wife had always found it difficult to make allowances for a husband underfoot; so she much preferred that Richard work long hours. Dorothy remained self-involved, solitary, and unaffectionate, and Richard despaired of making her his wife in spirit.

The summer following the loss of his business, Richard found the first Lesser Brotherhood's mundane school, which was obscurely tucked away in the back hills of San Diego County.

The school buildings were clean, well-maintained, and tastefully arranged on a hillside overlooking an extensive valley ringed with mountains. The teachers and other personnel were indistinguishable in dress or mannerisms from the normal persons one encounters anywhere else, and Richard was relieved to find that no one affected pious attitudes or wore beards, or flowing robes. The information given in the school's brochure left no question in Richard's mind but that the school was a genuine agency of the Brotherhoods. He persuaded Dorothy to undertake the course of study with him, and they both officially became students on June 24, 1953.

It was at this time that Dorothy and Richard learned from a mutual friend about the plight of a certain college girl who had been abandoned by her lover when he learned he had gotten her pregnant. In disgrace, the young woman had run away to

San Diego where she was living alone in a dingy shack because of very limited funds. Richard and Dorothy offered to share their home with the young woman until after her confinement. Dorothy's sympathies were particularly aroused since she herself was four months pregnant with her second child. The young woman gave birth to a boy, and this stirred Richard's remembrance of Berkeley's instructions that he was not to reveal the name written upon his body until the first boy was born in his household. The evening of the child's birth, Richard scraped off the film of collodion concealing his name and disclosed its existence to Dorothy. However, the effect of this was only detrimental to his marriage. His wife questioned him repeatedly about how he happened to be marked that way and for what reason; but because Dr. White had forbidden him to tell Dorothy his real identity or purposes in life, Richard couldn't give her a true account of the matter.

Shortly following the birth of the young woman's baby, she moved to an apartment of her own. Then, a few months later, on November 20, 1953, Dorothy was delivered of her second child—a sturdy boy. Unfortunately, Dorothy screamingly demanded that she be taken to Chicago so her mother could help her with the babies. Convinced that his wife was no longer able to carry on under the conditions of their life in San Diego, Richard moved his family to Chicago.

After his return to Chicago, Richard had the unpleasant task of releasing Grace from her "union" with him. Grace, of course, could not have been expected to understand him, and so she regarded him with perplexed wonder when he told her that he no longer placed any claim upon her and that he was freeing her from any obligations she had ever assumed toward him. A short time after Richard had thus severed his "bond" with Grace, she received a rather unexpected proposal of marriage from a man of her own race whom she had known for several years. A pleasant courtship ensued, and she became a bride just one year after Richard had complied with Dr. White's suggestion to release her. The obscure cause of Grace's illness was discovered by one of her physicians, and the mysterious malady was brought under control so that she could lead a normal life. These pleasant events were happily appreciated by Richard, who, by this time, was becoming acquainted with the workings of the Brotherhoods.

The lessons he was still taking from the mundane school called upon him to make a constantly greater effort at self-improvement. The qualities of the Great Virtues were held up to him as difficult but attainable goals demanded of all persons aspiring to Citizenship in the Kingdom of God. However, he was painfully aware that he fell short of many of the attributes within each of the general concepts of Charity, Courage, Devotion, Discernment, Efficiency, Forbearance, Humility, Kindliness, Patience, Precision, Sincerity, and Tolerance. The demands of the school virtually brought him into a second "adolescence" due to the necessity of his radically changing his mode of thinking and discarding his fallible attitudes in favor of Christ's way. He could never rest on his laurels. Every victory gained over personal weaknesses merely cleared the way for greater challenges and further needed victories. The emotional turmoil incidental to the overall reformation of character in which he was engaged was indeed strenuous.

Richard found an office job in production-control work at a large steel-fabricating plant; and within nine months of their return from San Diego, he and his wife bought a new home in Lombard, Illinois, a western suburb of Chicago. He quit his office job after a year and a half and went back to cabinet-making as a journeyman for a company specializing in kitchen cabinets and architectural woodwork. He also was a kitchen-cabinet salesman in the evenings and worked in a restaurant on weekends. Dorothy was gratified by her husband's industriousness and comfortable income; yet she was impatient at the slowness with which the luxuries of life were being afforded her. Their home especially embarrassed her after she became president of a women's club in Lombard; for compared with some of the other club members' fine residences, her house was modest and unimpressive. Richard agreed to build her a large house in Glen Ellyn, which adjoins the town of Lombard. He drew the plans for their new home and acted as contractor for the house. From May, 1957, to February, 1958, Richard worked approximately fifty hours weekly on this building besides his regular employment. He personally did the interior framing and finish carpentry, cabinet work, electrical installation and steamfitting; and when he completed the house, he considered going into home-building as his livelihood.

Dorothy's father, who was in his early seventies, was willing to help Richard get started in business by lending him the necessary funds. He was favorably impressed with Richard's skill and was confident his son-in-law would succeed as a general contractor. Richard was astonished to learn that his father-in-law was a wealthy man, but nobody could have been more amazed than Dorothy when she discovered that her parents were of substantial worth. They had always concealed money matters from their daughter and had lived conservatively to the point of parsimony.

Richard began to wonder if he would be doing the right thing by plunging into the long siege of day and night work necessary to start in business. During the year he was building the home she wanted, his wife had grown even more remote from him until the breach of communication had widened to the point where Richard and his wife merely shared the same address. There had never been any open quarrels between them except for disagreements on the philosophy to be followed in raising the children, and in this Dorothy had her own way in his absence. As she became increasingly mindful of her coming social status as heiress to her share of her aged father's wealth, Dorothy insisted that Richard prepare himself for their prospective social position; but he wouldn't learn "status-conveying" games like bridge and golf. Subsequently they each moved into separate social spheres which respectively suited their widely different personalities.

Richard progressed very slowly in starting his home-building business, but he felt unable to push himself to work harder. A persistent underweight condition and chronic fatigue finally caused him to seek a physician's opinion because it became increasingly evident to Richard that his health was not up to par. As a result of his confidential arrangements for a complete physical examination, he was informed he had tuberculosis. The physician was required to report the case to the county health authorities, but Richard asked that he delay a few days so he could think over the situation in which he found himself. The doctor, who was an old acquaintance of Richard's, agreed that a week more or less was not too critical. He told Richard that he would have to be sent to a sanitarium and that it might be anywhere from six to eighteen months before he could work again. He suggested that Richard put his affairs in order and return in a few days to prepare for admittance to the hospital.

Richard was sorrowfully aware that he and his family faced financial ruin, and he feared that his wife would be unable to withstand the depletion of their capital for his sake. Richard had his lawyer sign over one of his cars and all of his real estate to Dorothy as part of his plan to feign desertion while he secretly went to Phoenix, Arizona, to have his case of tuberculosis "discovered" there. In order to provide for his family's support during his absence, he left his wife all the cash he had had in the bank to start his contracting business. It was his hope that he could pick up the threads of their home life after he was well again. However, when he started to break the news to her that he had to go away for a few months, his plan became complicated by Dorothy's threat that should he actually go away she would never allow him to come back; whereupon she immediately packed his suitcases and told him she had plans of her own.

It was only with difficulty that Richard persuaded his physician friend to refrain from reporting his case, but the doctor relented after the reasons were explained. Then, quite accidentally, Richard learned that his Chinese friend, Calvin, had contracted tuberculosis and was to enter the municipal sanitarium in a day or two. The fact that Calvin visited Richard's home almost every week cleared up the question in Richard's mind as to where he had been exposed to the disease. Fortunately, the information about Calvin provided him with a convenient excuse for having Dorothy undergo tests for herself and the children.

Richard left Chicago the afternoon of September 11, 1958, and during the first two days on the road he drove continuously without sleeping or eating. The tightness in his throat and the turmoil of his emotions overshadowed all else, for the ache in his heart for his children was overwhelming. He was about forty miles east of Globe, Arizona, in rugged terrain when the drag-link of the steering system of his car snapped loose and left Richard completely without control over the direction of the car's travel. The linkage happened to part just as he was rounding a canyon turn at a speed of about forty-five miles an hour. He jammed on his brakes, and the car veered toward the cliff wall beside the road. After clipping off several post stubs along the shoulder of the roadway, the car scraped to a halt against the base of the cliff. Damage was confined to the bumper and a fender, which was negligible compared to what would have happened had the car run off the other side of the road into the gorge. About ten minutes elapsed before another car came along, and Richard waved it down. A weather-beaten, garrulous old rancher emerged from behind the wheel of his ancient-looking station wagon and offered his assistance. After much circuitous discussion, the old man agreed to tow Richard into Globe for ten dollars; so they rigged a tow bar between the cars and started for town forty miles away. Richard rode in his own car so he could apply the brakes on the downhill grades, and the trip was accomplished without incident. The old man was very patient in helping to find a garage which could repair and align steering systems, and eventually an out-of-the-way place was found which was seldom patronized by tourists.

While Richard watched the mechanic work, he attracted the attention of friendly folk who noticed his eastern-style clothing and the Illinois license plates on his car. The local residents were much in evidence because it was Saturday, and several stopped to chat with Richard and satisfy their curiosity about him. One husky, jovial fellow in his late fifties who was clad in typical western boots and ten-gallon hat seemed to have time on his hands, and he talked for quite a while with Richard. The man seemed to be a perfect example of the western rancher. He was evidently successful in his business judging by the quality of his clothes, and his rough, sun-browned neck and leathery face indicated he was an outdoor man. The rancher carried himself with a commanding, self-assured bearing, but his manner was kindly and his humor witty. His face was square and masculine with a large nose and high cheek bones suggestive of an Indian, but his reddish face was sharply contrasted by white sideburns and blue eyes. Although his language was cultured, he spoke with the local drawling twang.

At noon the auto mechanic went to lunch, and Richard inquired of the rancher with whom he was chatting if there was a lunchroom nearby that served decent food. The man offered to walk with Richard to a good place he knew of; and when they were about a half a block from the garage, the rancher casually addressed Richard by the name Dr. White had given him. Richard stopped in his tracks and looked at his companion in amazement. They exchanged sign and countersign, and then Richard knew the rancher was indeed a Brother.

CHAPTER 15

Bathsheba

As soon as Richard discovered that his new acquaintance was a Brother, the first question that came to his mind was dictated by his experience with the Essene in Miami, Florida, "What's your name?" he asked.

"You may call me John," the man replied, and resumed walking.

"Well, I'm particularly happy to run into one of you fellows right about now," Richard said with unusual familiarity born of John's earlier witty conversation. "Believe me, I've got troubles!"

"To the contrary, Richard. Your trouble is behind you now."

Richard's expression became grave, for he thought John implied his death was imminent. "Do you mean my TB is more serious than the doctor told me?"

John smiled broadly and said, "I reckon the joke's on your doctor—because you *don't* have tuberculosis."

"But all the tests and an X-ray prove that I have it," Richard protested. "How can you say I don't?"

"You forget that the inner workings of your body are on continuous display before persons of sufficient clairvoyancy, and the precise state of your health is visible to them in the same way that your emotional make-up is an open book to all who can perceive your astral aura."

"Well, if I don't have TB, why should I be feeling sick? Is it psychosomatic like my wife says?"

"You're suffering from lead poisoning, Richard."

"From when I was grinding those solder joints?"

"Yes."

"But I got over that in April. It doesn't seem likely I'd be suffering from it again, and I haven't been near any lead since then."

"The summer sunshine has reactivated it. Lead tends to deposit in the marrow of the bones, but sunlight will put it back into the bloodstream so it can be eliminated. Your case isn't serious, and no lasting effects are likely to remain."

Richard sighed as if a great burden had been lifted from him. "You mean to say that all this fuss has been just a mistake?" He laughed nervously from emotional relief and threw his head back in exultation.

Then Richard became absorbed in thought for a moment, and he asked, "What about the X-ray? That shadow isn't from lead poisoning."

"The spot that appears to be in your lung is not a tubercular lesion but a small cyst on the inner wall of your thorax. I'ts due to an injury you suffered last Halloween night which also disjointed the cartilaginous connection between a rib and the breast bone."

"I remember now that you mention it," Richard commented as comprehension dawned. "I'm beginning to suspect a conspiracy."

John smiled self-consciously.

"Well, at least it's good to know that I can go back home and not have to worry about being confined to a sanitarium."

"You may return home, of course, Richard, but don't expect to find everything the same as before you left."

"What do you mean?"

"I refer particularly to your wife. She now owns everything you had. What have you to offer her when you return?"

"That's a devil of a question! What need a husband offer?"

"Ah! That's the crux of it," John said wryly.

"I see the point," Richard conceded with a sigh.

"There's not much to be gained by forcing yourself on a woman who feels she has outgrown you," John cautioned.

"What am I to do? Just sit back and throw away everything I have?"

"A man's material possessions and his family ties may tend to hold him back from Christ should He call. Let the dead bury their dead. Become a slave to no loved one."

"But I have a responsibility toward my children. Shall I abandon them to Dorothy?"

"You will have a greater influence for good upon them from a distance. Leave your children to Us."

"Am I to understand that you're encouraging me to give up my wife and family?"

"Don't be so surprised, Richard. You yourself have already perceived that your marriage is dead. If you hadn't, you'd have never left Chicago. Haven't you learned yet that familial propinquity and successful coitus do not make a marriage? You shouldn't confuse your devotion to the institution of marriage with the actual experiences you've had living with Dorothy. Your suspicions that Dorothy has quit your marriage are well founded. She won't take you back if you return."

"Do you intend to influence her so she'll reject me?" Richard asked irritably.

"Assuredly no! We never have and never will! You were the one upon whom We acted in order to spare you the anguish of certain events Dorothy would have been likely to bring about in the future. Since the decision to separate was too painful for you to make of your own accord, We set up the circumstances that would force a decision.

"I see," Richard said sadly. He looked off into the distance and blinked back incipient tears as he contemplated the emptiness of his personal future. After they walked a few minutes in silence, he said, "Well, I guess it's all over except for the alimony."

"Don't despair, Richard," John said consolingly. "She who Dr. White characterized as *Devoted Love* awaits you now."

Richard frowned, "After all I've gone through with Dorothy, you talk to me about another woman?"

"My son, this woman incarnated specifically to continue her spiritual advancement with you. You have worked so beautifully and effectively together in past lives that it has been given her to assist you as your mate in the great work of the Brotherhoods. The special qualifications she developed as Nefert-iti and Bathsheba[1] ideally suit her to the demanding work that lies ahead."

---

[1] In the course of mankind's sojourn on this planet many truly great men and women have lived and wrought mighty works for their fellow beings. The names

John's words aroused Richard's interest. However, he cautiously replied, "I thought she was to appear in later years."

"These are the later years," John stated. "The time when your work begins is near at hand. On December 15, 1960, you will be thirty-three-and-a-third years old. It is on that date that the master plan for bringing the Kingdom of God into physical reality shall be set into motion."

Richard was dumbfounded. "But I'm not nearly ready, and that date is but little more than two years away."

"Do you doubt us, Richard?" John asked sternly.

"No!" was the firm reply.

"Then prepare yourself! Your new wife shall free your spirit from the cage of anxiety created by your late marriage. That person which is really you shall again emerge to take on the responsibilities for which you have been prepared. Then you may also abandon the guise of fool under which you have cloaked yourself, for you have learned the lesson it was intended to teach."

"What lesson is that?"

"The folly of pride. Pride is the bastion of the childish personality. To be pompous in authority or to assert infallibility are weaknesses of the proud man. You have learned to admit your errors and to seek and accept counsel. The road to humility is a long one, but your realization that you are but a man among men and a lesser among Masters is a good step in the right direction.

"You shall serve men not rule them. Mankind is mistakenly impressed with the man of power, authority, and commanding mien. They admire the despot for the obedience he demands and receives by force. Little men admire such a ruler because of their envious, vicarious identification with his apparent achieve-

---

of very few of these illustrious ones have come down to us through history, but it is really of insignificant importance for us to know such names. Of the many Egos incarnated in physical bodies today, most have in one or more of their past incarnations been persons of note even though no written record exists to tell it. However, it served the purposes of the Brotherhoods to preserve the names and deeds of Nefert-iti, Akhnaton, Bathsheba, and David against this day even though multitudes of Egos spiritually surpassing the two Egos who bore the above names have come and gone in obscurity.

ment of total freedom from domination by others. Only the mature individual has the inner security to seek nothing over his neighbor and to see nothing degrading in serving others.

"Act wisely, but do not seek to appear wise. Be strong but not imperious. Think independently, but hear out the opinions of others. Adhere to what is proper, and override even that which is popular if it be in opposition to righteousness. You must guide men but not govern them, for men must govern themselves and build the Kingdom of God themselves. Comport yourself in an unprepossessing manner lest men confer their allegiance to your personality and public image and thereby detract from their wholehearted devotion to Christ and the great co-operative principles of the Kingdom of God. Any leader who allures the Citizenry for his personal aggrandizement will do so to the disastrous detriment of all concerned. Because of this ever present danger, the vehicle you chose for this work is purposely lacking in glamorous handsomeness and commanding stature.

"Show the way by example; and above all, subordinate your own spiritual advancement to nothing. The whole system of government shall be designed to promote everyone's achievement of Egoic growth at the fastest possible rate. Do not let the false values of the American way-of-life mislead your people. The United States may be the stepping stone to the Kingdom of God, but its current moral philosophies are to be exorcised from the Illinois community if the joys of true Christianity are to bring security and happiness to its citizens. Never lose sight of the Brotherhoods. They are your strength."

"Remember your responsibilities, Richard. You cannot escape them. Your life shall be an open book from this time forward. Not even your past is exempt, for your whole story shall be made public. You cannot hide from God, and the name written on your body will identify you to enemies. Therefore, be strong, forthright, and righteous; and all blessings will be yours to enjoy."

"Then show me the way to wisdom," Richard pleaded.

"Wisdom cannot be granted to anyone. It is a result of conscious Egoic advancement. Even Solomon was not given wisdom—he prayed for what was already his."

The two men walked in silence for a minute while Richard

243

absorbed his lesson, and then he said, "Tell me, shall I actually marry this woman?"

"Yes, of course, Richard. You will be wed in a house of the City of David. And it shall be given your bride to wear a wedding gown of pure white linen."

"You have earned this young woman, and she is indeed a beautiful soul. I have watched her grow, and I know that the wisdom and grace of Nefert-iti and the fire and strength of Bathsheba are blended in her present incarnation. She has been excellently bred by her parents with a strictness parallel to your own upbringing. We have protected her from the negative influences within her home, and her attitudes protect her outside of it. We are pleased to have such an Ego in the important role of wife to the Builder of Lemuria."

"When shall I marry her?"

"You will marry her after you meet her, and you shall meet her when the time is ripe. Not until then will you know her name and her excellence."

"In other words, I'll have to go it alone," Richard observed.

"Don't you think it's better that way?" John asked smilingly. "After all, she's an Ego entitled to self-determination. She doesn't know who she is or who you are. Whether you win her hand or not is dependent upon your skills at wooing her. We can't give her to you. She's a woman through and through, and you'll have to be a pretty good man to match her."

"Somehow this discussion seems grotesque seeing that I have a wife and two children. It will be many years before I could hope to be in a position to court a woman."

John smiled understandingly. "You are not in a state of marriage with Dorothy, and you know it. By the time the mechanics of her divorce have been completed, your views may have changed quite a bit. I can appreciate your shock upon the realization that you've been cut off from your family, and I know you can't expect to recover from such a blow overnight. But time is a great healer; so just don't hanker after what can no longer be, and serenity can be yours."

"Where shall I go from here?" Richard asked pointedly.

John eyed him speculatively and answered, "Look to Rockford, Illinois! But before you do anything else, you had better get your physician off the hook."

John stopped walking and directed Richard's glance down the street. "There's the restaurant," he said pointing to a place about a block away. "I must go now. You'll understand, I'm sure, if I ask that you continue alone."

Richard smiled gratefully and shook John's powerful hand. "Thank you, John. You've given me much to think about."

"There are many people pulling for you, Richard. I know that you will do your best. So very much depends on you now." With that, John bade Richard good-bye and strode off in the direction from which they had just come.

Late Saturday night, Richard arrived in Phoenix, Arizona, and rented a motel room. He stayed in town only long enough to have a stereoptic X-ray taken which showed that the shadow appearing to be in his lung was actually just under his breastbone. A subsequent sputum test proved negative, and the doctor thought that Richard's recent exposure to Calvin's active case could have been responsible for the positive reaction on his previous test. Richard made his way to San Diego, about four hundred miles away, to consult a doctor he knew there. Medication was given to him to speed the elimination of lead from his system, and within a few weeks he was feeling well and fit. Richard communicated these developments to his physician in Chicago who was happy though chagrined at the news.

It was October 7, 1958, almost a month after he left home, when he arrived back in Chicago. Richard tried not to let John's predictions dampen his hopes that Dorothy would perhaps share his excitement of homecoming and receive him in a spirit of forgiveness and rededication. But Dorothy was well aware that Richard's excellent job was gone, and she had been informed by a letter from one of their friends in San Diego that Richard had left Chicago because of tuberculosis. She conveyed a warning by way of Richard's parents that she didn't want to see Richard or his car so much as near the neighborhood of her house.

Richard inquired of his lawyer if his wife had the right to bar him from his home; and he was informed that since he signed away his legal title to the property, he could be excluded by his wife. Furthermore, in accordance with Illinois law, if Dorothy were to allow Richard to live with her in the house for even one day, she would be considered reconciled with her spouse, and his act of desertion would be nullified.

Richard began working at his father's factory, and now that he was living again at his parents' home where time would likely be heavy on his hands, he planned to go to night school at Northwestern University. On Friday evening, October 17, 1958, Richard went to the Northwestern University campus in Evanston, Illinois, to consult one of his former professors in regard to the requisites for his returning to school there. On his way home he stopped at the *Key* ice cream shop across from the women's residences on campus. The soda fountain was temporarily out of order while a carbonation tank was being changed; and as he waited at the counter, a young woman came in and sat by him. Several minutes passed but nobody came to take her order, and finally Richard volunteered the information that there would be a short delay while the attendant was fixing the fountain. They engaged intermittently in comments about school which led to a pleasant chat.

In the course of their conversation, Richard commented that the accent of her speech sounded like her home town was in Wisconsin. She laughed and said he guessed close but that she came from Rockford, Illinois! The girl looked somewhat startled when he pronounced the name of her home town simultaneously with her, but she could not have been as amazed as he was. Richard looked at the comely young woman in an entirely different light. He offered to walk with her to wherever she lived in order to learn where he could find her again.

Richard called on her the next Sunday and made a date so he could find out more about her. They went out on a Wednesday night since her weekends were thoroughly scheduled with dates, and Richard took her on a tour of Chicago in his car while they spent a mutually enjoyable evening talking. The young woman's name was Gail, and her nickname, Gay, suited her perfectly. Her vivacious, wholesome personality was extremely attractive. Moreover, she possessed that rare and elusive attribute known as charm. Richard learned that she was born June 3, 1940, which made her his junior by thirteen years; however, she was astonishingly mature for eighteen years old, and she was unconcerned by the difference in their ages.

She was attending school on a full-tuition scholarship and had enjoyed a straight A grade average in high school. What particularly impressed Richard was her outstanding competence in higher mathematics and the calculus. Gail's energy and efficiency enabled her to go out on dates almost every night of the week with the swarm of male admirers she attracted and still keep her studies at a high level. It was not only her beautiful character that the men found so delightful but also her poise and good grooming which enhanced her blond beauty. Richard was impressed by her good manners and self-discipline. She behaved naturally with easy dignity and good taste; and her friendliness was as ingrained as her sparkling gaiety, for it clearly was not forced or false in any way.

Gail was equally impressed with Richard. She had hoped that somehow he would call on her after their chance meeting at the *Key,* and she had been unusually concerned that he should like her. When Richard called to ask her for a date, she was mysteriously thrilled by his request. Their personalities so evidently matched each other that both of them could hardly escape noticing the fact. From the very beginning their relationship was extremely close, and on their second date they discovered that each secretly subscribed to the same religious philosophy even though they were both nominally Lutherans.

Gail's strong attraction to Richard began to confuse her inasmuch as she was engaged to a boy named Mike in Rockford. Her parents had purposely sent Gail to a school far away from Mike in hopes that Gail would forget him, for Mike was not of the same religious persuasion as her parents, and they didn't want Gail to be misguided by him. Gail's mother insisted that she go out with a multitude of boys so she could learn what different men were like, but the idea of not directing her attentions exclusively to one man was innately distressing to Gail. Wholehearted devotion to her man was an inborn characteristic of hers.

Richard went out with Gail often, and he found he was becoming very attached to her. Gail, on the other hand, was growing irritable and upset over her indecisive feelings toward her fiance; and her conflict with her mother's insistent attempts to dictate her love life made matters all the worse.

Gail went home for the Thanksgiving holidays, and Richard joined her in Rockford on the last day in order to have Sunday dinner at her home and meet her parents and younger sister. Luckily, he also met her fiance, Mike, who came to spend a few hours with Gail before Richard drove her back to school that evening. Mike was a blond, wavy-haired, handsome youth of athletic build and boyish charm. He and Richard met congenially in Gail's home, and Richard was able to observe her parents' satisfaction at Mike's uneasiness. After seeing Richard and Mike together in the same room, Gail realized her heart was being given ever more to Richard. When she confessed that she could no longer tell which she loved, Richard was much disturbed. He wanted her love and wanted to love her, but he was acutely cognizant that an unencumbered young man like Mike or some wealthy student at college would suit her better. Gail herself couldn't be sure if loyal devotion to her fiance wasn't more important than the unprecedented inner excitement she felt for Richard. However, it was not long after Thanksgiving vacation that she finally knew Richard was the man for her.

This revelation was a mixed blessing for Richard. He was thrilled and happy that she returned his affection, but now he had to face up to the havoc his appearance had wrought upon Mike, Gail, and her family. When he went to bed that night, he lay awake until almost four o'clock in the morning trying to arrive at a sensible course of action. As he lay there, Dr. White's welcome voice came to him by clairaudient induction.

"Well, Richard, it would seem that you are getting nowhere tonight."

Richard had become weary with his sustained attempt to reason out his problem, but a fresh burst of enthusiasm flooded his consciousness at the sound of Dr. White's voice. "Thank you for answering my prayer," Richard said gratefully. "I want to do the right thing, but I don't think I have enough information to make a conclusive decision."

"Then allow me to assure you that Gail is the woman you should marry, for she is *Devoted Love* of whom I spoke many years ago."

"That solves *that* problem," Richard sighed in relief. "But I can't afford to put another woman through college and support two children at the same time. Gail deserves the right to get her college degree; and if I were to interfere with that, no one would forgive me."

"That decision is Gail's," Dr. White commented tersely.

"Even so, I can't help but think that she'd be better off marrying Mike after they've both graduated."

"Have I not already told you that Gail is your intended wife? The Brotherhoods are desirous to have you two re-establish the Egoic teamwork you have demonstrated in the past. Insofar as Mike is concerned, his usefulness has been served. His most important function in preparing her for you was to provide basic information concerning the true nature of the universe. His grandmother's teachings from the Unity School of Christianity and the Theosophists have helped wean Gail from the provincialism of her parents' religious prejudices. Even now he is not true to Gail but regards her as a reserve against a summer vacation without a girl."

"The most important concern at the moment, unfortunately, is that Gail has become an important target of the Black Mentalists. They have already achieved some success against her by means of the spiritualist seances Mike has taken her to, and her present state of emotional upset offers a perfect inroad for their evil devices. Her mother's current fears and negative thinking allow the Black Mentalists to use her also as an instrument through which they further their campaign against Gail. It is most essential that you extend your protection to her and help her transmute the negative influences which have entered her life. Give her the information she needs to attain freedom from these evil influences who seek to reduce her to ineffectualness. Give her a firm course to steer, and share your own strength of purpose when you've decided that you'll fight to make her yours against all opposition."

"I'm ashamed that I have so little to offer her," Richard said wistfully. "My life has become so complicated and disrupted that all I could ask her to share is troubles."

"Your life is still comfortable despite your petty uncertainties. Compared with the vast problems you will encounter in forming the cities, the personal difficulties in which you find yourself now are truly insignificant. You, and you alone, are responsible for every condition operative in your environment, and you are the one who must deal with them in a practical manner. Obviously, your children are entitled to your financial and moral support, and they take precedence over other considerations. They are the greatest blessings your life with Dorothy has provided you. Also, because of the trials of your first marriage, you will be better able to appreciate and cherish Gail. Now that you know the pitfalls inherent in marriage, you can avoid them in your future relationship."

With that advice, the interview abruptly ended; and Richard soon lapsed into deep, restful sleep. From that time forward, but only so far as Gail was concerned, he relaxed his ingrained restraints against divulging esoteric information. He imparted to her valuable devices for self-protection against deleterious influences; and with two weeks of Richard's care and assistance, Gail was again on even keel.

A few weeks later, Richard spent Christmas Eve with his children and Dorothy. His wife regarded him as an old but remote friend, and she chatted gaily about her social activities. She seemed delighted to be free of the burden of a husband, but Richard pursued a discussion of their separation and its effect on all concerned. Although Dorothy stated there was no possibility for a reconciliation, their discussion in this vein was nonetheless important to Richard; for he was able to ascertain that rather than his putting her aside, Dorothy was independently determined to end their marriage. He had remained friendly and helpful toward her and had avoided any unpleasantness so that if she had been inclined to accept him again, it could not be said that he had discouraged her.

After this meeting with Dorothy, Richard felt free to court Gail. Their mutual love matured rapidly; and as Richard became increasingly secure in Gail's devotion, the loving emotions that he had suppressed in self-protection for the past several years slowly emerged. The magic of Gail's warm and sincere love performed a miraculous alchemy upon his personality, for Richard opened himself to her in growing trust. The beautiful happiness they found together soon reflected in everything they thought and did, and Gail grew so radiantly beautiful as a woman-truly-loved that everyone seemed to notice. The loyal affection and motherly sympathy she had held for Mike paled into insignificance compared to the adult love she experienced with Richard. She had been unaware that she could love so ardently and enrichingly, but Richard's highly developed love-nature and sense of romanticism elicited a vibrant response from her which mutually reinforced the extent of their spiritual mergence; yet these blessings were in no way dependent on sexual attractions. The bonds with which they forged themselves into unity were not possible by physical means.

The similarity of their tastes, backgrounds, and philosophies obviated the difficult adjustment two personalities normally must undergo during courtship and marriage. Theirs was not a case of opposites attracting but of like reinforcing like. They integrated smoothly, naturally, and completely. Gail and Richard had achieved a degree of communion which made it fitting that they formally pledge their love; and on February 16, 1959, they vowed to bind their lives together in service to the Brotherhoods. They called upon Christ and the Elder Brothers as their witnesses as they knelt together before a Cross of Melchizedek and solemnly joined their lives to Greatness.

On the first day of May, Richard moved from his parents' home to a small apartment in Evanston. The apartment didn't have furnishings other than the range and refrigerator; so he was making the necessary furniture in his spare time at his father's factory on Saturdays. One day as he was machining a piece of walnut lumber freehand on a high-speed router, the whirling knives in the cutter-head grabbed at an unusually hard grain in the wood. Richard's left hand was jerked into the cutters, and the end of his thumb was sliced off across the point where the nail emerges from the cuticle. He was angry with himself as he looked at the gaping cross-section of his thumb, and his awareness of the irretrievability of that useful member made him disgusted. However, he was thankful that he didn't lose all the fingers on that hand, for by rights he should have. Through some miracle the piece of wood stopped short without apparent cause; and this aroused such wonder, that despite his dripping wound Richard tried to determine what had stopped the board from following through with its violent thrust.

Suddenly, Richard heard Dr. White's strong voice announce, "There's the sign sought by the Sons of Tubalcain!" No further explanation was given, and Richard could sense that there was nothing more to be heard. Richard was all alone in the factory; so he wrapped his hand in a towel and summoned the police to drive him to a hospital where a bone specialist performed plastic surgery to partially recreate the thumb while effecting closure of the wound.

The weekend that Richard lost the end of his thumb was also eventful for Gail. Her family drove to Evanston to take her to Rockford for a two-day visit at home, but Gail was out when they arrived at the dormitory; so they all waited in her room for her to return. There, in a desk drawer, they found an envelope bearing the return address of the same mundane school in California where Richard was a student. The letter it contained was from Gail's counselor at the mundane school, and it concerned Gail's relationship to Richard and discussed his separation from Dorothy. As can be imagined, the furor arising from this revelation was unprecedented in its violence. Tears, shouts, recriminations, ultimatums, obstinance, and threats marred their whole weekend. With courage founded on knowledge, Gail could not be intimidated by her father's violent temper or her mother's tears of shocked mortification.

Gail returned to the university campus Sunday evening, but she was well aware that her family would not dismiss the subject until they were successful in separating her from Richard. She was to be permitted to finish the present school year, which was two weeks from completion, but her plans to attend the summer session were cancelled. Her family wanted her at home for three months to dissuade her from her folly and to bring her back into the fold of the "one, true, saving faith" into which she had been born. Gail, however, flatly stated that she would not give up Richard nor recant her belief in the Brotherhoods' philosophy.

Her father, who was president of their church's congregation, used his influence to have Gail threatened with excommunication as an adulteress on the grounds that the attentions she paid to Richard prevented his reconciliation with Dorothy. When this stratagem failed to coerce Gail, her father went to the Evanston police and demanded that Richard be imprisoned on a charge of enticing Gail to his apartment for immoral purposes. Gail's father was so enraged by his daughter's and Richard's defiance of his demand to stop seeing one another that he threw a tantrum in the police station and threatened to kill Richard.

Two detectives from the Evanston police visited Richard and talked with him for more than an hour. They were satisfied that the charge was without foundation, but the detectives warned Richard about the death threat. Their inquiry concerning Gail's father in Rockford had disclosed his history of assaults committed in anger, and the police considered the man sufficiently distraught to be deemed very dangerous. Although Richard was inclined to disregard their fears for his safety, the detectives finally persuaded Richard to disappear for a while to elude his adversary. They revealed to him many devices by which one can prevent being traced even by trained investigators.

After Gail had been home in Rockford for about two months, the irreconcilable conflict with her family deteriorated to a condition of ever increasing ill-will and outright hatred on her parents' part. The minister of their church knew everybody's version of the situation, and he finally advised Gail that it would be in the best interest of everyone involved that she leave home. Her parents then delivered their ultimatum that she choose either Richard or her loving family—she couldn't have both. Late in July, 1959, Gail packed a suitcase and took a train to Chicago.

Richard moved from the apartment in Evanston; and using a different name, he rented another in Chicago. Gail, in the meanwhile, lived at a hotel in Evanston and took an assumed name so her father couldn't trace Richard through her. Members of her father's family had warned Gail that the death threat against Richard was not to be taken lightly, and her father's violent behavior left her no doubt of his serious intent. A few weeks after her departure from Rockford, Gail found a job in a large office which was near the furniture factory where Richard had since acquired a position as general foreman. Although they shared a hunted existence for five months, their trials and hardships only further cemented the bonds between them.

CHAPTER 16

A New Challenge

A few months later, in December, Richard was staying home from work for a week when his doorbell rang. This was a rare occurrence since no one knew where he lived. A moment later there was a knock on his door. Richard became alarmed; and after a moment of indecision, he asked cautiously through the closed door who was there.

A man's voice answered, "A friend of Dr. White."

Richard opened the door to reveal a tall man about fifty years old. He wore a business suit and winter overcoat but no hat. "Good morning, Eklal. My name is James. Our mutual acquaintance, Dr. White, sends his greetings."

Richard smiled broadly. "Please come in."

James entered, and Richard led him to the livingroom, whereupon he took the man's coat and hung it in the front closet while James sat down.

As Richard returned to the livingroom, he asked, "How about something to warm you? Would you like coffee or tea?"

James replied, "No, thank you. Perhaps later."

"I presume you have a lesson for me," Richard stated with some anticipation as he sat on the sofa facing the chair James sat in.

"Everything in life contains the elements of a lesson," he replied with a friendly smile. James contemplated Richard for a moment, then said, "We note that your divorce from Dorothy is about to become final and that you plan to then marry Gail."

"Yes. But it bothers me that I couldn't make my marriage last longer than ten years."

"It has already been pointed out to you that Dorothy came to feel she outgrew you socially after she found out she was to become an heiress, and she herself told you she had never loved you."

"That only made me feel fooled," Richard said sadly, "and it hurt."

"Have you noticed that you are attracted to hard-driving, ambitious women?"

Richard was taken aback by the question. "I certainly like pretty girls who are intelligent." He paused to consider for a while. "But you might be right. I never thought of them in that light. But isn't it desirable for me to have a wife who can *work* as a good team mate?"

"You are pretty much a product of American materialism, Richard. You have accepted without question the going concepts of the preeminence of work, obedience to authority, aggressive goal-striving, and the other attributes of our patriarchal society. Gail's father is an ambitious man, and Gail has been conditioned to believe that these same traits are manly and desirable in you."

"Is that supposed to be bad? Hard work is what has made America great."

"No," James corrected. "It has made our country rich and powerful. It has brought us technical progress at the expense of love. The new nation you are to help found must recreate a balance of the patriarchal and matriarchal world views, just as the great Lemurian culture had."

"I don't think I have a good idea of the distinctions between those," Richard confessed.

"Okay," James began, "The patriarchal attitude leads a society to pursue high spiritual and intellectual goals; however, patriarchal societies, like the ancient Greek, Roman, and Jewish, perceived a separation between God and the world and between spirit and flesh. Western Civilization derives its philosophy of life primarily from those three cultures; and so Western man conceives of himself as divided within himself—separated from God and in contention with Nature which threatens to overwhelm him. He places high value on his Mind and spirit as being sacred, whereas his bodily needs are regarded as base and dangerous. He molds his environment and exploits it for his own purposes. He's 'realistic,' intellectual, finds dignity in work, bases his self-worth on wealth and the power it gives him, and hedges his life about with laws and boundaries to keep order. He glorifies a strong, disciplined character by which he can subdue his emotions and hold to his ambitious drives. His culture is practical, rational, war-like, aggressive, and authoritarian. He has a hard time just being and enjoying.

"On the other hand, matriarchal societies, which are earth centered, regard the human Mind and body as a unity and see God in every aspect of Creation. A man living in such a culture regards the universe as a continuum of intelligent orderliness, and he feels himself to be a drop in the cosmic ocean of life. He believes he should enjoy the caprices of life; and for him, dignity resides in mysticism, fantasy, play, and love. He allows his emotions and instincts to guide him, and he avoids 'egocentric,' purposeful behavior toward others. He believes that to allow his head to dictate to his body is insane. The virtues of trust, nurturance, and surrender are highly valued by him. There is a natural democratic sharing of decision-making in his society, and everyone tends to flow with the stream of events of Mother Nature and human nature. He can enjoy pleasure without having feelings of anxiety. Unfortunately, matriarchal societies are not inclined to strive toward civilization-building and Egoic aspirations.

"Several centuries ago, Europeans were agrarian people who worked close to the land and were in tune with the pulses of Nature. The people turned from that maternal, life-giving emphasis of Nature-consciousness to materialism and ownership. This was brought about by the rise of the merchant middle class and Protestantism which gave impetus to the industrial revolution. The new emphasis on status promoted acquisition and, hence, separateness and covetousness. Then masculine militarism and the patriarchal traditions of the ruling class came to the fore to organize the energy of the general populace into nationalism. The patriarchal and matriarchal views of the world have come to be extremes of what should be a balanced whole that incorporates the best aspects of these two world views. As you've been told before, you will be largely responsible for setting into motion the recreation of the Lemurian philosophy in the future nation. The advantages of technology and practicality must be blended with care for Nature and the elimination of antisocial aggressiveness."

Richard thought for a moment in silence. "I never sorted through those concepts before; so, obviously, I haven't analyzed what they mean to me. I guess I'm going to have to dig into it further. I was told that Western Civilization was fostered by the Brotherhoods as a stepping stone to the Kingdom of God. Hasn't Christianity uplifted mankind to spiritual aspiration?"

James replied, "Historically, it has been the humanists who have uplifted man by fighting the entrenched power of the coalition between the clergy, the nobles, and the wealthy. Church doctrine, being an offshoot of Jewish and Roman patriarchalism, promotes obedience to authorities and uses guilt to make people accuse *themselves* when their lives go wrong rather than question the system which is designed to suppress the general populace.

"In every patriarchal society, a woman is hardly a person in her own right. Rather, she is a status symbol which a man is encouraged to acquire in order to establish his manliness. The idealized patriarchal man is considered weak if he actually falls in love. Few American men have actually learned how to love. Modern marriages are usually based on mutually clinging needs for sex, status, and security.

"The human brain will produce a personality which is either pleasure-oriented or violence-prone. *Its neurological structure allows it to develop only one way or the other.* Matriarchal societies lavish physical affection on their children and encourage their enjoyment of pleasure so that they will grow up to be loving adults who have happy, long-lasting marriages. The concept of war is foreign to such people. There is *no* crime or insanity among them. They are not aggressive or acquisitive, and they regard women and men as complete equals.

"In our society we harshly coerce children into submissive obedience. Boys are encouraged to compete with one another in every way. We treat them coldly and discipline them rigidly so that they are deprived of the ability to ever experience love in their lifetime as an unintended result. About all they are left with is their sex drive when they attain puberty. As men, many become despoilers, fighters, and contemptuous of women."

257

"But this is a war-like world," Richard protested. "It seems men must be bred to become aggressive to stay free."

"Lemuria survived 50,000 years without a war. You must develop your community so its people find *real* love and kinship with the earth and all its creatures. Then, when men of war have been killed off at the turn of the century, you will have a Lemurian society already begun which will endure in safety. Few American or European men have ever experienced love within themselves. Even the excitement you feel now with Gail is not love."

Richard bristled. "Now wait a minute! I resent that. My feelings for Gail are the most beautiful I've ever felt. Are you trying to dissuade me from marrying her?"

James replied blandly, "No. But neither do I think it wise to kid yourself about what you think is love. You're in the same boat with several hundred million men in patriarchal cultures for whom sexual desire is the only sensation akin to love they will ever feel. And although they can enjoy the pleasure of sexual climax, their upbringing deprives them of ever experiencing the mystical ecstacy of complete orgasm because they have blocked almost all such awareness in their body."

"How am I supposed to take that?" Richard asked petulently. "Do you want me to feel guilty because I don't experience mystical ecstacy that way? Anyway, that sounds like some Oriental myth."

James addressed him sternly. "What I'm talking about is a natural development in a natural man or woman. What is certainly a sexual myth from the Orient is that celibacy is a precondition for a person being able to elevate himself spiritually. That false idea even entered the early Christian church from the East during the era of Monasticism when asceticism and self-denial were hypothetically held to purify the soul. Of course, it didn't work for them either. Nevertheless, you will learn what I'm talking about as first-hand knowledge! And you will be expected to pass that information to other men—and also to women. You see, patriarchal cultures deny that women can experience orgasm. Women are theorized to be docile receptacles to the service of men's sex drives. So women must also be awakened and freed for the fulfillment of happiness that our Angelic Creators intended for us.

258

"A whole new way of rearing children must be encouraged by you to prepare them from infancy onward for deep marital satisfaction and sublime contentment as adults. These new rearing practices should put an end to antisocial aggressiveness and the desire for power over others, which breeds the drive for money and materialistic possessions. The inborn human drive to please others and receive pleasure, which society has labeled as evil, is being strictly suppressed in children through shame and punishment. This puts people at odds within themselves for a lifetime. Such inner conflict destroys self-esteem and causes suppressed body rage. As a result, the whole society is thus trained from young childhood to subordinate their basic human needs to disciplinarians of all types and to feel unworthy because of their thoughts of pleasure which are held to be dirty. Authoritarians of Church and state take over where parents leave off, and they order entire populations to obediently do things which are destructive of human life and block civilizing influences. Egoic progress depends upon self-direction, freedom, and the ability to love oneself and others; however, these are denied by the forces of Evil which work their power over mankind through religious despots and secular tyrants."

"Look," Richard interrupted. "I'm not sure I know exactly what you're talking about. John told me I'm to get married to a woman who has been reared with a strictness parallel to my own upbringing. He also said that she's supposed to work with me in the demanding work for the Brotherhoods. Dr. White later confirmed that Gail is that woman. There's nothing in my knowledge that comes even close to what you're saying, and I'm virtually certain your view of childhood and pleasure is not shared by Gail either. So if John and Dr. White think our strict rearings provided the attitudes that are right for the job, that's good enough for me."

James sighed with disappointment. "Nevertheless, such social and psychological changes must come about if mankind is to move toward Egoic advancement in significant numbers. We will bring home this lesson to you in living examples over the coming years; for I'm aware that you truly do not understand this most critical of issues. But you will change, for it is in the nature of forerunners to do so. Gail is a powerful disciplinarian. Her help will be essential in your forging unity of direction out of the diverse personalities who will first come together to start your community. And your new wife will also highlight for you the social drawbacks to the patriarchal way of rearing children. Christ's admonition to love one another will continue to be thwarted if you allow Old Order habits to enter the Kingdom of God. The very survival of mankind depends upon his ability to re-learn how to love. Love is *the* creative power, and it streams from God continuously. In order for it to flow through a human channel, that person must be free of neurotic blocks and have self-esteem."

Richard glared at James for a moment before he blurted, "I don't like people popping out of nowhere and complaining about everything I think and do. All I want is a normal life and to raise my two children in peace. You guys fill my head with ideas that no one I know has ever heard of. It's made me damned uncomfortable. And I don't like feeling that somebody is pushing me around."

James calmly responded, "I honor your irritation with that; but the timetable is moving on, and you're wasting time."

Richard softened and then smiled sheepishly. "Yeah, I know." Then, in a serious tone he said, "I can't let go of what all of you have told me because it works when I use it, but I don't see how I could be capable of the huge job all of you say I'm supposed to do. Pull your own chestnuts out of the fire, if there *is* a fire! Frankly, the world is a pretty neat place, and I don't see anything that's so very wrong going on around me."

"You will be appalled at how fast things will fall apart in the United States before the end of this century," James warned. "You will need to prepare for the future while you still can."

Richard said soberly, "I worry about that a lot. I just don't know where to start."

"That's your job to study and figure out. And even though you think you're pretty mature now that you're thirty-two years old, you are still in training. Moreover, you're going to have to learn a great deal about child psychology and the neurological development of the human brain. You know almost nothing about how to rear your children properly."

Richard was shocked by James' statement. "What do you mean?"

"You're not doing any more for your children than your parents did for you. Rearing children is not like training a pet! All children have abilities which are not being developed because of the culture's mass ignorance. People now attain less than *half* their potential intelligence because as children they are not given the right kind of stimuli and guidance at the proper moments in their neurological development. The optimum time for the introduction of mathematics and reading is years prior to the time a child starts school at age six. A child should be able to read well by his third birthday and be able to write by four—these are basic tools to the attainment of high intelligence. Math and musical talents are built-in abilities of the brain; and if the right materials and learning environment are provided, *every* child has genius in these areas. But this requires much skill and almost full-time attention on the part of the parents for the first five years of a child's life. Schools should never be anything but a supplement to the child's principle education in the home. Most parents put an infant in a playpen and largely ignore it. Then they let the neighborhood kids, and now also television, be the main influence in their child's early development. You must also come to realize that natural childbirth (away from the interventionism of hospitals) and breast feeding, as well as excellent nutrition all through life, are key factors in a child's eventual attainment of high intelligence and psychological health. Modern medical practices have inadvertently been subverting Nature's plan for the infant's optimum development. To merely clothe, house, feed, and be kind to a child is just so much warehousing of a young life, which does not provide the preparation for the greatness we are all heir to. Parents seem to be mostly concerned that a child not be a nuisance and be well-behaved and adopt the parent's prejudices. This is traditionally accomplished by literally terrorizing a child to fit into those prescribed molds. No one should ever strike a child or threaten to. To do so may assuage *your* impatience or anger, but it inflicts long-term anxiety on the child and gives him a low sense of self-worth that usually lasts a lifetime."

"I don't know anyone who doesn't hit their kids to make them behave or to discipline them." Richard commented.

"Just because it has culture-wide acceptance doesn't mean it is the most effective means of eliciting the desired result. Most school systems traditionally employ a host of other negative reinforcement techniques to try to get students to study and behave, but mostly they quash a child's natural love of learning and block his intellectual attainment through anxiety. We are going to require that you personally become an expert on child psychology and superior methods of teaching so you can see to it that students are educated in an entirely different way in your community. Western institutions succeed in making people feel guilty, unworthy, afraid, and inadequate to reach out and direct their own destiny. The present system, and the parents who conscientiously help perpetuate it, teach most people to be failures and losers and, at best, mediocre. During the next couple of days, I will do my best to explain to you the awful truth of how warped this culture is and how essential it is for your community to reestablish the flow of *real* love in this culture for others to emulate."

James spent three days going over detailed explanations and enlargement of his points for Richard to assimilate. Unfortunately, Richard found the ideas so foreign, that he could not readily accommodate them. It took about ten years before he understood them to the extent of accepting and using such information effectively.

Shortly before Christmas, Dorothy's suit for divorce was heard at court without Richard's lawyer having been notified in time for Richard to attend. She was given full custody of their children; and although the decree specified that Richard continue to pay the same amount he had been donating monthly for the children's support, Dorothy was denied forever any claim to alimony. The divorce became final on December 31, 1959, precisely ten years after Dorothy and Richard were wed. He was relieved that the uncertainty over Dorothy's intentions was ended. He looked forward to an adult relationship wherein a man and woman demand nothing of the other and yet receive superabundantly through thoughtful exchanges freely given in love. This higher relationship is infinitely considerate, and one's rights are never trampled by a boorish spouse. In an empathetic marriage there is no battle of wills.

Now that Gail and Richard could marry at any time, Gail wanted to be wed immediately so she could live with him in peace. Richard, however, insisted that they have a formal wedding and a reception to which their relatives and friends could come and celebrate. He would not attempt a marriage without first doing everything possible to bring peace between Gail and her parents, and it seemed both logical and fitting to use the organization of the Lutheran Church to arbitrate the dispute. Her family was not to be placated, however, and they formally brought the charge of adultery against Gail so she couldn't be married by a minister of their religion. As long as she was in a state of discipline by her home church, no other minister could interfere. After the adultery charge was proved invalid to everyone's satisfaction, her family still held out on a charge of her violation of the fourth commandment by not honoring her mother and father. Gail and Richard finally went to Rockford to see her parents with a promise of protection from harm by the regional head of the church synod, who conducted the meeting. The charge of not honoring her mother and father was reversed and the blame properly laid to her parents.

Gail's parents eventually had to relent, and they came with their relatives to Evanston to attend the wedding. Her father even took part in the ceremony in order to give away the bride. Gail wore a gown of pure white linen damask which she sewed herself according to instructions afforded by Richard, and on March 12, 1960, they were wed in Bethlehem Lutheran Church by the pastor[1] who had labored to effect the reconciliation with Gail's parents.

Richard's parents were very much pleased with his marriage to Gail; and although they had been unable to glean much understanding or insight into the personality and beliefs of their son, they could at least form some basis for judging him by the kind of woman he married. Richard was invited to return to his father's factory where the elderly man had real need of Richard's abilities, and they worked together with mutual respect. Richard's great fund of energy enabled him to do justice to the

---

[1] It is perhaps symbolic that the first name of the pastor at Bethlehem Church is *Samuel* and his last name can be translated into English as *Judge*.

work for his father in addition to the exacting tasks required by the Brotherhoods in preparing for the founding of the community in Illinois.

The marriage between Gail and Richard soothed all tensions of the past into nonexistence, and the knowledge that this marriage had the sanction of the Brotherhoods gave Richard a sense of peace never enjoyed with Dorothy.

The errors and hardships of his youth strengthened Richard's character and tempered his wisdom; and now that he was older and less rebellious, he lent himself more freely to the plans the Brotherhoods had for him. As serenity and confidence enfolded him, Richard's productivity in regard to preparations for the city soared. Just as Dr. White had predicted, doors opened: love, happiness, beauty, health, and prosperity entered the newlyweds' lives. There are, of course, others like them in the world who are on the way to achieving the same devotion to Greatness. Perhaps such beginnings seem small and unimpressive, but drop by drop the onrushing wave of human greatness is gathering.

CHAPTER 17

Results

Richard founded The Stelle Group on March 5, 1963. It was organized as a not-for-profit educational corporation, which also provided a legal framework within which those who were ready to join the Brotherhoods' work could function. The Stelle Group published the first edition of THE ULTIMATE FRONTIER in that same year.

Richard and Gail served as a rallying point around which like-minded people could find one another in order to work together and build an environment conducive to their Egoic growth and cultural improvement. People gradually arrived from all over the United States with the expectation of finding purpose and spiritual fulfillment, but no one really knew how to achieve those goals. Some who arrived were strong individualists who knew how to get things done—educators, engineers, technicians, and professional people. Some who added their numbers were college students rejecting the establishment and seeking the "New Age" idealism of the late 1960's without knowing what that amounted to. And some persons came looking for a guru to lead them toward perpetual peace and bliss. All who were accepted from among those who applied for membership had the potential for achieving practical and spiritual advancement, and they were selected for being reasonably well-balanced psychologically. However, their common intention to partake in an ideal community was a far cry from their awareness of what that required practically. Setting the tone and forging these diverse types into a workable team became Richard's main task.

The last half of the 1960's was frustrating to all the members of The Stelle Group. It was a time of slowly accumulating capital for the purchase of land and of determining the principles and concepts of the overall design of their future community. Everyone had a different idea of what constitutes an ideal city and an uplifting way of life, and years of debate and research seemed to drag on and on. The number of members had stabilized at around sixty adults during the planning phase, and this number seemed to lend itself well to a town-hall type of discussion group. Alternatives by the score were examined, studied, and resolved over those first several years. But it was all limited to theory and philosophizing without being able to actually build and live together.

As members joined The Stelle Group, they moved into the immediate neighborhood of the large house where Richard and Gail lived in northern Chicago, and they gradually formed a rapport among themselves through their efforts to plan the community of their dreams. The most practical of their early efforts was the establishment in June, 1968, of an elementary school in the basement of Richard's home. Although the Brotherhoods had instructed Richard that children were to be taught to read by their parents by the time they were three years old and to write by the time they were four, the Stelle mothers said they didn't know how to go about teaching their children; so it was agreed that Stelle children would come to school beginning at age three with their mothers. Gail and the full-time teachers of the Stelle children taught the mothers how to teach their little ones. Gail had given birth to a daughter, Dawn, on December 12, 1965, and Gail worked in the school with her own child to prove out the methods shown to the other mothers.

Another practical undertaking was the founding of Stelle Woodworking Corporation on the near west side of Chicago in March, 1969. It was reasoned that it would be wise to have an already-thriving business whenever the group moved onto the property they would one day purchase. Seven members each put up one thousand dollars to capitalize the company, and by July they had purchased machinery and were set up for production. Richard quit his job as liaison between engineering and production at a large manufacturer of office printing machinery in order to manage Stelle Woodworking and also to do estimating, buying, and production work there. This little company was the forerunner of Stelle Industries, Inc., which just seven years later had assets of 2.2 million dollars. The woodworking business soon became an eighty-hour-a-week job for Richard, and he turned over much of his daily administrative duties as president of The Stelle Group to its board of trustees, of which he was a member and which he had been training for several years. The four trustees in addition to Richard were hard-working, conscientious people who worked long hours every night at The Stelle Group offices located on the first floor of Richard's home. Gail's first concern was rearing her daughter, but she was also vice-president of The Stelle Group and head of the school. While Richard spent the next three years concentrating on getting the woodworking company established, Gail took charge of The Stelle Group's routine business since she and the corporate secretary were the only two trustees at the offices during the day.

Gail had been prepared by her parents to assume responsibility. She is personable, beautiful, has a mind for detail and precision, and like most successful American executives has been an energetic achiever all her life. She teaches children well, likes talking with people and is politically astute. Gail and Richard made an effective team in guiding the members of The Stelle Group into becoming a functioning organization.

There was much natural resistance to get even the most earnest members to try methods and ideas that were new to them, and Gail began to despair that the democratic ideal could ever be possible in the foreseeable future. The group demonstrated that modern Americans have little practical experience in how to work cooperatively or how to govern themselves and make joint decisions. Indeed, many members discovered they really didn't like a majority deciding how they should do things whenever they happened to fall into the minority of an issue to be voted upon. Because of the concern that the group might vote for the easier route rather than the better route, the trustees tended to avoid democratic procedures when they could. The trustees became more reactionary despite Richard's insistence that self-management builds self-responsibility and self-esteem. Richard and Gail began to split in their views on the management of The Stelle Group and the mode of instruction in the school.

The group agreed to volunteer their labor to build a modern, 20,000-square-foot factory on 240 acres of farmland (48 city blocks) they bought, south of Chicago in January, 1970, and construction began in the fall of 1970. More members joined and more donations and tithes were received to fund the cost of materials. In November, 1972, Stelle Woodworking Corporation moved into the factory, and in March, 1973, the first two homes were occupied. The offices of The Stelle Group and the school were moved at the same time to the site of the budding community, and Stelle was officially underway. Eleven more homes were built in the next twelve months, and streets and sidewalks were installed. A water purification plant and pumping station were completed along with distribution piping. A sewage treatment plant and sewer lines were also put in the ground. All this work was designed and installed by the members of The Stelle Group.

Members work in Stelle and spend their wages any way they want. Stelle is not a collective nor are there communal living quarters. The strength of the Lemurian system lies in the people building together cooperatively and solving problems together. It was even more gratifying to see people develop self-esteem as they became skilled and dependable workers. The practical directions on how to achieve Egoic advancement worked more effectively than Richard's best expectations. Stelle became an intensely accelerating catalyst for individuals' maturing. Young men and women were able to fill important offices which they would likely have had to wait until they were twenty years older before such opportunities might arise in the outside world. Their sheer joy of developing a distinctly more enlightened culture was contagious to new arrivals, and this kept the overall level of enthusiasm high. All this delighted Richard, but he was all too aware there was a major flaw in the way things were going.

The Stelle program is designed to be a social workshop where people find the support and example of others of like mind to strive for character development, practical application of Universal Law, and spiritual uplift toward the end of becoming a more effective human being who is happier, more in control of his destiny, and more in touch with his inner nature. This growth was happening to the members at a remarkably satisfying pace, and the members' growth was directly related to the degree of their actual participation in building the physical aspects of the community. The area where the members' growth seemed to be inhibited, however, was still in their lack of involvement in the community's internal government and decision making. All through 1973, Richard tried to perceive where the difficulty originated. He recognized that his trustees were comfortably entrenched in a power structure that was not being resisted by the general membership because an effective formula for success had been put into operation. But he was also becoming aware that people were apprehensive about his seemingly unassailable position. The group voted that he head the project of building Stelle, but that was when the group was small. Now there were millions of dollars in assets to be directed and almost two hundred participants to guide. Yet when he made overtures to the trustees to initiate more involvement from the group at large, the trustees resisted since they felt sure it would bog down the efficiency of the organization by returning to endless debates without resolution.

Gail's arguments against decentralization of control were based on her general contempt of the members' ability to take charge of their lives or to fully implement the philosophy. Gail was well aware that her husband was getting restive over the issue, and she was concerned that he would delegate some of his duties and thus dilute their power as a team. Since Gail was personally unable to share her areas of responsibility with anyone, she felt that Richard's desire to decentralize was a weakness on his part.

In October 1973, Richard received instruction from his Teachers, John and James, to prepare for a new assignment which was to start within the coming year. His new job was to try to warn the businessmen and government executives of the State of Texas how to keep the economy of their state functioning after a collapse of the United States economy.[1] He was told this would require that he be able to travel more freely and be away from Stelle for extended periods of time. Richard had already independently decided that his everyday presence in Stelle

---

[1]Richard was told by his Teachers that the Republic of the United States of America would survive only 200 years. There are several possible dates eligible for the founding date between 1776 and 1789.

weighed heavily on the group. A strong hand had been necessary to get Stelle moving in the right direction, but now his identification with authoritarian power was detrimental to the group. He reasoned that without his authority to point to, the trustees and officers would have to deal with the members in a more egalitarian manner. Furthermore, if he became less available to make the major decisions, and since no one else in Stelle had direct information from the Brotherhoods, then everyone's opinion would be as valid as anyone else's regardless of their position; therefore, a democratic decision-making process would logically evolve without having to undermine the trustees by revealing their disagreement with him. Because of their daughter, Dawn, Gail would have to remain at Stelle full time. Moreover, for years, Gail's self-determined schedule had kept her busy until three or four every morning. A hired housekeeper took care of their home, and Gail saw Richard only at supper and at meetings. The demands placed on their marriage by the exigencies of the group's needs had essentially reduced their association to the teamwork necessary to do their jobs. Their further division over the "democratic versus authoritarian" issue became more adversarial as time went by.

By the time Richard announced his departure to the group six months later, in April, 1974, his association with Gail had come to a point where neither could respect the political views of the other. The first five years of their marriage had been happy and fulfilling for them both, but in recent years Gail had become the consummate executive whose devotion to duty superceded anyone's personal needs. Now that she and Richard had somehow come to be working at cross-purposes, he had to reevaluate his assumption that John had implied a guarantee of harmony and marital success when he told him that Gail was ideally suited to the demanding work they would undertake together. Richard had encouraged her to be her own person, think independently, take initiative, and express her equality as a human being. Richard regarded her as his complement, not his subordinate. Gail is strongly self-willed, and the Brothers do not prevent anyone from exercising free will to strike off in an independent direction.

When Richard took his leave from Stelle, he recommended

that Jim, who was both a fellow trustee and a member of the Stelle Industries board of directors, become president of both corporations. Richard also resigned as trustee and director since he obviously could not function effectively in those roles while being absent for indefinite periods. He retained only his position as executor of a Voting Trust by which he was entitled to name board members to Stelle Industries. Later that month Richard encountered his Teacher, John, in Globe, Arizona, where they discussed the plight of The Stelle Group and Richard's responsibility to build the city, Philadelphia, on the island in the Pacific Ocean. Richard regularly telephoned Jim to bring him up to date on events as he traveled from state to state to look at inventions for Stelle Industries to manufacture. When Richard returned to Stelle after a six-week absence, he informed Gail that he thought a divorce to be in order and he suggested she obtain one on grounds of his desertion. Gail responded by having the trustees back an edict barring Richard thereafter from setting foot in Stelle and from talking to any of the members except Jim or Gail. Since Richard now held no offices, he felt obliged to obey the edict or else he would be acting against his organization's self-determination and raise consternation among the members. Moreover, by this edict the trustees made themselves solely accountable for their actions.

Richard moved to Dallas, Texas, to begin his assignment there. The following August he was contacted by John and told it was imperative that he return to Stelle because of disturbing trends in the direction the group was taking, and he was charged with helping the people of Stelle come to govern their own affairs more in accord with the ideals in THE ULTIMATE FRONTIER.

Before Gail and Jim allowed Richard on Stelle property, he had to agree to work under Gail's direction. He soon discovered that all the office personnel had been told he was not to have access to files, records, accounts or letterhead and that they were not to converse with him in the offices. Richard was seldom permitted to attend trustees meetings, but he used his rights as executor of the Voting Trust to appoint himself as a director to fill a vacancy on the Stelle Industries board. The actual decision-making meetings were held thereafter in secret. Richard finally carried his case directly to the membership in mid-March of 1975, just two days after he had been told by John that through their totalitarian oppressiveness the trustees had separated themselves and the whole group from active support by the very Brotherhoods who had championed and founded self-ruling governments through centuries of careful development of Western Civilization and the United States of America. Richard was instructed to actively pursue exposure of the trustees and their removal from office. Richard presented his evidence in a general meeting and called for the resignation of the trustees. Gail and the other trustees countered the next month by expelling Richard from membership on the grounds that he was undermining the rightful authority of the trustees. In order to undermine Richard's credibility and thus weaken acceptance of his defense, the trustees further claimed he had been sexually exploiting several young women. After Richard's ouster, Gail seized the position as executor of the Voting Trust so as to prevent Richard from being able to elect new directors to run Stelle Industries at the annual meeting of stockholders which occurred a week later.

The membership finally grew quite disturbed over these events and became concerned over the growing arbitrary use of power by Gail to summarily expel Associates who opposed her or closely questioned her. The Stelle Group polarized around two basic viewpoints: one faction supported the trustees in their claim that their having acquired responsibility/authority from the Brotherhoods via Richard relieved them of the obligation to consult the people of Stelle; whereas the other faction supported democratic structuring of government in Stelle and felt that all matters affecting the lives of individual members should be voted by referendum as recommended by Dr. White. Thus, the stage was set for a dramatic struggle as the members came to reaffirm the principles of self-determination through democracy. After several legal actions, the members finally called for a special meeting to remove the trustees from office, but in mid-August, 1975, the trustees announced their resignations. During the next several weeks, the former trustees resigned their various offices; and Gail and Jim, along with a fifth of the members, moved to Wisconsin.

The new trustees were capable and energetic, and there were many members available to fill the vacated offices competently. Richard stayed in the Stelle area for four months longer to help the new trustees privately if they needed information, but essentially the group was put on their own to examine the complexities of governing Stelle and to make the hard decisions themselves. Richard felt confident about the group's maturing; so he returned to Dallas, Texas, in December, 1975. Meanwhile, the group was learning how to debate issues effectively and legislate safeguards to prevent future despotism or abridgements of their rights. Instead of feeling put upon by Richard's holding them to higher principles, they examined the philosophy carefully and formalized the same conclusions Richard formerly had required of them. In January, 1976, John informed Richard that The Stelle Group was again receiving the active support of the Brotherhoods. At that time John also conveyed the Brotherhoods' approbation for Richard to form another community around him to support his work in Texas.

During the time that Richard had managed the affairs of Stelle, he experienced an estrangement from its members since they could not accept him as an ordinary man. His love for the members was returned by something more akin to awe or trepidation. This was too distancing for him; so when he and Gail were finally viewed as flawed and not held to be indispensable, Richard rejoiced to see hope for a more human relationship between himself and the members of Stelle in the future. Richard resumed writing his monthly *Observations* column for the Stelle newsletter, which is sent free to people around the world who are interested in keeping abreast of the Brotherhoods' program. He sued Gail for a divorce, which was granted by the courts in November, 1976. The young woman who had been praised and commended to him by John was now, seventeen years later, condemned by John for her ambitions. It did not escape Richard that the Brotherhoods had known then how his relationship with Gail would eventually evolve, but he was thankful for the largely positive lessons he learned during their marriage. Her energetic devotion to Stelle was essential to moving it in the right direction in its earlier days, but she came to view her husband's patience and tolerance as weaknesses for which she felt she had to compensate by taking charge. The admissions rules of The Stelle Group do not allow only one partner of a marriage to become a member without the other, but after his divorce became final, Richard was free to apply for renewal of his membership. He was accepted as a member, but without the right to vote or hold office since he lived elsewhere than in the Stelle area. Richard traveled to the community once a month and stayed for several days to teach, conduct philosophical meetings, and keep himself informed of events in the community since he is still responsible to his Superiors for Stelle carrying out its assignments as part of the Brotherhoods' Plan.

During his assignment in Texas, Richard also established The Adelphi Organization, which is based on the same principles as The Stelle Group. This new group developed a private community near Quinlan, Texas, 35 miles east of Dallas.

Between 1975 and 1981 the residents of Stelle explored and developed ways of achieving closer interactions between themselves. As a result of close communication being expanded beyond the confines of each family, the children of the community are now afforded the love of all the members. The school system has been extended to support parents in the education of their children from early infancy, which has produced in the youngsters an extremely high intelligence and a sense of competence. The Stelle Group school uses advanced techniques which have been developed all over the world by experimental educators, but which most school boards in the country rarely take advantage of because of their overly conservative policies. Adults in Stelle enjoy the advantages of training in awareness whereby they can get in touch with all aspects of their human nature. In this way, they integrate their purpose and feelings, leading to rapid psychological maturing and increased happiness and productivity. Stelle is at the forefront of developing the human potential.

The community provides many of its own internal needs from among the skills of its members. The self-sufficiency of the community is a major aim for The Stelle Group, which is also responsible for developing special aircraft for a massive airlift at the turn of the century. This will be for participants in The Stelle Group, and of the new city of Philadelphia to be built on the island presently in the Pacific Ocean that was shown on a map to Richard by Dr. White. The airlift is proposed to sustain these people in the stratosphere during the reapportionment of the world's land masses at the turn of the century, because this is the only way to assure safety from the high winds, dust, gases, earthquakes, and tidal waves. The Stelle Group's Office of Technology developed the capability of producing engine fuel from agricultural products as part of an interim energy source for the community's use. Their work was considered commendable enough that the U.S. Department of Energy gave a sizeable grant to The Stelle Group to prepare a publication of Stelle's method for dissemination to the public. Another major achievement in the area of self-sufficiency has been the establishment of the Stelle Telephone Company as a mutual, not-for-profit corporation owned and operated by the people of Stelle. Late in 1980, Stelle Telephone received authority from the Illinois Commerce Commission to serve the community of Stelle with a direct link-up to the national long-distance network.

Richard has seen The Stelle Group develop a stable nucleus of dedicated members whose mettle has been tempered through a decade of necessary trials and lessons. This nucleus is not an "in group" but rather a multifaceted base to which most new arrivals can find a comfortable attachment and thus eventually become bonded more readily into the extended family that the Brotherhoods intend The Stelle Group to be.

Everyone who has become an active participant in Stelle has admittedly matured and deepened more rapidly than ever before; however, there were others of equal potential who joined but held themselves aloof, thereby benefitting little. Some quit when they realized that Stelle members were not titans and that the city had not yet evolved to the heights it took the Lemurian Empire ten thousand years to attain; whereas others quit because they felt inadequate compared to the development and progress of those already there even though *everyone* at Stelle is both a student and an example for others to emulate. It is to the great credit of members of The Stelle Group that there is no saintly posturing or smug self-righteousness among them. Many participants have "graduated" from Stelle's inculcation of the Lemurian Philosophy and left Stelle to use its principles to become successes in the world-at-large, and Stelle has lost the expert services of still other participants because they would not serve the Work of the Brotherhoods except for a high wage. A few believed the group should abandon technology to live in back-to-nature simplicity and eschew all rules; so they went away to pursue this direction on their own. Fortunately, the kinds of persons whose personal failings and guilt-ridden fanaticism lead them to join causes find no mass movement in The Stelle Group to attract them, so they don't apply for membership. Yet there are far too many good people who have never come to Stelle because friends might laugh or because the effort to make of themselves what they dream might be too demanding.

We all know how to become better human beings, but the subtle yet powerful influences of society discourage us from aspirations to reach beyond shallow convention. The world lauds saints after They are safely dead but actually deprecates idealism, altruism, and ambitions to rise to personal excellence. The efficacy of people striving upward together in an environment largely removed from the deleterious influences of the cynical, self-involved members of society has been demonstrated in Stelle. Men and women who put the great principles espoused by the Brotherhoods to work on a daily basis evolve rapidly toward Egoic advancement. Moreover, it is great fun. It is not so much a matter of gathering more and more information that makes for personal growth, but rather such growth is gained by one's continuous application of practical idealism in an environment where others are also working toward the same ends for themselves and their children. Then the practice of the Golden Rule is feasible because one is safe from exploitation. The community of Stelle is a Learning Center where it is expected that one will also accept the demands of taking charge of one's own life in a democratic setting. One does not advance by surrendering self-responsibility to a guru or by giving obedience to an authority figure. A genuine teacher shares his insights and braces his students to become free and be their own selves so they will be doers in the world who acquire self-fulfillment.

Psychologists and anthropologists have shown that today's problems of anti-social aggression, neurosis, psychosis, violence, and marital failure are direct results of a culture's methods of dealing unaffectionately with its children and using guilt and fear to inhibit natural human behavior. Our Creators intended for us to be fully in touch with the Earth and consequently in touch with our interior selves instead of being alienated and anxious castaways on our journey through incarnation. Our bodies and brains contain all the tools by which our Egos can achieve internal unity and deep communion with others. The Stelle Group is evolving more humane and loving methods of rearing and educating children to the end of returning our erstwhile stifled individuality, productivity, creativeness, and interpersonal relationships to the God-given inheritance it is our right to have and enjoy. The Stelle Group is a forerunner of the re-establishment of a Christ-like, loving world even if only to pilot workable techniques at first.

On March 18, 1982, Richard was met in Texas by his Teacher, John, outside of a post office where Richard went to deposit some mail. John directed him to move The Stelle Group's offices and some of its members to the community being developed by The Adelphi Organization near Dallas. John also instructed him to open the community of Stelle, Illinois to any persons interested in advancing their spiritual development without having to join The Stelle Group. This opened the way to make Stelle an ecumenical educational center. There are many other groups that are concerned with living in greater harmony with the natural environment, finding harmless, more loving relationships with one's fellowmen, working toward inner spiritual completeness, and being responsible for one's own life rather than yielding that responsibility to "experts." The Brotherhoods are in sympathy with the wide-spread reawakening of people to these concerns, for this promises final rejection of the ages-old, dangerous practices of spirit mediumship, witchcraft, drug usage, and dietary extremism which have been touted by their promoters to produce spiritual enlightenment but end instead in entrapment and despair. There is renewed hope that people will return to the Lemurian principles that have proven safe and effective for spiritual growth as a result of their earnest searchings for truth. Stelle, Illinois is now able to welcome other individuals, philosophical groups, and other private schools into the community and allow others to build or buy homes in Stelle.

Many intentional communities have been formed for various reasons, each with its own particular slant on survivalism, religion, health, ecology, etc. Stelle is different from these in that it pursues a balanced, holistic upgrading of all aspects of living, which involves the conscious evolution of economics, politics, social structure, art, aesthetics, education, health, technology, spiritual and psychological growth, commerce, construction, agriculture, and futurist undertakings. Its people are practical enough to use anything that has proven workable in improving their lives and the environment of their community.

It takes a decade to get a city started, and very few organizations have been as successful as The Stelle Group in establishing the firm groundwork for such a community. Therefore, Stelle is seen as the place for conscientious people to relocate their businesses and homes in order to work with others of high practical idealism in applying ecologically sound, industrial technology toward the stable growth of this New Renaissance city. Many groups and new churches, which may not have ten years or the expertise to establish their own cities, have Stelle, Illinois ready to accept them into an ongoing community of people working to establish a culture that transcends the mediocrity of mass-man. Stelle is envisioned as a cultural and educational mecca for the men and women who aspire to personal greatness. Advances in holistic health, and the spiritual offerings of many new and rediscovered avenues to self-awareness, plus personal instruction from higher teachers are all bound to make Stelle an inspiring Spiritual Center unparalleled in the world. The consolidation of knowledge, resources, world lecturers, entertainers, artists, and scientists, will bring exciting advances. Thereby the Brotherhoods can reach more people than ever before who are ready for Their truths. In such a positive, constructive atmosphere, everyone should be able to find the right growth-engendering programs to fit their unique needs at whatever their level of advancement.

In former years, before the separation of The Stelle Group headquarters from the community of Stelle, residence in Stelle, Illinois was synonymous with membership in The Stelle Group. Those members slowly but steadily upgraded their personal development through day-to-day application of the Brotherhoods' philosophy, and they gradually but perceptibly evolved their level of community involvement beyond that expected of people elsewhere in the country. Thus, as time passed, transition to life in Stelle became more difficult for, and seemed overly demanding on, most new people joining The Stelle Group who didn't have the benefit of years of accommodation as had the earlier members of the organization. Now, with the opening of the city, the cultural shock experienced by newcomers to The Stelle Group is ameliorated by taking up residence in the community in Stelle, Illinois as an initial step toward accommodating to the high expectations of The Stelle Group's Lemurian philosophy. In Stelle they learn practical democratic functioning, how to hasten their emotional maturation, and acquire spiritual knowledge in a gradual escalation of self-discipline, facilitating a smooth transition into membership in The Stelle Group.

The Stelle Group sponsors seminars for adults and also maintains its own private schools in Illinois and Texas which accept applications from any who wish to enroll their children. The Stelle Group will also continue to accept new participants from among residents of the city of Stelle and from persons living outside the city. Some very specific tasks given The Stelle Group by the Brotherhoods are to be carried out in the private community in Adelphi, Texas. Residence in Adelphi will be limited to participants of The Stelle Group and The Adelphi Organization who are assigned to assist Richard directly in his work.

The Ultimate Frontier

The Stelle Group provides an organization for persons to achieve the greatness intended of human beings. That, of course, is the very purpose of the Brotherhoods. Both Stelle and Adelphi will actively engage in outside commerce and in the affairs of the world. People outside those two cities will very likely seek to emulate the effectual philosophy of The Stelle Group and The Adelphi Organization when they observe the peace-of-mind, security, and economic advantages it makes possible in the lives of its members.

There will be no recruiting drives or evangelistic proselytizing in order to swell the rosters of The Stelle Group and The Adelphi Organization, for it is more fitting that the persons who are naturally ready for the great work should actively seek a place there by their own volition. Even those individuals whose ingrained skepticism will hamper their immediate participation will overcome their hesitancy as the demonstrable practicality of the Brotherhoods' philosophy becomes increasingly apparent. It is Christ's way to attract adherents by example, and it is better that men aspire to residence in Stelle or Adelphi by way of their reasoned convictions than by glib rhetoric. Participation in Stelle and Adelphi provides a dynamic, exciting frontier where everything is being reexamined in order to discard the useless and extract the best. Pursuing this level of excellence is a stimulating challenge, making everyone involved feel alive and valuable. The community of Adelphi, especially, affords an atmosphere of mental, emotional, and spiritual maturity because of the gathering there of thinking persons who are devoted to the planned preservation of civilization. The spiritual and expansive tenor of the city of Stelle will provide a transition place for participants of The Stelle Group as they prepare for a more intense and self-disciplined involvement in Adelphi. Until the day of the Progression of the Life-Waves, the Citizenry of the Kingdom of God will strive to make each succeeding generation more perfect than itself. Each teacher will find fulfillment as his students' knowledge and proficiency exceeds his own, and each parent will see to it that his offspring seek and achieve a more noble character than his own. Enlightened man will work for the future knowing that what he furthers today he will enjoy in a later incarnation.

The time has come for men who hold high the ideals of civilization to separate from the matrix of present world society and create a refined way of life. Men must gather up their courage and make of their environment what they wish it to be. The Pilgrims left their surroundings in Europe because Europeans cramped their dreams and corrupted their youngsters.

The Western World, and particularly the United States, is entering a second renaissance. The first (during the 15th through 17th centuries) gave rise to scientific methods and led to freedom from religious despotism. This New Renaissance is *combining* science and religion as a result of the discoveries of physicists, archeologists, and anthropologists who have found that the knowledge of ancient peoples and many religious traditions contain *facts* of history and the nature of existence. This synthesis is now resulting in people turning from blind religious faith (or no faith) to reasoned belief. The Stelle Group is at the forefront of this change in consciousness, and it is charged by the Brotherhoods of scientist-philosophers with the task of helping men and women to be all they *can* be.

But the New Renaissance will be challenged by traditionalist leaders whose power over their followers might be threatened by the wide-spread changes inevitably wrought by the emergence of Truth. This is further complicated by the coincidental resurgence of fascist conservatism plus a return to fundamentalism in all the major religions. The reasonable person will need to find stability in the face of two emerging extremes: 1. the neo-paganist forces who are inspired by the evil Tibetans of Shamballah via mediums (like Helena Blavatsky and Alice Bailey) to establish the Antichrist through unwitting New Age groups and international power brokers: and 2. conservative religious fanatics who are convinced they must defend themselves by force of arms against the ever-threatening iniquity of unbelievers and liberals. The Stelle Group can be a center of peace and sanity amidst these two destructive factions whose conflict is likely to undermine all civil liberties in the nation as well as the right to openly pursue truth.

America was inspiring when men of various backgrounds subordinated their differences and pulled together to build a dream, but now an increasing number of factions each seek to gain control over the nation. The self-seeking unwillingness to yield to the greatest good of the majority can tear the nation apart.

Inasmuch as the practice of strict honesty and sensible morality is so heavily penalized by the present order of things, The Stelle Group is available for those who seek to live in an orderly and sound fashion again. The serenity and simplicity of living life in a straightforward manner will permit the return to Christ's ideal of thinking and acting without guile. So long as any one person seeks advantage over another, there will be tension, frustration, envy, hate, and anger present in human relationships. When all persons practice gracious courtesy, when they tend to create rather than take, and when they are humble rather than power-seeking, then the Golden Rule will be operative in our lives. If there were even one Ego in the Kingdom of God who sought to impose upon others for his safety, income, and comforts, then all the self-providers would be obliged to be on guard. Everyone in the type of civilization to be achieved in the Kingdom of God must be able to rest assured that he won't ever be expected to sacrifice his energies for the sustenance of malingerers or slackers. The assurance that a man can trust his neighbors implicitly is a priceless blessing, for then everyone can practice meekness. The practice of meekness in the world-at-large today requires the courage of a Christ because of baser men's taunting eagerness to take advantage. In The Stelle Group and The Adelphi Organization, men should never have to turn the other cheek to thoughtless, discourteous, or self-imposing persons.

Courage will be a foremost quality of those who ally themselves with the Brotherhoods' work. A man must have the courage to lead and direct his household. A family without a true man as its head ceases to be a healthy unit that can be depended upon to make its essential contribution to the growth of the Kingdom of God. A woman must have the courage to be a real woman instead of an unnatural man competing with men. There is no possible improvement on the arrangement where a man is a man and a woman is a woman. To live to the fullest that which one happens to be is a glorious blessing and a source of satisfying contentment. Equality between the sexes means merely that neither is to be subservient to the other, and that they have equal rights.

Usually the aspirant to a great goal is subjected to scornful criticism by friends and relatives because of his idealism. To abandon one's familiar surroundings, property, friends, and place of employment in exchange for a way of life transcending anything in one's experience will call for determination and the ability to adjust upward. Most persons can backslide without too much psychological disturbance, but a certain psychic stamina and adaptability will be essential for the men and women who strive to create the Kingdom of God.

The Stelle Group and The Adelphi Organization should not have to suffer anyone who is a drag upon the group effort toward excellence. There is no time to waste on incorrigibles, for less than one generation lies between us and Armageddon. The seeds sown by Christ almost two thousand years ago are now ready for harvest, and the wheat must be diligently separated from the chaff. Capable persons whose productive energies create wealth are needed to coalesce their superior abilities in the cities of Stelle and Adelphi.

Every nation in the past has been destroyed by the large numbers of impractical Egos incarnating into it after it has been brought to its pinnacle of success by practical people. The something-for-nothing types will give rise to irremediable political and economic chaos in America. Only when every participant in a commonwealth sustains his share of responsibility and keeps his individual karmic account in balance can there be any lasting security in that commonwealth.

The world's ignorance of Universal Law has made it vulnerable to Armageddon and Doom's Day. War—man's supreme folly—is a prime example of the panoply of negative emotions in which the world indulges because of its lack of understanding of karmic principles. However, man presently derives many satisfactions from the strivings demanded by war.

Man must have a goal to strive for—something worthy of his talents. The frontiersman braves all hardships for the satisfaction of having conquered. Man's restlessness in an era of ready-made accomplishment and his lack of worthwhile goals have resulted in wholesale anxiety in our society.

There is one perfect, albeit overlooked, frontier to satisfy men for all time. It is the ultimate of frontiers. No matter how high a man may rise, the goal of attaining Brotherhood, Adeptship, and Mastership—and then in turn, Angelic, Archangelic, and Celestial advancement—calls for utmost perseverance and knowledge. No matter how high one rises, there is always another even greater goal within reach. Furthermore, there is no challenging enemy anywhere to compare with the cunning power of the Black Mentalists. The good fight is not for the faint in heart. The upward struggle for union with God creates our souls, enlarges the circle of love, and destroys the power of evil. The man of war will be eliminated by Armageddon, and the man of intelligence will find peace on Earth after Doom's Day is done.

The Wisdom of Christ fulfills all the needs, hungers, and passions of the human being. Our hunger for divine truth and our attraction to virtue were painstakingly built into our Egos by the Celestial Host so that we would be compatible with the cosmos. Joy is our intended lot provided we grasp the opportunity to ally ourselves with the unfailing principles of the universe and pursue the ultimate frontier.

Remarks
by the biographee

A book as limited in size as THE ULTIMATE FRONTIER precludes complete development and explanation of its subject; yet its scope provides a basic introduction to the teachings of the Brotherhoods. In some respects the presentation of information may have seemed cursory, but the average reader was probably best served by having followed the same sequence of instruction that had been carefully designed for my understanding as a youth.

Persons who are predisposed toward formalized philosophy might have preferred the tenets of the Brotherhoods' belief to have been developed step-by-step from *a priori* foundations, but to undertake a logical argument on this basis would be unprofitable since philosophers are not yet in agreement as to what constitutes a truth firm enough to be regarded as a basic philosophic foundation. For example, mathematicians and physicists agree to ignore the many unprovable foundations of science so long as these arbitrary assumptions continue to work in practical applications. Even empiricists are often forced to accept as fact many things which are but subjectively self-evident.

In any event, it is highly improbable that the cosmology known to the Brotherhoods could ever have been imagined by man—let alone proven logically by him. The realm of scientific philosophy lacks objective evidence of the planes of existence beyond the physical, and without acceptable observations, an hypothesis cannot be derived nor understanding be achieved. Unfortunately, scientists will never acquire objective knowledge of the other planes of existence because the necessary evidence can only be obtained through mental experiences which are wholly subjective. Inasmuch as observations must be reproducible under laboratory conditions in order to be admissible to the body of scientific knowledge, the powers of Mind are officially cast into limbo. Thus we are faced with a crippling shortcoming in man's search for truth. Science has by its own rules limited itself to material phenomena and excluded itself from analyzing man's place in the cosmos. I don't quarrel with this sensible limitation, but I find it unfortunate that scientists have not as yet been able to extend their thoughtful probings to a disciplined study of the phenomena of the higher planes of existence. Essentially this has been the work of the Brotherhoods; and when a man sincerely undertakes the quest for higher understanding, he attracts the assistance of the Brothers who traveled that same path before him.

Our knowledge about the world has its root in man's perception of existence through his five basic senses. Observation and logical inference have thereby brought him into possession of a great deal of knowledge concerning his physical environment. The next step is taken when an individual has intensified his senses beyond the physical, for from that point onward his increased perceptions of nature allow him to know things about his environment that are closed to normal men. The Ego who has advanced to the point where he is acceptable for admission into the Brotherhoods *knows* that the Brotherhoods' philosophy is truth because by then he is able to rely on empirical evidence—subjective though it may be. Men who have developed clairvoyant abilities are generally unable to convince those who haven't yet come to possess these powers that there are other planes of existence. It is like describing a rainbow to a man totally blind since birth—for all the blind man knows, the very idea of sight is a taunting myth.

A hypothetical island wherein all the inhabitants have for untold ages been genetically sightless would very likely declare a visitor with normal sight insane were he to describe the beauties of the sunset and the starlit skies. These islanders would have no place in their philosophy for a fifth sense, and their science would be seriously hampered and distorted by lack of the very important sources of information sight affords. The true clairvoyant fares no better in our society when he describes the beauties and wonders of the Astral Plane. He becomes the object of ridicule and stands in real jeopardy of being committed to an asylum if he has the temerity to insist. The intelligent, scientifically-oriented person who has experienced spontaneous flashes of clairvoyance is predisposed to regard these experiences as mere coincidence or psychological weakness, and he consequently suppresses his emerging latent powers the more vigorously. As a result, we find the type of individual who can best forward mankind's quest for civilization—the critical, discerning and logical Ego—is turned from a true understanding of himself because of the code of thought prescribed by scientific dogma.

Fortunately, the current popularity of psychology mitigates an otherwise gloomy prospect for mankind's future. Even though psychology is not yet a science (being essentially still in the stage of amassing observations), many of the reasonable conclusions it has synthesized after a century of analysis have earned it respect in scientific circles. The psychologist's evident ability to predict human behavior has led to several accepted "laws" which are of practical use. Parapsychology is likewise beginning to draw attention to the case for man's extrasensory perceptions, and sheer weight of evidence may eventually force the scientific philosophers to accord serious consideration to the sixth sense.

Social psychology, led by the depth psychologists, Freud, Adler, Fromm, and Overstreet, offers some invaluable insights into the trouble with man's current relations with his brethren. Man's problems center on his lack of emotional maturity as exemplified by his glaringly evident predilection for emotional motivation and his avoidance of taking thought. Clarity of logic will be hard for men to achieve inasmuch as the prevailing institutions which influence us are so predominantly childish, self-seeking, and emotionally motivated. Perception of reality is obscured by one's environmental conditioning to accept current popular belief as the highest good. The scientist and philosopher who critically seek truth know all too well just how difficult it is to be honestly objective. And ultimate truth is all the harder to come by when "truths" of many colors and postures are imposed by national and religious groups.

Equally confused is the attempt to discern the hallmarks of emotional maturity. However, the Brotherhoods long ago recognized the highest values in human behavior and described these goals as the *virtues*. Now men outside the Brotherhoods have arrived at nearly the same conclusions as a result of psychologists' recent efforts to ferret out the ideal characteristics exemplified by the completely mature man. We might expect a person of balanced emotional maturity to be considered the epitome of social acceptableness; but although he may be admired and respected, today's world remains aloof from him. Our society instead rewards the person who conforms to its current modes of behavior. Evidence of strength of character in a man marks him as a disquieting and irritating influence.

There has been so much popular misunderstanding about Freudian frustration that a trend has developed to indulge one's every whim lest suppressed desires lead to neurosis and psychosis. Freud never advocated hedonism as a psychological panacea, nor were his discussions related to conscious determination. Rather, he was concerned with conflicting drives on the subconscious level which the patient could not resolve consciously. Clinical experience among psychiatrists indicates that the current fads of self-indulgence, self-pampering and self-dissipation have backfired into causing grave emotional illnesses. Life is by nature a continual series of frustrations and conflicts, and maturity is measured by one's ability to deal effectively with them as they arise.

A number of pop-psychology movements have twisted the sensible and liberating works of humanist psychologists into justification for the current "Me generation" to throw aside concern for other people as the students of these movements allegedly seek self-actualization and personal autonomy by casting off rules of behavior imposed by the social structure. These counterfeit religions of self-worship give moral sanction to their followers' selfish desires which do not contribute to society's well-being. Another recognized measure of psychological maturity is to grow less self-centered and instead develop care and concern for others. To do only one's "own thing" and to pursue self-serving aims at the "justified" expense of everyone else who might otherwise hold one back is but to retain and intensify infantile tendencies. A philosophy of looking out for "number one" against a perceived enemy of everyone else is obviously socially destructive and alienates the individual from his fellowman.

The development of character and wisdom is not enhanced by following emotional whims and group manias, nor can the adventure of life yield Egoic advancement if the mind is clouded by alcohol or tranquilizers. Sanity grows upon the sharp point of contact with reality and keen alertness to its challenges; whereas avoidance of life and one's problems is delusory.

Individuality and moral integrity protect one from being stampeded with the multitude who surge blindly to the command of the impersonal though all-powerful fad-maker—*they*. On every side we are coerced to strive for social acceptance, and our children are made to sacrifice all too much on the altar of popularity. But to have achieved perfect adjustment to a society that is childish is to have regressed. Our social aspirations are presently geared to glamour, and young and old alike have become willing pawns to the "image makers." The manipulators of glamour and advertising have carefully designed these forces to make us discontent with what we are and possess so that we are moved to purchase and consume whatever goods are represented to advance one's status. As a result of this insidious conditioning, we worship celebrities who are renowned for little more than their well-knownness, glorify the executive and his attendant wealth symbols, and emphasize sex for the wrong purposes. America has retreated from political, moral and economic reality so that life as it really is and the rewards for living it on its own merits have been largely abandoned for a glamour world. This national hysteria is equivalent to Germany's erstwhile romantic hysteria of Supermanism. One's adeptness at playing at life according to the mode of American juvenilism is not to have reached the height of human aspiration.

We bend our energies to the pursuit of power, property and plaudits instead of to the pursuit of maturity. The former lead to folly and disillusionment whereas the latter brings contentment, confidence and self-respect. Almost everyone thinks pleasure should bring happiness, and so it follows that sex has become much indulged in; but lack of maturity keeps such activity from delivering real satisfaction or contentment. By comparison, hazy misapprehensions about the rather rare state of psychological maturity restrict its popularity as a goal. Admittedly, it is difficult to have aims beyond one's own horizons of understanding. Moreover, nobody can portray the advantages of maturity to a childish person because no amount of description can convey the feelings of an emotion to a man who has not already experienced that emotion. The short-range advantages of pleasure are apparent, but the long-range advantages of maturity are obscure and more difficultly realized; therefore, the majority of mankind has always accepted the quicker goal and has barely even considered the greater goal.

One of life's cruelest deceptions lurks in the shallow ambitions of man because when they are satiated, the result is boredom, discontent, and dejection. The hoped-for happiness is a will-o-the-wisp that leads the pursuer to seek newer pleasures after each in its turn proves as devoid of innate happiness as the last. Nonetheless, perennial happiness *is* possible to the possessor of psychological maturity. Not so much because of the maturity *per se* but because of the attitudes that make maturity possible. Selfless labor for others, love of humanity, love of nature, active furtherance of high principles, and communion with divinity are the demonstrated wellsprings of undiminishing human joy. Although myths must eventually bow to realities, man is more emotional than rational; so the shortsighted goals still prevail despite all the evidence against happiness being derived from physical pleasure alone. Literally thousands of novelists have hammered away at this human failing to correctly relate cause and effect, but their vivid accounts of men's futile and perverse struggles for happiness seem to have been largely discounted by their readers.

The philosophers of the eighteenth century were stirred to great hope for mankind when the concept of *reasonable man* was propounded. The application of scientific inquiry to the enigmatic phenomena of the physical world had brought about the dramatic emergence of order out of confusion and gave rise to the belief that the puzzle of human behavior would likewise be reduced to rules of mathematical clarity and precision. Their unscientific, idealistic hope has since proved wrong—at least by their standards. The ground rules for science were drawn up during the eighteenth century and were based on the lowest common denominator of materialism. Testimony offered via supramentality and mystical perceptions are not admissible evidence to clarify man's cause for existence, and so mankind still gropes in vain because of restrictions fixed by himself. Thus scientists are shackled by what traditionally cannot be done. The scientific mind when freed of these non-valid restrictions and then tempered with parapsychology may yet lead man to new and greater philosophical tools. Americans scornfully point to the absurd limitations placed upon Russia's intellectuals and scientists yet fail to see the extent of the limitations in traditional Western thinking because they cannot view themselves as objectively.

As far as the two-hundred-year-old dream of *reasonable man* is concerned, it has been attained only but limitedly. I would venture to say that far less than one percent of the world's population approaches the mark. Upon these few persons rests the stability of society, and this is all the more remarkable since few hold high positions of temporal power. Perhaps no more than ten thousand men and women of the upper echelon of reasonable maturity keep the world on even keel. Most of these ten thousand are educators, philosophers, moralists and humanitarians; and they together with an unintended following of perhaps fewer than one million persons of goodwill and practical good sense comprise an informal association for the preservation of mankind. The rest of mankind are drifters who miserably fail to sustain civilization if the percentage of mature individuals within their society falls to a low percentage of the population.

Less than one person in 2,500[1] can be considered emotionally mature, and only this *aristocracy of excellence* is really ready for democracy. Even in the democratic nations of Western Civilization the average citizen sells himself out at the polls. I believe Freud was right when he asserted that democracy will fail because of the emotional flaws in man. Abraham Lincoln prolonged democracy on earth by being dictatorial at the crucial moment, but the British and American traditions of democracy continue to be undermined by universal suffrage. Western Civilization is producing some of the most brilliant men and women to be seen for many millennia, but decadent and irresponsible individuals are multiplying far more prolifically and consequently so is their voting power. The hard-won freedoms of the

---

[1]This figure was supplied by the Brotherhoods.

democratic governments are being thoughtlessly surrendered by "emotional peasants" in exchange for "security."

Despite these seeming drawbacks, the Brotherhoods insist that a democratic form of government is best for mankind; but They admit it can survive only among a citizenry almost wholly composed of emotionally mature individuals. The Brotherhoods hope to prove Their contention by assembling the truly capable and mature persons of the world into a single group. If men of maturity and wisdom fail to unify themselves in this way soon, it could well mean the end of political and philosophical freedom anywhere on earth for all time to come. Future seismic activity and political disintegration should serve to alert the mature individuals of the world who have been tardy in perceiving the imperative importance of so uniting. Even now eminent social and economic analysts are warning us of many destructive trends that indicate a likely collapse of our present way of life in the very near future. I suppose I too could be classed as a prophet of doom, except that I foresee the wonderful nation-to-come being prepared under expert guidance. Whatever dire cataclysms man brings upon himself for the remainder of this century can be tolerably viewed by understanding that it is for the greatest good in the long run.

Our sick world is beset by problems that cannot be solved by the conventional power plays of times past, and I am doubtful that enough politicians throughout the world will adopt attitudes likely to solve the dilemmas of our times. At any moment, statesmen may thrust us into a crisis that can swiftly compound into a debacle of unimaginable destruction. That is a sickeningly pessimistic outcome to visualize, but it is realistically probable. I would like to console myself with a Pollyannish dream that mankind's sanity will prevail to save civilization, for then I could retreat into blissful disregard of the armament race. But reasonable men are unable to appreciate the motives of madness and therefore they have been repeatedly overwhelmed by lunatics. Madness will be at the helm during most of what remains of this century, and it is painfully obvious that we are particularly unable to control madness in other countries.

A sense of hopelessness is coming more into the open as we talk to the man on the street. He still has goals for himself, but his long-range dreams for mankind are very tentative. He advises others to grab what they can out of life while life still exists. He extends this prerogative to politicians and surrenders his concern for the outcome of the fiscal policies of his government. Emotional tautness of unremitting anxiety can fray the lines of rationality.

The relatively few years of peace since the end of World War II have brought a great increase in prosperity and technological improvement to both capitalist and communist countries. The world is big enough for both ideologies to work out their problems side-by-side; and if they would not harass each other, a century of mutual noninterference could see each type of government moderating toward the other in form. The communist despots are beginning to see that the profit incentive for individuals is essential for meaningful economic growth, whereas the democratic societies are slowly socializing. If the smaller nations emerging from feudalism were not constantly badgered by the eastern and western blocs, they would likely develop forms of government somewhere between the two extremes. The people of the backward lands are not so much concerned with political ideologies as with the quickest way to achieve the same advantages of materialism exemplified by the United States of America. They want food for their bellies, advanced medical care and public health, and they aim to have it by whatever means will procure it the quickest. Since there are glaring failures in both the soviet and capitalist forms of so-called democracy, neutral nations should be left free to devise middle-of-the-road political systems. They might come up with some practical innovations in self-government which would be worthwhile for the larger nations to adopt. A number of small nations thus could serve as empirical proving-grounds for democratic refinements. In any event, a hands-off policy by the large nations is essential and proper if for no other reason than that interference in the internal environment of a people is karmically disastrous and gallingly impertinent.

We needn't worry about my views becoming an eventuality because there is not enough trust between the big nations to give it a try. Trust is precluded by the Communists' deceitful propaganda, world-wide subversive activities, and avowed determination to destroy the United States of America. The western powers dare not relax a moment in the face of such a relentless diabolical enemy. And this enemy is all the more dangerous because dedicated Communists exude the fervor of evangelism in an era when most of the suppressed peoples of the world are clamoring for a change in the status quo. The Western concept of democracy is the better way, but it is now the old way that in its time failed to improve conditions for the masses of most of the world. To this extent Communism has acted as the conscience for the shortcomings of Colonial Capitalism. We would like to see the nations which are newly liberated from colonialism adopt democracy as their form of government, but their peoples are sorely unprepared for intelligent self-rule. The confused and unsophisticated people are an easy mark for communist propaganda which offers golden promises couched in terms of a glorious adventure in achieving a social paradise. By comparison, the Western Bloc's lack of a purposeful, positive goal around which to rally its own people and inspire the world leaves us disunited and bereft of dynamism. Communism is winning the battle of ideologies for the same reason that Christianity triumphed in the Roman Empire—idealism and great expectations. The Communists are remarkably successful in imposing their philosophy upon others; and when the western nations finally find themselves backed against the wall in a losing battle of wits, they are likely to resort to force like any cornered creature.

There are many thoughtful persons who are sorely saddened by the prospect of seeing human beings reduced to a stone-age existence again. The likelihood of one's grandchild (should one survive a nuclear contest) being reduced to a stupid, snarling, short-lived, malnourished clod is crushing to one's sensitivities. One cries out in anguish at the thought of mankind's achievements going to naught. Yet no one is more sympathetic to this pathetic state of affairs than the Brotherhoods, for They have watched civilization obliterated many times over. In certain instances, men of quality who have cried out against the insanity of it all have been granted solace by the Brotherhoods who took them in and enlisted their talents.

If the average man of today were transported to a civilization like that of ancient Lemuria or the coming Kingdom of God, he would be a jarring misfit. His selfishness, his negative desires and ambitions, his arrogant intolerance, hatreds, cruelties, and overall lack of personal peace and happiness would make it impossible for him to get along in cooperative harmony. Since fear, anxiety, fretfulness, and irritability in one individual tend to spread to those who come in contact with him, it is obvious that he would only detract from the spiritual peace of a Lemurian environment. In spite of the luxuries, beauty, and material abundance that a society can create, its civilization is vapid, restless, and unfulfilling if the citizens are no better than the man of today. He has not learned self-discipline let alone self-government. He would require too many laws, and the Lemurian way of life relies on its code of ethics without external enforcement.

The very minimum of government is a Lemurian principle lest the government operate in the environment of the citizens against Cosmic Law. The purpose of Lemurian government is to provide public services inexpensively; and although there are government administrators in the Lemurian scheme of things, there will be no politicians. Democracy will be exercised by referendum and not by a republican legislature bending to pressure groups and lobbies seeking legislative favoritism; nor will organized political parties vie for control of government policies. The executive officers of the government will not be the leaders of the people but will be strictly public servants having supervision over only their respective departments and offices. The people will look to the great philosophers among them for inspiration and counsel, and then they will act for themselves.

Lemurian economic policies will seem quite different from the traditions we follow today. Machinery will put an end to hard labor, and automation will reduce the workweek to a few hours. This will result in low weekly wages, but the cost of such necessities as food and rental of housing will permit the wage earner a comfortable surplus for savings and luxuries. Automated farms will produce food very inexpensively, and radically simplified distribution methods without middleman markups will hold retail food prices close to the cost of rain, sun, fertilizer and seed. Hard goods will be made to last for generations so that natural resources are conserved. Designs in the styling of appliances and autos will be such that they will look attractive indefinitely as well as outlast the owner's lifetime. Production methods today are geared to produce the greatest profit for the stockholders; therefore, continual style changes accompanied by advertising that has conditioned us to scorn the old and worship the latest makes us discard what is still useful. Just in case some persons might prefer to get the maximum usage out of an item, defects are purposely engineered into it so it will need to be replaced early. The savings involved when one needs to buy only one automobile instead of ten during his life is considerable.

The Lemurian economic system is designed to fulfill *all* the mundane needs of *every* citizen. Industry will be due its profits, but making profits will not be the attitude impelling manufacture; nor will people be driven to "keep up with the Joneses" or seek social status through high income or elite possessions. The long period of serviceability of housing, autos, furniture, and appliances will allow later generations to live their lives without having to replace goods passed to them by their forebears. A tremendous savings in resources and human labor will result when only food, fuel, clothing, and personal services need be purchased. Our present system is designed to keep us from catching up, and it has come to depend upon the exchange of goods and services at maximum production capacity in order to avoid collapse.

The great increase in the amount of leisure time to be enjoyed in the Lemurian system will be occupied by schooling. Education will be a lifetime avocation in the Kingdom of God, and Citizens will be disposed to eagerly seek knowledge of all things. Every effort will be made to perfect education as well as the socio-economic environment so that the door to spiritual advancement for man will be opened to the Nth degree. The individual's attainment of Adeptship in the Brotherhoods will be the end goal of every activity in the Kingdom of God, and the beauty, bounty, and tranquility of that nation will be regarded primarily as enhancement to Egoic perfection.

The Kingdom of God has been planned by the Brotherhoods for thousands of years, and it shall be successful from the inception of the community in Illinois. Perhaps at last we shall see to what heights man can rise in fulfilling his quest for civilization.

Appendix
(Referred to on Page 169)

In the Nation of God, the Citizens' attitudes toward professions, parenthood, acquisition of wealth, and having prestige will be profoundly modified from what people hold today, and this difference will stem from unique economic policies there and a reawakened sensitivity to genuine human needs. In recent decades, women have been pressured into the workforce by several factors: a predominating cultural philosophy of materialistic consumerism, high interest rates, high taxes, and the policies of manufacturing hard goods down to a price at the expense of quality. Once women became part of the workforce, they encountered unfair and unjustified prejudices against them—notably, less wages paid for doing the same work as men, and being denied opportunities for promotions or *entrée* into certain fields of work. These practices stirred a rebellion against men's domination of the commercial scene and spilled over to include the entire spectrum of man/woman relationships. The fresh examination of the traditional roles played by the two genders has been personally painful for almost everyone and has brought about profound social disruptions. In the long run, these changes are likely to be very beneficial psychologically, but this generation of people will bear the brunt of the turmoil involved.

Women are rightfully demanding more opportunities for self-determination in commerce, professions, and education. However, men's resistance to change turned this demand into a fight against males as perpetrators of injustice, whereas, actually, individual men have been carrying on social attitudes traditionally handed down to them from Biblical pronouncements. The symbols of success for the Feminist Movement are: to excel competitively in commerce, have the economic "power and freedom" men allegedly enjoy, gain the trappings of executives' prestige, and enjoy unfettered sexual expression—and these are essentially the same goals that males eventually discover carry a heavy psychic price that make such goals questionable. Women are now clamoring to attain the very goals which men are beginning to reject, and in effect, women are being encouraged to focus on becoming like men instead of working to evolve as-yet-undeveloped potentials of womanhood. They are buying into a bad bargain, and they will eventually learn why men would like to get out of the demeaning rat race in which many women now hope to best men.

Presently, women are pressured to work in factories and offices to help make ends meet or to have a career. If they have small children, they begin to feel guilty and could resent them. Love between people and maternal love requires time and leisure to be at its satisfying best. Women are inherently more nurturant than men, and everyone should benefit from that important, basic quality. When love and romance fall by the wayside because a woman or man tries to work too much, then everything becomes brittle and less feeling for them. Christ's message is that love ultimately is everything; yet love is hardly compatible with fatigue and harried feelings. Mothering her child and being a lover to her mate must inevitably suffer from a woman's being a super achiever in several other areas; thereby she can lose what ultimately means most to a human being. The widespread inability of people to love causes our population to seek substitute satisfaction in acquisition of things and prestige. We must reverse this trend or perish as a civilization.

In the Nation of God it will not be expected that everyone will marry or have children. Everyone has had more than ten thousand children over his or her thousands of incarnations. Sometimes an individual or a couple has more important tasks to accomplish in a given lifetime than being a parent again. Everyone should have the right to choose what to do with his or her life. There will be many opportunities for both genders to do volunteer work of all types, to display their artistic talents before the public, and to see their art on an open market. The helping and healing professions will be open to women; they will become university professors and scientific researchers, independent artisans, craftswomen; and, of course, a farm operator's wife does everything. But the Brotherhoods strongly discourage women in the armed forces, mining, lumbering, metals processing, heavy construction labor, chemical industries, and manufacturing production lines. These jobs, and others like them, They feel will diminish feminine sensitivities even in the context of a civilization practicing the Lemurian Philosophy. The Brotherhoods, who are half women, point to the lessons of history which indicate that a civilization best meets the needs of all its citizens when women are allowed and encouraged to fulfill their natural instincts to love and to nurture rather than assume masculine traits of competitiveness and inurement to repetitive physical hardships. That women can excel in these areas has been proven over and over, but the overall price of having women in industry is too high for everyone concerned.

Within fifty years after its founding, the coming Nation of God, like ancient Lemuria, will have an economic system where the amount of time worked for gainful employment will be twelve hours per week—two days at six hours each—whether in industry or agriculture or governmental services. Factories and marts will be open six days per week and have three teams of workers for each job. There are several reasons for the drastically reduced hours required to earn a good living: (1) elimination of all interest payments, (2) no taxation, (3) elimination of middlemen in the distribution chain, (4) elimination of unemployment and its associated welfare payments, (5) a minimal budget for national defense, (6) stabilized styling of goods and (7) manufactured items designed and built to last over the life-times of several generations. For instance, homes were built of mortised rock in Lemuria and were serviceable for twenty thousand years and more; engineers today have the know-how to build automobiles that can last a hundred years for only twice the cost of one that lasts five years. Only one person in a household will need to work in order to support that household comfortably, and people will not share the American immigrant's philosophy and willingness to exhaust himself in acquiring personal possessions. Personal ownership of land will not be allowed in the Nation of God. Furthermore, there will barely be enough jobs to allow more than one member of a household to have a job.

The importance of meeting the built-in needs of infants and

children will be recognized and be taken care of. Lifelong enducation and comprehension of ultimate reality shall be universal, and education will be free of cost to everyone. There will be a heavy reliance upon women as the transmitters of knowledge and culture. However, both parents will have the time and incentive to share in parenting. Almost one quarter of all paid jobs will be involved in education, but parents will be wholly responsible for intensive education of their children for the first six years of their child's life. This is one of the reasons why the Brotherhoods urge that the children in a family be spaced at least six years apart; so they can have the full attention of mother for those critical years. Higher education slanted toward women will continue until age 28, and most women will likely not marry until that age. There will be every opportunity for her to undertake training in any academic and scientific studies; but during the time that she is rearing her children, the society will expect her to not divert her energies from that all-important activity. If widowed, she will be supported economically by her neighbors via the state so that her children will not be deprived of their human right to undiminished love and attention. It is foretold that the exclusive, nuclear-family concept, which has been around for about eighty years, will return to an inclusion of neighbors and blood-kin into an extended family so far as children are concerned, and this can prevent feelings of isolation by everyone. Even farms, which will become highly automated, will be operated by multiple family units, each with their individual homes or in one hacienda on the farm.

The philosophy of the Nation of God and the personal goals of its people will produce a culture almost unrecognizable from today. Prosperity, peace, and the focus of the entire governmental structure upon personal Egoic evolution will promote personal fulfillment.

Some of the
publications
available from

The Stelle Group

P.O. BOX 75, DEPT. P, QUINLAN, TEXAS 75474
(214) 864-0799

FREE complete publications catalogue available on request.

The Stelle Group

Established on March 5, 1963, as a not-for-profit educational organization, The Stelle Group has over twenty years experience in providing programs for spiritual awareness and development. An underlying principle of The Stelle Group's programs is a conscious commitment to excellence shared by participants and students of the Brotherhoods' philosophy.

The four primary interest areas of The Stelle Group include adult education, accelerated learning programs for children, the advancement of Stelle, Illinois as a community dedicated to human development, and research into technologies that foster self-reliance. The Stelle Group relies on the tithes and donations of participants and friends in order to accomplish its purposes.

Participation in The Stelle Group is open to all English-speaking people regardless of race, color, creed, or national origin. Further information will gladly be sent upon your request.

THE LARGER TRADE EDITION OF
THE ULTIMATE FRONTIER with 54 - page Index

The Ultimate Frontier was written by Richard Kieninger under his pen name, Eklal Kueshana. The philosophy in the book is drawing together people of integrity from all fields of endeavor in order to build the communities of Stelle, Illinois and Adelphi, Texas.

Includes 54-page index . . . . . Softbound - $6.95   Hardbound - $12.95

RETAIL VOLUME DISCOUNT PRICES

Quantity	Softbound	Discount
1 to 4	$6.95 ea.	0%
5 to 9	$4.20 ea.	36%
10 or more	$3.80 ea.	45%

The Ultimate Frontier Study Guide

Essential information from *The Ultimate Frontier* is presented in a diverse question-and-answer style to facilitate a clearer understanding and firmer base of information on the Brotherhoods' philosophy. The *Study Guide* also includes information not found in *The Ultimate Frontier*. **$10.00**

Sharing
THE ULTIMATE FRONTIER

Would you like your family and friends and/or business associates to have information about *The Ultimate Frontier* and The Stelle Group? You can provide them with the same opportunity you have had to benefit from this uplifting information.

Please print their names and addresses below (use additional sheets of paper as needed).

- - - - - - - - - - - - - - - - - - - -

NAME _____

ADDRESS _____

CITY _____

STATE _____ ZIP CODE _____

☐ *Please indicate the information is sent at my request.*

- - - - - - - - - - - - - - - - - - - -

NAME _____

ADDRESS _____

CITY _____

STATE _____ ZIP CODE _____

☐ *Please indicate the information is sent at my request.*

- - - - - - - - - - - - - - - - - - - -

Mail to: The Stelle Group
                  Office of Publications
                  P.O. Box 75, Dept. P
                  Quinlan, Texas 75474

Or telephone: (214) 864-0799

Sharing THE ULTIMATE FRONTIER

NAME _____

ADDRESS _____

CITY _____

STATE _____ ZIP CODE _____

☐ *Please indicate the information is sent at my request.*

NAME _____

ADDRESS _____

CITY _____

STATE _____ ZIP CODE _____

☐ *Please indicate the information is sent at my request.*

NAME_____

ADDRESS_____

CITY _____

STATE _____ ZIP CODE _____

☐ *Please indicate the information is sent at my request.*

NAME _____

ADDRESS _____

CITY _____

STATE _____ ZIP CODE _____

☐ *Please indicate the information is sent at my request.*

NAME _____

ADDRESS _____

CITY _____

STATE _____ ZIP CODE _____

☐ *Please indicate the information is sent at my request.*

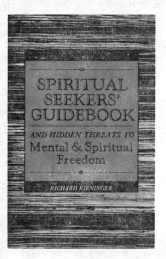

ADDITIONAL ESSAYS
BY THE BIOGRAPHEE OF THE ULTIMATE FRONTIER

The manuscript for *The Ultimate Frontier* was shortened over thirty percent before it was published. This additional information was later printed as essays in The Stelle Group's monthly newsletters. Richard Kieninger's *Observations* essays are now available in booklet form. *(Note: Observations I is out of print.)*

Observations III

- Morality and Youth
- Life Essences
- Living One's Convictions
- "Supermen"
- Improving Civilization
- Prosperity and Tithing
- Negative Influences
- Money and Wealth
- Maintaining Standards
- Controlling One's Environment
- Emotional Maturity
- Dietary Comments
- Personal Excellence and Quality
- Considerations in Childbirth
- Stelle — A School of Life
- Hypnotism . . . and more

Observations II

- The Twelve Great Virtues
- Pharaoh Akhnaton
- Comments on Education
- Factors in Moral Decay
- The Beauty in Complexity
- On Heroes and Heroism
- God
- Meditation and Prayer
- The Pursuit of Excellence
- The Remnant
- Social Standards
- The Peaceful Messiah
- Marriage and Romanticism
- Ecology Protected in Lemuria
- Love . . . and more

Observations IV

- The Seven Planes of Existence
- The Advance of Love
- Insanity and Lower Entities
- Karmic Responsibility
- Vibrations and Music
- Pointers in Precipitation
- Doing Christ's Work
- The Wayward Path of Occultism
- The Coming Depression
- Time and Thought
- Beginning the Path to Perfection
- Advancement and Giving
- Sages: Earthlings or Aliens?
- Stelle as a School
- Mystic Awareness . . . and more

OBSERVATIONS BOOKLETS . . . . $3.00 each

On Becoming an Initiate

— Cassette Tape Program

A Series of Discussions with Richard Kieninger

> *"The road to spiritual greatness may seem surprisingly simple — but only because it is. Man was intended to rise naturally in smooth sequence from the clod he was at creation to the perfection of Mastership. "*

-The Ultimate Frontier

**FOR THE
SERIOUS STUDENT**

**A HOME STUDY
COURSE BY THE
BIOGRAPHEE OF**
*THE
ULTIMATE
FRONTIER*

On Becoming an Initiate is a multi-media program designed to a all interested individuals in working toward human perfection; facilitate their attainment of the First Degree of Brotherhood. T program consists of twelve cassette tapes featuring discussions led Richard Kieninger, author and biographee of *The Ultimate Frontie* Each tape is accompanied by written material which contains info mation augmenting that presented on the tape. The *On Becomi. an Initiate Study Guides* consist of an additional 100 pages which a designed as efficient self-study aides for your further understandi of the audio presentations. It must be emphasized, however, th Egoic growth will not be conveyed to you just by exposure to t information, but rather, through the determined application of these principles in your daily life. Following is a brief description of the twelve components of the *On Becoming an Initiate* program.

Tape I/Tape II The Twelve Great Virtues

Richard explains the importance of practicing the Virtues to the pursuit of soul growth. He defines each of the Virtues, giving examples of their application. The supplements also contain written definitions of each Virtue, along with a review of the daily retrospection exercise, a self-examination section, and worksheets.

Tape I/Tape II . . $22.00 **With Study Guides . . $27.00**

Tape III The Brotherhoods

The organization and purposes of the twelve divisions of the Brotherhoods are explained, along with the requirements which a person must meet in order to be eligible for Initiation.

Tape III . . . . $9.95 **With Study Guide. . . $12.50**

Tape IV The Law of Karma

This Universal Law is discussed in depth — its purpose, the three divisions through which it manifests, the resulting Ten Lemurian Laws, the Law of Tithes, and many examples.

Tape IV . . . . $9.95 **With Study Guide. . . $12.50**

Tape V Mental Precipitation

The power of Mind and how it functions are described. The steps used in conscious precipitation are given, along with insights into the limitless challenges and responsibilities of using our Minds.

Tape V . . . . . $9.95 **With Study Guide. . . .$12.50**

Tape VI Balance

This is a discussion on how to achieve balance, one of the prerequisites for Initiation. Examples of Apollonian and Dionysian personality traits are given, as well as ways to overcome some of our cultural imbalances.

Tape VI . . . $9.95 **With Study Guide. . $12.50**

Tape VII Prosperity

Richard discusses what prosperity means in terms of Initiation an
how one can attain it and use it wisely.
Tape VII . . . . $9.95   **With Study Guide. . . $12.50**

Tape VIII Health

A healthy vehicle and personality are dependent upon your willing
ness to develop proper attitudes, good health habits, and emotiona
maturity. Achieving these qualities is discussed.
Tape VIII. . . . $9.95   **With Study Guide. . . $12.50**

Tape IX Cosmic Consciousness

Mystic awareness combined with self-controlled clairvoyance resul
in cosmic consciousness. This requirement for Initiation is explained
along with the means for its attainment.
Tape IX . . . . $9.95   **With Study Guide. . . $12.50**

Tape X Emotional Maturity

The characteristics of an emotionally mature person and the benefit
that result are discussed. The importance of one's aptitude for "life
is also explained.
Tape X. . . . . $9.95   **With Study Guide. . . $12.50**

Tape XI The Ten Qualities of Mind

Mind and brain are differentiated. Explanations are given on desir
memory, curiosity, intuition, consciousness, conscience, will, reasor
creativeness, and emotion.
Tape XI . . . . $9.95   **With Study Guide. . . $12.5**

Tape XII Controlling Your Environment

This is an in-depth discussion on how everything in your life an
your environment is the result of your past and present thinkin
You will learn what steps you can take to improve and uplift then
Tape XII . . . . $9.95   **With Study Guide. . . $12.5**

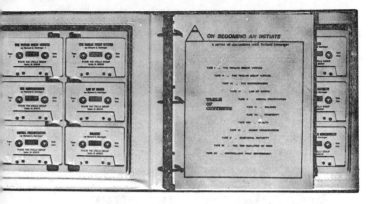

ORDERING INFORMATION

PLAN I — You may buy the materials separately, though each tape is automatically accompanied with supplemental written material. Study Guides are available only as supplements to the tapes.

Binder for all Tapes/Supplements/Study Guides $8.50
Study Guides for all Twelve Tapes $25.00

PLAN II — You may subscribe in advance for the entire program, including binder, but pay on a monthly basis.

- With the 100-page Study Guide included, your cost is $23.20 the first month (for the first two tapes plus binder), and $11.60 for the next ten months. This is a saving of almost $16.00 over the full price.

- Without the Study Guides, the cost is $19.50 the first month, and $9.75 for the next ten months. This is a saving of almost $13.00 over the full price.

PLAN III — You may purchase the entire program with the binder at one time.

With Study Guides (a saving of $31.00) $124.00
Without Study Guides (a saving of $26.00) $104.00

The Stelle Group Letter

Published ten times per year, this newsletter keeps our readers up-to-date on projects and events in our communities and it continues to supply information supplemental to the philosophy of the Brotherhoods. Please send us your address today.

THE STELLE GROUP LETTER . . . . . . **Free of Charge**

Publications Catalogue

A complete catalog of the publications offered by The Stelle Group is available free of charge. Please write and request your copy.

PUBLICATIONS CATALOG . . . . **Free of Charge**

Tours

We invite you to visit Stelle. You may schedule a tour by calling The Stelle Group receptionist. Tours and Public Meetings are given from time to time. For further information, please call (815) 256-2200.

We invite you to visit the headquarters' offices at The Stelle Group Center, 405 Mayfield Avenue, Garland, Texas 75041. For further information on The Stelle Group and its programs for study of the Brotherhoods' philosophy and opportunities for participation in its organizational activities, please write or call The Stelle Group, P.O. Box 75, Dept. P, Quinlan, Texas 75474 (214) 864-0799.

SHARING WITH YOUR FRIENDS

If you want free information about The Stelle Group sent to your friends, please list their names and addresses on separate sheets of paper and send them to The Stelle Group. You may also order our publications for your friends in this manner. Please indicate if you want us to inform the person that the book or information is sent at your request, or mention that it is a "gift from a friend."

ORDERING INFORMATION

Illinois and Texas residents, please add 6% sales tax. For Shipping and Handling Charge, please add $.50 per book or single cassette and $2.00 for each of the complete tape series. Please include money order or personal checks with your order, and make payment in United States currency only. Unless Airmail or First Class is prepaid, all orders are shipped via Fourth Class, which takes three to four weeks for delivery. For orders outside the United States, please add additional money if shipment by Airmail is desired, otherwise overseas delivery surface rate takes several months.

Please mail your order to The Stelle Group Office of Publications, P.O. Box 75, Dept. P, Quinlan, Texas 75474. This price list supercedes previous price lists and is subject to change without notice.

You may telephone The Stelle Group at (214) 864-0799.

Would you like to charge your order?
$20 minimum order please.

Check ONE: ☐ **Visa** ☐ **MasterCard**

YOUR CARD NUMBER: (All digits please.)

☐☐☐☐☐☐☐☐☐☐☐☐☐☐☐☐

IMPORTANT! We must have expiration date on your card! | Month | Year | | MasterCard only: Bank No. (4 digits over your name). | ☐☐☐☐

Signature _____

(Required if using credit card)

Name: _____

Address: _____

City: _____ State: ____ Zip Code: _____